LOVE BECOMES HER

A FABLE FOR THE AGES

Yun Rou

Love Becomes Her

By Yun Rou

ISBN-13: 978-988-8843-63-3

FICTION

EB213

Published in Hong Kong by Earnshaw Books Ltd.

For Nobuko,
my treasured companion of 31 years

Author's Note

Traditional Chinese culture rests on the shoulders of three men. The first is Confucius, who codified the requirements of a harmonious society, the second is the Buddha, who advanced the notion of karma, and the Pure Land (Heaven) and taught how to best to endure the inevitable pain and suffering life brings. The third, a Daoist sage known simply as Lao Tzu (The Old Master), took nature as his teacher and in turn shared advice on how to live in accordance with it.

Confucius, born Kong Qiu, expounded voluminously on etiquette and social mores. Many of his lessons are presented with commentaries from scholars of the time; Buddha spoke many sutras that were copied and spread across the Eastern world; Lao Tzu, however, penned a mere five thousand characters to teach us how to live meaningfully, effectively, and with the least effort. His slim volume, *Tao Te Ching, (Classic of the Way and its Virtues)* has been translated and read by more people than any book in the world save the Western Bible. If Confucius is China's conscience and the Buddha is its heart, then Lao Tzu is the wild spirit of that most august "Middle Kingdom".

All over China, indeed all over Asia, temples celebrating Lao Tzu still exist, and all are replete with representations of turtles. Shelled reptiles are everywhere in Lao Tzu's legacy. Alive and kicking, they swim in temple ponds; carved from giant stones, they guard temple doors; and penned in ink, they adorn classical commentaries on Lao Tzu's *Tao*. This is the story of how Lao Tzu might have become enamored with a particularly special turtle, and the life and death they might have had together.

And apart.

1

The sword-edge of life still slices my hard parts even here in the frigid darkness. My heart beats barely a hundred times for every cycle of the moon, yet I continually hope to feel less, to know less, and to experience everything less sharply. Pinpoints of light in a dirt-bleak sky, my memories both torture and sustain me. They are images of the man I love holding me, cherishing me, feeding me, doting on me, his devotion around and through me even though, some centuries ago, I felt what was left of him dry to bones beneath me.

My yearning to be with him remains unrequited. He circles me; I know he does, but we cannot quite touch—not really, not fully, not in a fashion that satisfies. It has been ever thus, the two of us so close we breathe each other's air yet separated forever by natural law. Even so, I accept him as the one and only source of warmth and light, ironically keeping me alive to some end I cannot imagine. Across the millennia, my love has pulsed steadily with recollections of my sage's glance, his touch, his words, the way his face bore age, the way his nails curled, the way his earlobes hung low, the way his teeth gleamed and finally fell. Even now I hold him like a fragile bubble that might at any moment give way, desperately afraid that I will lose him even as I yearn to join him by winding down and fading away.

It is so dark. It is so cold. I am still so in love.

2

Eons before European whalers spread news of the sweet taste of giant tortoise meat clear around the world, a ship of the Eastern Zhou Federation sailed into a quiet bay on the leeward side of one of the volcanic Galápagos Islands. Ding Lok, the bearded, barrel-chested captain, startled a bottom fish by nudging a bronze anchor overboard with his foot. He had the thick legs of a dwarf, the torso of a satyr, and was rumored to have single-handedly killed an entire regiment of barbarians from beyond the Taklimakan Desert escaping with merely a slice to his buttock. He always chose chaos over order because in chaos could be found the opportunity for profit.

"I only see black and barren rock here," he said, licking his rotting teeth.

"Don't worry," replied his navigator, a young apprentice shaman named Wang Yi. "If my master back at the court says there is treasure, then treasure there is."

The sailors had been at sea for months and were suffering terribly from scurvy. Eager for fresh fruit but wary about being bitten by the hammerheads and gray-reef-whalers churning the water around them, they kept their hands high on the pole oars and rowed ashore. Scampering over the barren landscape, they found giant turtles and called the news across the bay.

"Who cares about turtles? Where's the gold?" Ding Lok

yelled back.

The men cared. Sustenance was treasure for them, at least in the short-term. Elated at the prospect of a meal, they lit beach fires and set to slaughtering the creatures with their swords. "Turtles are a sign from heaven," said Wang Yi, trying to mollify his captain. "Remember that the most famous of all shamans, our great Ancestor Yu, saw the Lo Shu pattern on the back of a giant turtle, and from that, learned how energy flows in the world."

Ding Lok smacked the gunwale with his fist. "Forget legends and show me something that's going to make me rich!"

"Legends remind us that marvelous things can happen at any moment. Anyway, a man is often confused by all the things he could have and would be, but a tortoise is precisely a tortoise— no more and no less."

The captain snorted. "You are full of the same nonsense as that mystic master of yours."

A boat returned with turtle meat and cactus flowers. An apple-sized baby tortoise crawled out of the pile and Ding Lok scooped it up. "Ah," he cried. "An appetizer."

Acting as if it could somehow understand, the hatchling stretched its neck and bit the captain on the nose. As the victim stomped in anger and blood gushed, Wang Yi grabbed the animal and pretended to lob it overboard, while actually dropping it into his tunic.

As the first mate sewed up Ding Lok's wound, others of the crew dove for seals, gathered fruit, chased ground iguanas— the marine variety were too foul-tempered and quick to dive— beheaded blue-footed boobies for sport, and killed and ate more tortoises. They sampled the local penguins, too, but found the flesh oily and repellant. The island's exotic light and beautiful angles so enchanted the sailors that decades later, some swore

3

they still felt its tug on their blood.

Trying to coax his secret pet to eat, Wang Yi noticed celestial flecks in its eyes and wondered whether the pattern might not be some kind of omen. At the same time, the captain, still smarting from his wound, made a big business of personally beheading a dozen of the tortoises the crew had brought aboard.

"I hope every one of them is close family to that little biting bastard," he cried.

Wang Yi kept the turtle hidden until a few days later when the captain announced his intention to turn the ship around and head home.

"We've been duped," he chafed. "There is no treasure, and there never was."

"My master had a dream," Wang Yi countered.

"I had one too. Nine virgins attended me. I don't see them here, alas."

"You are not my master."

"Your master is a fraud. Instead of riches, all any of us have to show for half a year of sailing are tongues stinking of turtle. It has been a fool's errand all along, and now we must sail back empty-handed."

Wang Yi puffed his chest and tried to project the authority of the court's odd and forbidding magician. "My master predicts floods, flies like a dragon, and reads the truth in clouds. He doesn't send men across the sea without purpose."

The captain snorted. "That scheming eccentric holds the whole court under his spell."

"You speak ill of him, but it is his power that has protected us on our long voyage."

"Then use your own power to burn the shell of that little biter you're hiding, and tell me the location of my treasure."

Wang Yi hesitated. Cracking the belly scales of turtles with a burning poker and then reading the geometry of the resulting spread of lines in divinatory terms was a common practice, but it rarely left the turtle in prime condition.

"I'm saving the baby as a gift for my teacher. I'll burn an empty shell instead."

"Burn the baby. I insist."

Having no choice, Wang Yi heated a poker in one of the small cooking fires on deck. "Hear me, Ancestor Yu," he intoned. "I seek to know the truth of our mission now."

The hatchling writhed in pain as Wang Yi applied the hot poker to its plastron. Salty tears flowed from its eyes, and cracks appeared around the burn. One scute curled and smoked. Wang Yi frowned.

"Well?" the captain demanded.

Wang Yi burned another scute only to reveal the same message. He took a deep breath. "We can head home."

"So you admit there is no treasure?"

"On the contrary. We have found it."

"What?"

"This baby is the treasure. It is written in the lines."

If the crew had not suffered so deeply and for so long, the assertion might have been comical. As it was, there was a stunned and disbelieving silence before the men finally erupted in fury. They would have thrown Wang Yi overboard had Ding Lok not protected him, afraid to make the arduous journey back across the world without the assistance of the young shaman's remarkable navigational skills.

Later, alone at the stern, Wang Yi watched the islands recede with the sense that something truly important really had come from their visit. He regretted that he was unable to think of a way to memorialize the fact that the first human feet to touch the Galápagos Islands were those of a bunch of ragtag explorers on an impossible ocean mission for a powerful sorcerer from a land across the sea. The little turtle, incapable of such sophisticated associations and ambitions, was simply filled with a pulsing ruby of longing for a home it would likely never see again.

3

This Earth has blood and veins and chasms between her bones. She has lungs, too, which I know because I hear her breathe. Her inhales are long and slow, and sometimes she gasps, shivers, and shakes as she exhales. Her rivers take her poisons away to the sea, and her pulse, like mine, is so slow that someone whose ears were not so very deep underground and so tightly pressed to her might not hear it. That pulse, the flow of those fluids, and the expanding and contracting of her stony rib cage, all take patience to hear.

My life force scavenges for the few tiny pockets of yellow fat that remain inside my shell. Fueled anew, and with measured contemplation, I turn my attention to the dance between Heaven and Earth. Even through the layers of dirt, I can feel the moon's gravity and measure her cycles, which, in combination with tiny changes in temperature, reveal months and seasons.

Can you imagine how sensitive I have become after all this time, doing nothing but paying attention? Very recently, I have come to notice a new vibration, one lacking in nuance and originating far closer to me than any heavenly body. It is a delicate, small, and repetitive melody, and yet somehow vaguely familiar. Gradually, I recognize it to be the arrhythmic working of a shovel in human hands.

Up there in the vernal forest that I remember so well, and under the warm sun of spring, someone is digging.

4

Outbound from what would later be China, the trade winds had conspired with the South Equatorial Current to push the ship along briskly. On the return voyage, however, zigzag tacks were required to get anywhere at all. Slow progress put the crew in a foul mood, and they eyed the baby tortoise, symbol of their pointless trial, with increasing ire. Even so, Wang Yi remained confident that procuring the tortoise had been his master's plan all along. He guarded the little creature carefully and ministered to its shell with herbs.

As the ship continued west, the change of seasons brought disquieted currents that raised plankton to the surface. Small fish followed, as did larger ones and ones even larger than those. Early one morning, in a steady wind, a pod of orca whales, each fully as long as the ship, drew close enough to bump the hull and set the timbers aquiver.

As the spray from their blowholes soaked the deck and their piercing, high-pitched wails dropped the terrified sailors to their knees, Wang Yi grabbed hold of the anchor station, draped himself over the prow, and extended the hatchling out over the water as an offering. The little turtle kicked in the wind like a sprinter, and one by one the whales closed in for a better view. Always a superstitious lot, the crew was astonished to see the whales veer away. In the face of such talismanic power, the men allowed that the little reptile might have some importance after all. As a reward for likely saving the ship, Wang Yi offered up a piece of dried cactus he'd been saving, and the turtle took its first bite of food since leaving home.

Two days later, the crew spied the distant shores of what would later be called Banaba, in Kiribati, off to the starboard side. The beckoning isles were a tonic after so long under sail, and Ding Lok worked the tiller and sail to bring them closer. The men hooted and cheered at the sight of the perfect beaches, but Wang Yi found troubling omens in the ripples on the water and in the way certain seashells aligned on the bottom.

"I don't like this place," he said.

Ding Lok fiddled impatiently with the band of yellow silk he used to cover his damaged nose. "It doesn't like you either."

"It's not safe," Wang Yi persisted.

"Then go along and stand watch against whatever it is you fear."

Ashore, Wang Yi found the men netting nesting seabirds, cracking coconuts, and collecting pandanus, breadfruit, and pawpaw. He watched them fall asleep to the moans of wooing shearwaters after gorging on the fruits, and stood sentinel as he had been bidden, keeping marauding crabs away from the hatchling with his foot. Less than an hour later, he heard a suspicious rustling in the bush.

"Get up," he whispered in the ear of the first mate.

"Leave me alone," the man grumbled.

"You have to wake up and take the men back to the ship."

"Why?"

"I hear bad noises."

The mate turned over, eyes still closed, and put his arm under his head as a pillow. "Go away."

A band of Polynesian warriors in breechcloths and bright

face-paint suddenly burst from cover. Despite the superiority of their own bronze swords, the sailors, thick with food and sleep, were overcome by the natives' marlinspikes. Scattering, they swam desperately for the ship, the pursuing natives shrieking and hurling spears. The blood in the water drew sharks, and a few men met ghastly ends.

Throughout the attack, Wang Yi remained hidden in tall grass. When the warriors retreated, he slipped out, tortoise in his tunic, and scissor-kicked across the bay, his progress so gentle even seaweed let him pass.

"Four dead," Ding Lok announced when he clambered aboard.

"I warned you," Wang Yi replied, working a thorn from his foot. "Now let's sail quickly as I fear we have not seen the last of these savages."

Polynesian war canoes did appear on the horizon at midmorning, but they gradually fell behind. In the days that followed, the ship passed slowly beneath what would later be called the Marshall Islands and then the Carolines, on a diagonal course through the coastal waters of Micronesia. Off the equator, the nights turned cooler and the color of the sea changed. Wang Yi strove to understand currents complicated by the presence of the islands and to navigate properly.

Where the open Pacific had been a violent, howling beast capable of destroying the ship at any moment on whim of wind or tide, the passage south of the Philippines and into the Celebes Sea was an intricate wonderland of sounds, smells, and opportunities. The ship sailed past the mouth of the Moro Gulf and came around the horn of Mindanao, through the narrow passage at Zamboanga, and into the Sulu Sea, where descendants of the Nesiots—plying routes between their Barangay city-states, Irian Jaya and Sulawesi— offered trade and ready liaisons with easy women.

Malaccan islanders too were hungry for commerce with the Zhou ship. It would be at least a thousand years before Islam arrived and nearly as long again before the Spanish set a standard price of Mexican silver for their spices, so Ding Lok negotiated strongly and was happy with the result. Commerce was just as lively at Iloila and Pandah and the tiny Calamian Islands, where the Zhou offered silk in return for cotton to patch the ship's tattered sails, and ploughshare iron in exchange for a stunning array of fruits to banish scurvy, along with pepper to enliven the palate, cinnamon, nutmeg, cloves, medicinal buds, seeds, berries, wood bark, and ornamental ginger. Specifically to impress the court, Ding Lok also procured items from the Far West, including intricately carved gold, durable pottery, rhinoceros ivory, and huge saltwater crocodile skulls he and other Zhou traders took for the bones of dragons.

Like his famous master, Wang Yi was interested neither in wealth nor trade; rather he dwelled in an interior world full of presages and signs. Encouraged by the gentle rocking of the ship in sheltered water, he meditated in pursuit of the rhythms of nature, using them to aid in positioning the ship between sea and stars. He had in mind the threat of the summer typhoons known to arise with barely a whisper of warning in the stretch of water around what is now called Taiwan, so he watched even seedpods on the wind and leaves on the water for early signs of trouble.

When his eyes were not on the sea and air, they were on his charge, which he fattened with island delicacies including red, blue, purple, and yellow flowers that resembled those of the Galápagos cactus the sailors had called prickly pear. Increasing in weight and size, the tortoise had grown tame as a dog, letting its keeper scratch the soft skin under its neck and wipe the morning fog from its face with his fingers. Shamans have always been interested in animals and their spirits—it was said that the great Yu had been capable of shape-shifting into a bear—so while it would be too much to say that Wang Yi loved the tortoise, he certainly felt affection for it.

The young navigator's primary shipboard duty was to point the way, but, like his oracular master, he was also responsible for reading omens, healing the crew, inviting spirits, making rain, and interpreting the messages of the mind at night. Early one morning, as the ship sailed past what would one day be Fujian Province and down nearly to Fuzhou, the captain asked Wang Yi to explain a dream.

"Recount it for me," the young shaman ordered.

The captain sighed heavily. "I have been on the island of turtles again despite the fact that the memory of the place shames me. I saw a group of those black diving lizards working together to carry my mother to the ocean. She held out her hand, but when I tried to reach her, I couldn't."

Until that moment, Wang Yi had not been sure the captain's eyes were capable of producing tears.

"You miss her," he said.

"I'll never see her again, will I?"

Wang Yi knew that the woman had died but did not wish to confirm it.

"I'm sorry," he said. "I sense a storm coming and must prepare."

5

Small rocks shift, shrinking the space around me and compressing the ancient, leathery bellows of my soft parts until breathing becomes a chore. I twitch my tail and wriggle a bit to open some space around me. My love's fingerbones crunch beneath my shell. Once those fingers worked ink brushes over scrolls, expertly guided sharp blades against evil, and caressed my flesh like butterflies. The spade music above me slows—presumably due to tired arms—but soon resumes, removing overlying rocks and soil. Soon, I feel light enough to float straight up toward the spring moon.

At length, the moon retires. I feel her retreat because we have been friends ever since she washed me clean on my island, a bond only strengthened when my sage gave me her name. Her flaming husband follows her, and his heat stirs the creatures of the dirt—the crusty crawlers and the wiggling worms that have tortured me by exploring my inner channels. Long past caring, I have accepted their expeditions as much-longed-for company. Now, as the soil churns, I sense their elation as they zip between the particles of sand and mica, gorging on rotting plant matter. Through the last few feet of ground, I can sense the warmth of the sun as strongly as if I were in an oven. The feeling is overpoweringly sensual.

I feel a swoon coming on.

The rhythmic ticking of the digging continues. The anticipation of being unearthed is almost too much to bear. The will to stay alive is testament neither to my invulnerable anatomy nor to the magic still brewing inside me but instead to the power of my love for my sage. I wonder what this new world will look like after all these years. Will his teachings have so enlightened the world that even the fantastic sun seems dim by comparison? Will shelled creatures like me have risen to the fore? Will the house of Zhou still rule the land? A thousand questions come to me, queries I now have reason to hope will be answered.

I expect the digger is a grave robber. Whoever he is, he must think me a rock, for rather than seeking the outline of my shell, he hacks at my shell as if it were stone. I fear for the inscriptions that have become so integral a part of me, executed by the loving hands of my lord. I can almost feel the blade violating their delicate lines and curves. The digger ceases, pauses, and resumes with a vengeance, excited and breathing hard.

He scrapes the hard-packed dirt off my shell in chunks, then lowers himself into the hole with me. I feel his knees touch my shell and the warm, human contact; the soft, yielding skin brings back my love's touch so strongly my dry eyes ache to cry. Unearthed, the sun is on my skin. I can feel it, but I cannot see it. After so long in the darkness, I have fallen blind.

6

The typhoon was beyond any mortal ability to dissuade — a child of a spinning Earth and a roiling sea. The center was far to the south, but the storm's arms reached a great distance, creating a swell that pushed the Zhou ship closer to the treacherous outcroppings east of the tiny islands by Dongtou, near what would much later come to be called the Chinese city of Wenzhou.

Wang Yi watched the rhythm of the enormous waves and reached into the water to gauge the temperature before licking his fingers to read the concentration of salt. Sensing the storm and a need for safe harbor, he had the men stow the sail and row at a fearsome pace while the captain, still brooding over his dream, merely watched as the ship plunged down the face of the massive troughs and climbed up again.

Through all this, the tortoise stayed calm. It knew little of the danger of storms, because they do not occur in the Galápagos Islands, and did not understand the panic of the crew. Its primitive reptilian ears were not built for balance, so it felt less seasick than the men did and did not sense the shuddering of the hull and the groaning of the mast. Insofar as it could cogitate on contingencies, it figured that if the ship sank, it could always swim.

A funnel of spiraling air to the east wobbled, twisted, and cohered into an orange dragon of a waterspout that sucked up a shark from the surf — black-eyed and thrashing with a rockfish in its mouth — then veered over land to rip birds from their nests and draw aloft scrub trees, their roots dangling like beards dripping dirt. The ship achieved an unnatural velocity, drawing so much water that even dolphins gave way. It raced around the horn of Yuhuan and through labyrinthine coastal passages up to Ningbo, finally finding calm water off Hangzhou Bay. The men's spirits lifted as they lay down their oars and let the sail carry them north, drinking island brew, belching and laughing. Ding Lok issued a flowery speech about the warm reception they would receive once they were home with their loot.

"My master's power kept us ahead of that storm," Wang Yi told the turtle as he rested in his bunk. "He can communicate with animals too, and he knows the heart of a thing merely by asking. You are healthy and growing quickly. He will be so happy with you."

Satisfied by the prospect, the shaman fell asleep and stayed that way as the ship passed the future site of the frothing city of Qingdao and rounded the Shandong Peninsula. Finally awakening to the sound of an anchor dropping into a cove off the Yellow Sea, he donned a bearskin cloak and climbed to the deck, where icicles dripped from the mast, and the captain, wrapped in the pelt of a tiger, issued orders to the first mate, wearing fox, and sailors clad in sheepskin. Left alone and torpid on the frigid wooden bunk, the tortoise longed deeply for a soak in volcanically heated Galápagos mud and for the comforting company of its brutally-butchered clan.

7

He jabs at my head with his shovel, and I draw back. Startled by my movement, he leaps away, leaving me with only a salty shower of his sweat. Drops sizzle on my hot shell and trickle into my mouth making me suddenly achingly thirsty.

"What kind of monster lives in a tomb?" he cries.

His rough and flat-toned speech tell me that people have moved away from nature and no longer tap into its natural rhythm and beauty when they speak. The word music of the Zhou is gone, replaced by a poor facsimile in which rising and falling tones stand in for a depleted vocabulary. The underlying intelligence of the old speech — its foundational insight into and appreciation of the natural world — has been supplanted by a pervasive thread of agenda and enterprise. This is a language of getting things done rather than savoring the doing, a language of entitlement rather than gratitude. In this new tongue, it is difficult even to express how thirsty I am.

"No monster at all, but a turtle. Ha. It's no surprise you're thirsty. You look like you've been down here forever."

I am as shocked by his pronouncement as he is by the fact that I am alive. I struggle to comprehend the notion that he can hear what I'm thinking. Despite the thousands of years I have lived, countless miles I have traveled, and the hordes of pilgrims, monks, penitents, and disciples I have met, only two men could hear my thoughts as their own, and both are long gone.

"Open that crusty beak of yours, and I'll pour in some water."

I do my best to comply, but over the eons, worm slime sticky as hoof-glue has sealed my beak. While the man works it open with the tip of his spade, a butterfly alights on my nose, startling me with the wind from its wings and the play of its tiny legs.

"I'm worried this shovel is going to crack you, so I'm going to use my fingers. Just promise you won't bite me."

I promise.

He steps back as if he's seen a snake. "Did you just talk to me? Of course.

"And I heard you. In my head, at least."

Yes. Unexpected for us both.

After some poking and prodding, his fingertips get in. I patrol them with my tongue.

"That's disgusting. Don't do that," he says.

I stop, but reluctantly. His flesh has the taste of life.

I hear him produce a something from what I take to be a satchel and feel him angle it into my mouth. Drop by agonizing drop, the water flows from my nose to my toes, turning the prune of me to a plum. My tail fills as do my shrunken, shriveled eyes, the brittle tympani of my ears, my bones, and my soul.

"That was fast. Here's another bottle. Take it slow."

Are you a grave robber?

He pulls the bottle away. I am still blind to the world but I feel his irritation. "This mountain is a tourist site."

I ask because you were digging up a grave.

"There was a huge rainstorm and a piece of the cliff fell away. I saw a stele sticking out of the mud. I couldn't read the characters, but I know someone famous is buried about a hundred yards away."

"*So you dug.*"

"Digging into things is my specialty."

Images accompany this declaration. One is some sort of flat glowing screen with shifting symbols. It seems ominous and magical to me as if, perhaps, it is a portal to a world beyond my comprehension. I wonder if this means that this digger, too, is a shaman but of this strange and modern era. Another is of a giant metal bird that roars steadily, flies without beating its wings, and carries those it has eaten inside, where they sit in quiet, orderly fashion. The last is of huge bugs that carry people quickly over land on soft, spinning legs.

"My name is Athens, he says. "Athens Li."

Li is a lovely name. Athens hurts the ears.

"Thanks very much."

Certainly. Do you hail from Qin?

"From China? Only on my father's side. My mother is Greek but raised in America. Now tell me, what are you doing buried in this hole?"

A long story.

"I will try and figure that out. My guess is it's been eons."

My bowels loosen at the thought, releasing a painful, putrefying mix of rotted fruits and leaves and the chitin of all the insects that have lived and died within me.

"That's just wrong," Athens clucks, his hands flying to his nose.

Please excuse me. There are circumstances. And I'm hungry.

"So let's get you some food. What do you eat?"

I surprise myself by telling him I crave cactus.

"No cactus here. But I have an apple."

He puts it under my nose. The aroma is the world to me. It goes on and on, note after note, like a show of girls dancing for an old king.

"Go ahead and try it," he says.

I do. One bite and I'm back in Long Ears' garden, the very place where the change began.

8

War messages for the Zhou Federation were commonly relayed over vast distances by the thick black smoke of wolf dung fires. The day the ship carrying the tortoise drew near, one such fire was visible rising from Jie Shi Mountain, whose peak at the western mouth of the Bohai Sea—near what is now Beijing—still bears a temple to Liang Liang, goddess of the ocean. Having been long without news from home, the incoming sailors construed the smoke as a sign of welcome as the shoreline came into focus.

To the north lay Shanhaiguan, the Ocean Gate. Dead ahead was Golden Beach, an expanse of clean sand as long, if not as warmly inviting, as any the crew had seen in the tropics. The aroma of cooking filled the air with mouth-watering smells. Villagers banged drums in welcome. Anchoring close in, the captain supervised the off-loading of the cargo. Some of the men paddled around the familiar water while others went in search of loved ones. Wang Yi took his clothing and his talismans and stepped off the ship, the tortoise tucked under his arm.

"I'll see you at the baths," Ding Lok called to him. "I have to pay my respects to the local headman, and I want you to guide me."

The shaman waved in agreement even though he had no intention of waiting. As soon as the captain was out of sight, he made straight for the marshy Yellow River at the edge of town.

He found a fat man sleeping in a shallow-bottom pole boat and nudged him awake with his foot.

"I need you to pilot me to the river."

The man scrambled to his feet but, looking Wang Yi up and down, saw only a scraggly sailor.

"In a rush, are you?"

"Very much of one, yes. Could we leave at once, please?"

"You don't look like you have money."

Wang Yi flashed a coin. "I am just in from across the world."

His compensation assured, the boatman pushed off. After an hour of watching just in case Ding Lok decided to pursue him, Wang Yi fell asleep. When he did, the tortoise set about exploring the boat. Discovering the boatman's black and pungent toenail, it took an experimental bite. The result was a reflexive kick that sent it sailing into the marsh.

Galápagos island mud is boiled clean by volcanoes, and tortoises love its soothing properties. The tortoise noticed that this marsh mud—ripe with insect eggs, trickled-down minerals from the high moraine, salty marine seepage, and the exoskeletons of marine animals—was another thing altogether. Splashing, it attracted the attention of a circling marsh eagle. The bird dove with a high-pitched scream. The cry woke Wang Yi, who jumped into the water, fended off the bird with an oar, and shoved the tortoise back inside his cloak.

"Make a wake," he told the boatman. "I have come far but still have far to go."

The Yellow River, with its frequently shifting course and tendency to flood without warning, has always been China's sorrow. Wang Yi had to contend with choppy water, crosswinds, deep channels, and no less than three portages through stinking muck before transferring to another boat. Alert for eagles, the tortoise put its front claws up on the gunwale and watched the parade of oak, birch, elm, ash, linden, and maple trees along the convoluted waterway.

"What a cute little girl," the new pilot observed.

"What makes you say it's a girl?"

"You can tell by her shell's flat bottom."

"Someday she will be larger than this coracle."

The pilot laughed. "Turtles that big are only in legends."

"She's a legendary gift for my master, the wizard of Luoyang."

"You don't mean Long Ears?"

"None other."

"You're lucky," the boatman sighed. "I've always wanted a teacher. If someone could tell me which mistakes to avoid, I could soar through life like a crane instead of crawling like a snail."

After three days, the travelers transferred to a barge pulled upstream by oxen. Castles of sand, built by the tide, rose and fell as the tortoise snuck bites of fried, spiced insects and sampled green, red, and yellow apples brought aboard by local passengers. She discovered pears and persimmons too, along with the tart taste of kumquats and the glorious sweetness of Clementines.

"Grow as big and strong as you can during these warm months," Wang Yi advised on the morning of their arrival at the capital city. "Summer here can be hotter than you know, and winter is colder than you can imagine."

He gave her a big pink bloom to chew. She gnawed her way into its pollen tube, inhaling the magical scent all the way to the ovule. With fragrant dust on her beak, she felt not a care in the world.

"You'll have a life like a peony now," Wang Yi told her. "It's the flower of Luoyang, and you shall be, too."

9

My eyes have finally begun to process light, rendering the world with increasing clarity. Even though it is now late afternoon, there is no color that does not shine for me, no edge that does not glow, no shape that fails to evoke a remembrance, no shadow that does not pierce me to the quick. It is a revelation to me that a pulsing fabric of energy pervades absolutely everything. The power of that perception bolsters my ability to interpret the details I see, the first of which is the face of Athens Li.

His brow evokes an imperial guardsman I knew, his cheekbones a woman of the court. The bridge of his nose reminds me of a child who brought me water in the last, old days of the mountain hamlet, and his lips, pleasingly plump, favor that fat old general Sun.

Yet it is Athens' eyes that slice me; they bring back strongly the eyes of Long Ears, that long-dead sage who lives on in my heart. Truly, they are impossibly the same pair of peepers, a gentle, almost rheumy softness surrounding centers of solid ice. If my love were any less, I might distrust such an ancient memory, but as it is, I know those eyes even without the glorious earlobes that once framed them, even when they are filled with more seeking and yearning than wisdom. I am disoriented, distrustful of the world my senses bring me, and unsure of which way is up.

Tell me again who you are?

"I am, at this moment, passing my days as a monk."

I am still unbalanced by the fact of his voice in my head and mine in his.

Yet you say you're in exile?

"I ran. I'm here. I'm not running now."

But you're hiding.

"At least I'm not in a hole. It's going to be dark soon. It's time to get you out of here."

Opposing forces threaten to pull me apart. I am simultaneously desperate to explore this world and terrified of leaving the dust of a love that has sustained me all these years.

Where will we go? What will we do?

Athens looks me over carefully. "You've been underground a long time."

I have.

"Well, you're back from the dead now. Let's get you tanked up and cleaned up and free. We'll keep going until this dream is over. Sound like a plan?"

What dream do you mean?

"This one. If I'm hearing a turtle's voice in my head, I'm obviously dreaming."

I consider his proposition. My mind has been playing tricks on me for centuries. Could this unearthing be one more?

But I hear you as well.

"I find that rationally symmetrical. How else could we have a conversation?"

If your dreams are rational, you're missing the point of dreaming.

"You're confusing rational with feasible. I've eaten square bananas in dreams, put my thumbprint on the moon in dreams, and now I've had a conversation with a resurrected, giant turtle. Dream or no, there's no point in you staying in your hole, so let's get you out and see what happens."

I find the causal, forward drive of his thoughts exhausting. He seems to be taking in the world in giant steps with angry bees behind him. Perhaps it is his brutal butchery of the Zhou language that keeps him constantly thinking of cause and effect and perpetually pressing forward.

Before I climb, I'll need more water.

He gives me some. Surprisingly quickly, my tail recovers its curves, and the soft hollows around my limbs—long covered only by gossamer skin bearing the imprints of stones—begin to fill. Still, it will be a while before I am once again as plump as in the rich days of attendants and kings, floors of fruit, and gardens of edible flowers.

"Ready now?"

Yes.

He circumnavigates the pit, developing an extraction strategy. Out of touch with his body, he moves as if he spends all his time in one position and is lost being out of it. He seems an old, young man. He's the opposite of me in this: ancient yet suddenly young and awake to the possibility that my story might end up breathing in air, warmth and light rather than suffocating in cold darkness. I smell his vaguely familiear sweat as he constructs a ramp of packed earth and notice that behind it there is a tapestry of scents far richer than the dank soil in which I have been forever confined. I inhale so deeply my lungs push against my shell and ache.

"Come on out now," he says.

I try. Nothing happens. My limbs are thin as cricket legs and make about as much power. He urges me on.

"The sun is going to set soon. The longer this takes, the more likely you'll be in there until tomorrow. If I wake up and the dream ends, you'll never see the world outside."

I remain unconvinced that this is his dream, or even a dream at all, but I try harder to relieve my frozen joints and revive my moribund muscles.

"You can do it," he says. "The journey of a thousand miles begins with one step."

I've heard that one before, and it makes me smile inside. I lift my head.

"There you go. That's the way."

Assessing the incline, I come up on my columnar limbs, briefly feeling as magnificent and strong as any conquering hero. A moment later I wobble and collapse, plunging my beak into the dirt once more. Athens gently wipes my face and helps me up. Again and again I rise and again and again I fall. At last, as a result of a series of modest steps, I crest the edge of the grave and am rewarded with the murk of twilight.

"Too dark to climb down the mountain," says Athens, stretching out beside me in the dirty grass. "Now we get to see what happens when I dream about being asleep."

10

Wang Yi had gotten into the habit of talking to the turtle as if she could understand him. "Feel the anger and smell the wine," he told her as they entered the city's southern gate. "I don't know how it is with turtles, but having children is the most important thing for any man. Since the King still has no heir, the people don't respect him and local strongmen scheme to make the dynasty their own. My master is the only one keeping things from breaking apart."

A horse-drawn chariot bearing a fresh, legless corpse, a warning to would-be thieves, rolled past as the pair headed to a market in the eastern corner of the city. Wang Yi purchased a robe decorated with crocodile dragons, then soaked his tired body in a sandalwood tub at the town baths. Only when he was clean did he seek entrance to the palace.

"One can never gain access the same way twice," he told the turtle. "Guards close and open gates at random to keep invaders and assassins guessing. Inside, there are hallways leading nowhere, doors with bricks behind them, and large, important rooms with tiny entrances. The whole place is about secrets and tricks."

When at last he found a way in, he identified himself to a palace guard and was escorted through breezeways and told to wait, surrounded by black swans, in a pavilion built over a pond.

He had no sooner sat down than a muster of peacocks burst into view, followed by maids-in-waiting and the queen's swaggering guards. A former princess, Queen Qin Jiang was neither willowy nor voluptuous, neither elegant nor sensual, neither merely graceful nor athletic, but a blend of all those qualities, a whole much more than her parts. Wang Yi dropped into a kowtow, and she caught sight of him.

"Ah. The apprentice returns. Ding Lok's smoke signals say he sent you with a turtle for Long Ears. I confess I'm surprised. I was expecting a mountain or a dream. May I see it?"

Wang Yi produced the animal slowly so as not to alarm the guards.

"You sailed across the world for that?" the queen laughed.

"She's special, Your Highness."

"I would hope so."

"She grows very large and will live a long time."

"Then we'll have years to enjoy her company. Take her to Long Ears now. I just passed him meditating under his favorite maple."

Wang Yi obeyed with a mixture of excitement and fear. At the sight of his apprentice, the court wizard struck a bronze, chevron-shaped bell that hung from a clasp on his robe.

"Welcome back, dear boy," he said after the piercing tone subsided. "Are you well?"

"It was a long trip, Master."

"I see you are too thin. We'll get some palace cooking into you."

"Thank you, Master."

"Shellfish and cow meat, but not too much. And fruit for what is left of your mouth sores. Your new beard shows that sailing with Ding Lok was a growing experience."

Wang Yi worked his mouth for a moment, trying to decide

what to say to his teacher. Only when prompted by a small smile of understanding encouragement did he venture to speak.

"Not everyone sees the world as we do, Master."

"Indeed they do not. Tell me more of what you mean."

"I seek to build bridges to all the forces of nature, to ensconce myself ever more deeply in the flow of Tao," Wang Yi said carefully.

"And?"

"And to avail myself of the motivation found in all the bumps and bruises I receive, to learn from my mistakes, to absorb the energy of others, including their hatred and scorn, and use it as fuel for my own elevation. Others remain tied only to material manifestations, to low thinking and base appetites."

"The world of men," Long Ears muttered. "What else have you learned, my boy?"

"That despite the fact that your body remained here at the palace, you were always with me, present in every wave and, especially, in every cloud."

"That says as much about you as it does about me."

"That I deserve your watchfulness?"

"You do," Long Ears smiled. "But surely you have learned more of yourself than just your just desserts."

"I've learned that I am the same far away as I am at home."

"Wherever we go, there we are," the sage nodded. "A wonderful lesson indeed."

"I also discovered that there are many different kinds of treasure."

The sage smiled. "Let me see her now."

Wang Yi pulled the tortoise from his robe and set her on the ground. Being a tortoise, she did not think, as many in the kingdom did, that the man before her must hang rocks from his ears to give him such lobes, nor that he looked too young to be wise. She did not find anything preternaturally wild in the thick, shining luxury of his black beard, nor did she judge his cloak to be too plain for a man everyone feared; in that first moment, she merely noticed that he smelled like the forest.

"Ding Lok slaughtered her family, and she bit him on the nose. Then she stopped eating for many days. There is stubbornness in her and a sense of justice too."

"The night sky is in her eyes," Long Ears murmured, bending low for a look.

"She has *ling xing*," Wang Yi said, referring to the tortoise's deeply spiritual nature.

"You are well to see that."

"She's only a baby, but she will be half as wide as a water buffalo someday."

"Good. That means she is as she appeared in my vision."

"Your vision? You mean you saw her?"

"I did."

"And sent me across the world to retrieve her?"

"Yes."

"May I ask why?"

Long Ears considered his answer for a time. "You know that I have seen and done much with beasts of Earth and sky."

"Yes, Master."

"You know, for example, that I have heard the cries of leaves as they fell."

"Yes."

"And watched the joyous dance of snowflakes, the tearful happiness of a mother squirrel delivering her young, the sneaky triumph of the hunting mantis at prey, and the intimate intertwining of mating cranes?"

"So you have told me."

The wizard nodded. "Too, I have revealed to wolves locked

in combat that they were father and son, and heightened the skills of a catfish so he could safely find his way from a shrinking pond."

"I was with you at those times, Master."

"And, yet, for all that I have seen and done, I have never come across yin as pure and strong as I sense in this tortoise."

"Pure yin," Wang Yi repeated.

"That is why I sent you to retrieve her. Every crag and crevice in and on the earth, every rivulet and eddy and stream, every breath of breeze, and every living being from a worm to a flower, a camel to a cod, is a contrivance of naturally balanced, opposing energies and matter. There is nothing that is purely one thing or the other in the world anymore, or, at least, there are very few such examples. Such objects, and, even more, such beings are powerful because of the effects and possibilities inherent in such unalloyed and concentrated energy. She is truly the treasure I sought, and more."

"What will you do with her?"

"Can you guess?"

Wang Yi had thought about the question for months. He had an idea, but he dared not speak it. Looking embarrassed, he shook his head.

"Go ahead," Long Ears urged.

"Might you be planning a feat of magic only our ancestor, the great Shaman Yu, has attempted?"

"I might," the wizard smiled.

"Really, great lord? You are going to attempt *Dian Hua*?"

The sage nodded. "Total transformation. As the purest yin energy to be found on land or sea, she was born to be a woman."

11

Out of my hole and on the edge of the world, I contemplate the sleep of Athens Li. Twitching like a dreaming dog, he lies curled on a bed of branches with a strange strapped bag for a pillow. There were times when my sage's dreams were known to me and times when I could read the dreams of other men, too, but the sleeping mind of my rescuer is opaque.

Far below me I see pale stars, trapped and blinking on the valley floor. Overhead, I watch bats in predatory pursuit of moths, enjoying the gliding, the swooping, and the final, extinguishing snap of jaws. In the the same fashion that Athens speculates that everything must be a dream, I wonder if I have not in fact died.

In anticipation of morning, a life's worth of memories play in my head. At times, I almost believe I can smell volcanic mud and count the creases at the edge of my true love's eyes. At last, a tiny change in temperature says the sun is scouting the horizon for a door. I turn to face it and wait patiently. Soon I feel the marvelous sensation of its rays on my scales. They wash over Athens' face. He awakens, climbs slowly to his feet, and looks around as if seeing me, and the mountain, for the first time.

"You're still here," he says.

So are you.

"Oh boy. What's going on here?"

I talk to him as if to a child.

There was a storm. The earth broke around me. You dug me out with your shovel.

He points down into the pit. "I know all that. Now tell me, whose bones are those?"

Before they turned to dust, they gave structure to a sage named Long Ears. He was a living legend. The most powerful spirit of his time, the most amazing mind, the most astounding heart. A kingly wizard whose only crown was twigs, whose most compelling speeches were conducted in silence, whose only god was nature, and whose truest love was me.

"All legendary wise men in this crazy country have long ears. When did this legendary sage of yours live? What dynasty? What year?"

He served the kings of the Eastern Zhou federation.

Athens thinks for a minute. "Eastern Zhou. Hmm. First came the putative Xia, then the Shang, then the Western Zhou...."

After that. After the capital was moved in from the provinces.

He counts things off on his fingers. "So you're saying this guy lived three thousand years ago."

Five hundred less than that.

Athens nods slowly. "And you know that how?"

I know it because I was there and because I've been counting the phases of the moon since I was buried atop him.

He swallows, then grows pale. "I can't be dreaming this. In a dream, the mind works with what it knows. I've never read anything about giant turtles, never seen a movie. You're the first I've known."

I was frozen. You thawed me.

He pops down into the pit and scoops dirt with his hands. What is left of my love trickles through his fingers. "You say he was famous, but there's nothing here."

I'm here.

34

"I mean no swords, no gold, no statues."

He was the simplest of complex men.

"And how, exactly, did you end up in his grave?"

A family issue.

He nods. "I know all about those. So, if I want to understand this guy, this sage of yours, in a sentence, how would I do that? What would his message be?"

As he asks this, his thoughts tell me that this new world is about getting answers fast rather than finding them out in due course. It's a new brand of self-indulgence and greed, and it looks as if I'll have to get used to it.

Follow Tao.

He pinches his nose, then wipes his face, his hands leaving a trail of chalky dirt. "So he was a Taoist sage?"

The original.

"I'm hiding at a monastery down the hill. The monks are devoted to the sage Lao Tzu, the founder of Taoist philosophy. Do you recognize the name?"

I answer carefully.

It means the old boy or the old master.

"Every time my father tells me I'm wasting my life, he quotes Lao Tzu about the way of the superior man. When I had to run, he hid me here, no doubt hoping I'd become one. All that's happened is that I've grown to hate rice porridge."

Ah. Jook. I would love some right now.

"I think the grave where Lao Tzu is supposed to be buried is empty and that I've stumbled across the real one."

Interesting theory.

"The legend says he came to this mountain to teach, died, and was buried here."

"But you don't believe that?"

"I didn't used to. I used to think he was a fictional character

35

like Buddha or Moses or Jesus—a myth made up to gain followers. Now I don't know. Maybe all of them were real."

If I don't eat something soon, I'm going to faint.

"So, there are only two possibilities. One is that being stuck here has finally gotten to me, and I'm dreaming about the character everyone around me mentions day or night."

And the other?

"That I've found the lost grave of one of the most famous men in Chinese history and, with it, some kind of magical creature who knew him."

We'll see about the magic.

I think we should get down off this mountain."

Yes. We have a long way to go.

"We do?"

Yes. Now that you've saved me, you're going to have to take me all the way home.

12

No living being can clearly perceive the limits of its reality, but as the wizard worked his magic, the little tortoise's stage deepened. Her hearing — long too indistinct to register anything softer than a wave thundering ashore — suddenly grew keen enough to catch the click of insect wings in the garden. Her vision sharpened until she could make out the veins in the leaves of trees across the courtyard and the glint of the sun reflecting off a distant sentry's sword. She felt each clump of earth and stone beneath her feet with new acuity and took in the thousand aromas of the palace — the kitchens, the flowers, the women and their men — as a powerful, fragrant wind.

Her thoughts reverberated as never before. Confused, she swiveled her head back and forth, looking for the source of so many complex concepts. Most of all, however, she struggled with her ability to communicate, but slowly grew more competent with each idea she tried. It took her a while. Following false fits and starts at consonants and vowels, she came to understand first the very notion of words and then the challenge of stringing them together in that endless literary quest, the correct and coherent sentence.

Eyeganearu.

"I can hear you too," Long Ears smiled.

Observing, Wang Yi heard a hissing sound from the turtle's

mouth but could discern no sense.

Howizdispozibel?

"All is possible inside Tao."

Budjudiditdume.

"You did it yourself. I merely helped."

Wuddisdisdao?

Long Ears laughed out loud at the question. "What was obvious to you when you were a turtle will require some work for you to understand when you become a woman."

Wudizwoman?

"You'll find out soon enough.

Eyewandononow.

"Impatience won't speed the process."

Ievlozdmyberrings.

"Your bearings will come back to you. All you need is time."

The tortoise took a few tentative steps then stopped and sagged on buckling legs.

"Is she alright?" asked Wang Yi.

"Transforming takes energy. She needs to rest."

Wadizyurname?

"My family name is Li, and my given name is Dan. Some folks call me Long Ears, and you can see why. Your friend over there is Wang Yi."

Eyewandaname.

"You don't really need a name. When we name things, we separate them from the way of nature."

Eyestilwandaname

Wang Yi cleared his throat. "May I say something, Master?"

"Of course."

"You say she is the quintessence of all that is feminine."

"Indeed, some day she will be the queen mother of the world."

"Then why not simply call her Yin?"

"You've grown wisdom along with those hairs on your chin, Wang Yi. Yin it is."

Yin rose on her legs until she was as tall as a footstool.

Ifeeldadandreeming.

"Certainly this is a dream," said the wizard, "and yet we are wide awake."

Master and apprentice watched Yin for a period of time, long enough for shadows to appear in the garden and then to deepen. They watched her as the temperature dropped a bit and as daytime fliers in the trees around them were replaced by the winged scavengers and predators of the night. Wang Yi wondered how much of what they had endured together she remembered, and he tried to divine. He couldn't really tell, although he did notice several convulsive fits followed by periods of restful quiescence and a peaceful expression in her eyes. At length, she stumbled to Long Ears' feet and took in his eyes with hers.

Ifeyeamduhmoonyuarduhsun.

The master bent down and kissed the top of Yin's head. When he did, a clear, bright spark crackled between them.

"What happened? What was that? Did it work? What did she say?" Wang Yi demanded, losing his customary obsequiousness to the excitement of such a magical event.

"She said that if she is the moon, I am the sun."

Overwhelmed by all the miles he had traveled and dangers he had braved in order to bring about this union, Wang Yi burst into tears.

13

Athens camouflages me with branches and heads off to look for sustenance. Even here at the top of the mountain the air is so foul it's hard to discern distant detail. What I can see with my slowly-returning vision is that all up and down the slopes, the graceful trees that once swayed like sleeve dancers have been replaced by weeds and shrubs. I wonder if this is a harbinger of what I'll see down in the valley. The loss of everything familiar leaves me bereft and sad.

Athens returns an hour later and shrugs his satchel off his back. "This is called a knapsack," he says. "I figure I should start familiarizing you with common items of this new world."

It smells like heaven.

He reaches into the satchel and with a flourish produces the fragrant items.

"These dumplings were made in the monastery kitchen for some visiting dignitaries who think they are living dangerously when they eat monk food. Of course, in the city they drive their Maseratis a hundred miles an hour in traffic, visit five hookers a week, and use enough drugs to put down a racehorse."

I want to ask him about the word Maserati, The word hooker, too. But when I close my eyes and put my nose to what he calls dumplings, I become entranced by their arom and lose my train of thought.

"The chef was a celebrity in Shanghai before his business partner stole his fortune. Now, in the wake of a nervous breakdown, his life is a meditation with a cleaver."

I recognize the flavor.

Duck.

He nods.

"Very good for warming the insides. Smoked and cooked with garlic, scallions, ginger, and five-spice too, which is mostly star anise. There are mushrooms in there as well. The monks say they are the medicine of the forest."

I have long eschewed eating flesh, but starvation has changed my sensibilities. I take a tentative nibble. By the second bite, I detect eleven layers of taste.

Pure heaven.

"Here's some oolong tea for energy."

The only thing that can tear my attention away from dumplings is the promise of tea. Athens pours it from a tall container into a bowl. I plunge my head in, drink, and feel the steaming river course through me.

"You can't protrude your tongue, can you?"

Not a thing turtles can do.

"Here. I brought these garden shears for your toenails. You'll keep teetering until I trim them down."

My nails have indeed run amok over the centuries, becoming spirals thick at the base and tightly wound at the tip. Athens angles his blades and makes a tentative snip. A chunk of nail drops away.

"I had a poodle when I was a kid," he says conversationally.

A what?

"A fancy dog. I used to cut its nails and make them bleed by going too close. Raised hell with my mother because it would leave a red trail on the white couch and the white living room rug. Eventually, I learned to do it right. Yours are tougher and so black I can't see the quick, that's the place where the blood vessels end, but I'm doing my best. Please let me know if it hurts."

It doesn't. I keep eating as he works. The duck makes my muscles swell, my ligaments tighten, my tendons thicken, and my bones grow hard. It would be easy to see this process simply as the reversal of starvation, but there is more going on. A magical element is at play, the rapid resumption of a process long halted.

You mentioned you are on the run and in hiding. Did you start running far from here?

"Oh yes."

Usually, when one has to run far away it is because one has offended a king.

"Not a king, exactly."

But somebody powerful.

"You could say so."

So royal guards are after you.

He smiles. "Something like that."

That means you're a criminal.

He stops snipping and puffs a long piece of air. "Judgments. Terms. Names. Everything depends upon perspective, doesn't it? Speaking of names, it says online that giants like you come either from the Seychelles or Galápagos archipelagos. Which is it?"

I slurp more tea.

Online?

"I'll explain later."

I left when I was little and nobody thought in names.

"But you remember what the place looked like, yes?"

Vividly. And I miss it every day.

"Were there mountains there?"

Great black ones.

42

"Galápagos, then. The Seychelles are flat. How in the world did you get all the way to China?"

On a small ship full of cruel and stinking men.

"So early in history? There's no record of such a journey, and the Chinese are famous for their record-keeping."

Oh, there's a record alright.

"Well, I haven't seen it.

That may be. Now I have a question for you. What is that terrible smell?

"A chemical plant in the valley. Another one for weapons and tanks. For a long time nobody cared about the air. Everything was unregulated and corruption was the rule. Things finally got so bad they had to addressed, so all that is changing now."

The dumplings bring me back from the brink of death, but they are so rich they make my guts roil. I break wind violently, but Athens doesn't react.

"Returning you to the Galápagos is a preposterous proposition," he says. "Money, laws, logistics, everything is against it. Luckily, I specialize in things that can't be done."

Since we will be traveling together, you should know I'm called Yin.

14

The divining ceremony took place in the great hall of the palace, which was created from wood, forced earth, and tile. In later dynasties, special orange lanterns—fetish objects among some members of China's ruling class—would light the space, but in those days, with a waning 800-year dynasty in contention, torches illuminated every corner so as to leave no shadow in which an assassin might hide. Queen Qin Jiang and her king sat on adjoining platforms. Across the aisle was a row of beautiful concubines. Yin hid behind the curtain made by their gowns.

A eunuch, slight in stature, began the ceremony with a sandal licker's ode to his monarch: "How fortunate we are to have so valorous a ruler as King Ling. Heaven has smiled on us by issuing our dynasty a mandate and filling that august requirement with such a singular family lineage, replete not only with wise and just kings but with the beneficent hero who now sits on the throne today. His steadfast protection, brilliant military mind, and piercing poetry make him the most gifted ruler of this or any other land…"

"Yes, yes. Let's get on with the show," the king interrupted.

On cue, the entire chamber came alive with movement and sound. A troupe of dancing girls began whirling in diaphanous silk, their gyrations birthing tiny worlds of promise within their gowns. Court musicians played lutes and rang bells while soldiers struck gongs and drums. Yin beheld the show with wonder. She had no idea that the music was intended to summon the ghosts of important ancestors and that the dances represented the five elements: earth, water, metal, fire, and wood. Nor did she know that Long Ears, as master of all royal ceremonies, was the supreme scholar, a living repository of a tradition—recorded in countless dialects and languages—upon which he drew to predict, prognosticate, prefigure, auspicate, and augur all future events that were to occur in the kingdom and surrounding lands.

King Ling's contribution to the proceedings was somewhat less, as indeed was his contribution to the machinations of rule. He had dark circles under his eyes because his kidneys craved water and his liver was assailed by large quantities of alcohol. He had a soft belly because, despite all the nonsense about him being a great warrior, he was, in fact, a worrywart and a homebody whose idea of exercise was to allow his concubines to pleasure him as he gorged himself on bird nest soup and marinated meats. As the dance reached its crescendo, he raised his bronze scepter in approval.

"Where is the oracle of the court?" he bellowed.

Long Ears' red robe shimmered, and his black beard glistened as he proceeded across the hall. When he reached the royals, he dropped to kowtow. The drumbeats fell away.

"Tell us what you see in the world today, my wizard," the King commanded. "Please tell of my subjects, my land, living nature, and the sky. How may we prosper and prevail against our enemies? Do you have the news for which I have so patiently been waiting?"

The King was, of course, referring to an heir and the fact that despite all his appetites and indulgences—and the legions of virgins who had suffered his favor—there had been no child. Ministers prattled on about the sorry barren wombs of the queen and courtesans; the royal physician blamed unpredictable energy meridians, the state of the moon, and the need for more shellfish in the king's diet. The sage saw things differently and had waited for just the right time to help the monarch with his problem.

"Indeed I do, Sire."

King Ling beckoned his advisor to approach. The sage's court rank, *zhu xia li*, referred to the fact that he alone could get closer to the King than bodyguards, fully as close as could a physician or a concubine.

The monarch leaned forward, no easy feat given the fat about his middle. The sage leaned in, too. Leaning was easier for him because his body was soft and supple as a baby's. Except for the encumbrance of their bulky robes, they might have been crows conspiring over carrion.

"You have something confidential to share?" the King whispered.

"The ship you sent across the world has returned."

"From the rumors I hear, that strongman in Yan has had first crack at the treasures of the voyage."

"The best treasure is already here, Sire, and she is a giant."

"I am ready for a woman of any size so long as she has a fruitful womb."

"Your Majesty may recall the turtle who introduced us to the way of the elements and nature by bringing the Lo Writings of Fu Xi to ancestor Yu?"

"I know the story, yes."

"Our giant is such a one as Yu's, Your Highness, and so powerful a fertilizing agent that her mere presence in the palace has already given you an heir."

"Really? She has that power?"

"She does, My King."

"I thought that such creatures were pure fancy."

"She is pure, Your Highness, but no fancy at all."

The King nodded thoughtfully. "All right then. When shall I see this prince?"

"In nine cycles of the moon, Sire."

"And who is the mother? I know so many willing girls."

"The most frequent beneficiary of the techniques I taught you, My King."

"Ha ha! Queen Qin Jiang. Your exercises brought forth *her* hidden talents as well."

"It is my counsel that you name him Prince Shen, Sire."

"Shen? Why so?"

"The name will suit his nature."

"You foresee it?"

"I know it."

"You are sure? Names are important."

"Absolutely, Your Highness."

"Very well, then, Long Ears. Prince Shen he shall be."

"Excellent, Sire. May I tell the court?"

"You may."

Raising Yin high in tribute, Long Ears made the announcement. Instantly, the hall was filled with the snapping of fans and the stamping of feet. Eunuchs schemed, nobles changed allegiance, generals and captains anticipated new responsibilities, eyes were cast downward, ambitions were thwarted, and a few fists were tightened.

Yin waved her legs in confusion and protested though none but the wizard could hear her. *Wadeaminit. Eyedidnddoanyting.*

The queen smiled a pregnant woman's unique, satisfied smile. The king fantasized about sharing his love of food and girls with his son, secretly wondering at what age the boy could assume the reins of power so that his own responsibilities would be discharged, and he could turn full-time to the hedonistic life.

So it was that in a single evening, the tortoise of the Kingdom of Zhou became a legend.

15

We descend the mountain through the thicket rather than on the primary path, as Athens doesn't want people he calls tourists to see me. He applies this term to strangely clad men and women carrying glowing devices that enslave them in theaters of mind. Long ago, when children were similarly possessed—speaking to demons and dreaming of ghosts—their mothers brought them to Long Ears for curing. He was so effective in doing so with his physical and meditative practices that the king finally made him stop helping because it distracted the wizard from matters at court.

Tell me about your king.

"Where I come from, he has the title 'president.' He's controlled by what you would call rich noblemen."

Eunuchs.

Athens laughs. "They would resent the term, but you're not far off. China has its puppet masters, too. The current dynasty toppled a long line of kings by promising to reconstruct the country according to a utopian, German book in which everyone works together and shares everything. It was, in part, a lovely idea but ignored the manic violence and narcissism in human nature. In any case it was a legitimizing banner only, never actually tried. In the end, the rich just got richer and tens of millions starved. The newer generation of leaders has no interest in ideals; they're just brutal with greed."

I don't know what Germans are and, in general, find Athens' ideas confusing. Perhaps this is because the effort of climbing down the hill exhausts me.

"You'll walk more easily once I hose all that hard dirt off your shell," he says, sensing my fatigue.

I don't notice the dirt, but the soil underfoot is more slippery and less fragrant than I remember. The undergrowth becomes denser at lower elevations, and we are finally forced onto a well-worn trail. We walk along a low rock wall. Sensitive as I am to changes in temperature, I feel the heat stored in the stones and pause to press myself against it. Instantly, I am overcome by a memory of my mother's dark, heavy shell against me. I haven't thought of her in centuries. Like candles lighting a stove, I decide, events in this new world can spark long-extinguished memories from the old one.

We follow the wall to the back door of the monastery. I see an unnaturally smooth road. On it, in various colors and apparently sleeping near the back of the building, are some of the giant bugs that carry people around. I want to ask them how human proclivities may or may not have changed during the last two thousand years, but when I cozy up to their black, round legs their cold, unresponsive silence tells me they will not share with me what they know.

Athens gestures fiercely for me to come through the door. "Hurry. We don't want anyone to see you. If the abbot finds out about you and Lao Tzu, you'll never make it out of China."

The smell of garlic is overpowering, but the kitchen is clean, with a long metal preparation table in the center, a series of stoves against the wall, and pots and pans neatly hanging on hooks. The floor is earthenware tile, and the grout lines are full of oil and scents. Athens pushes piles of carrots and broccoli under my nose along with apples, persimmons, and pears. The world falls away as I feed in enormous bites. In time, I feel a certain pressure building.

"You can't go here," he says, pointing at my twitching tail. "Not through that door either. That's the dining hall."

I try to work my increasingly mobile features into an indignant look. It's easier than I expect.

"I got a whiff of you earlier. That was plenty. Now out you go."

While I do my business against a tree, Athens brings me a bucket of water. I dunk my whole head. Tiny bubbles caress me, and I feel a momentary relief from gravity as the water buoys me. I open my eyes and see a cascade of shiny flakes of dirt released from my pores. The pattern they in the soil reminds me of river bottoms I've seen and currents I was once taught to read for their secrets.

"I'm going to bring you to the temple of Dou Mu," Athens says. "It's a perfect hiding place. Nobody ever goes there. It's up some stairs. Do you think you can climb?"

If we go slowly. Who is this Dou Mu?

"She's the Taoist mother of the world."

If she so claims, she lies.

"Why do you say that?"

Because I am the Taoist mother of the world.

He holds his hand up in submission. "If you say so."

We round a bend in the path and encounter an old iron elm. I remember it somehow and stop to sniff it.

I used to stand beneath this tree in meditation with Long Ears, although it was not nearly so tall back then, nor so inclined.

"How can you remember a tree?" he asks. "And how could it be the same one from thousands of years ago?"

You were raised in a city, yes?

"New York."

Never heard of it. But if you had been raised in nature instead, you would know that every tree has its own unmistakable energy and scent. I know this tree, or at least its lineage. Voices rise on the path ahead. We move into the underbrush and hold our breath as a train of monks passes. Once again, the giant elm gives me shelter.

"The good news is that the monks stick to their routines," Athens whispers as we resume our climb.

At the temple entrance, the stairs are so steep and sharp I scrape my shell negotiating them. A clod of hard dirt falls off and clatters down like pottery. Athens stares at the exposed area.

"You're carved."

My shell is, yes.

"Lao Tzu's work?"

I prefer the name Long Ears.

"I've got to get the rest of that filthy mud off you."

I drink in the fragrance of a patch of jasmine at the top of the stairs. My wizard eschewed it as an intoxicant saying that it clouded the mind, but in the late years on the mountain, I would disappear for hours among those bewitching white flowers. I suddenly miss him so badly my legs nearly buckle.

"Just a few more steps. I'm going to put you in that garden shed over there while I concoct an escape plan."

The sound of laughing monks floats our way over the encircling wall.

It's good that they're happy following the teachings of my sage. He bore so many responsibilities but still found joy in everything.

Below us, the yellow lights of the monastery flicker on in the growing dusk. Ahead, an incense cauldron smolders in the temple courtyard. As the heat and smoke waft our way, I ask Athens to tell me of his crimes.

He crosses his legs and drops down next to me on the cool stone.

"While you were sleeping, a lot happened. For now, let me just say that in addition to growing the population and murdering nature, technology gave birth to worlds within worlds. These exist in the form of energy trapped in boxes and wires and cables and boards. Together they create something known as a Web that connects the whole human race through fingertips, ears, and eyes. The process is advancing now to create or tap into something even larger called the metaverse."

You are a master of these worlds, yes?

He shrugs. "The concept of mastery doesn't mean much anymore. There are so many options and titillations available, most people don't stay with anything long enough to achieve the skills you're asking about. It's true, though, that my abilities make certain people nervous."

What did you find so disappointing about this material world that you seek refuge in that flat, cold space?

"I'm not sure I know the answer to that, although it is much more than a flat space. It has depth and diversity, attractions and excitement, discourse and experience that sometimes even encourages and challenges. Still, it is a pale rendering of this world a place I'm far from finished exploring."

How so?

"Well, in my short life I've already topped my class in college, snowboarded, skied, hit balls high with a racket, motorcycle raced, and shot tack-size bullets out of an Olympic target rifle. Traveling as a kid with my parents, I've seen the Parthenon, the Coliseum, the falls at Victoria and Iguazu, the Buddhas of Bhutan, and the snows of Kilimanjaro. I've bought dinner for my favorite girl atop the Eiffel Tower and kite-surfed the swells off Ho'okipa Beach on Maui. I've published a few essays and been admitted to a top graduate school in computer science, although I'm sure now those doors are closed. I've...."

Who was the girlfriend?

He shrugs. "Long gone," he says. "It doesn't matter."

I received beautiful images while you were talking.

"Of the girl?"

The sights. Now please tell me of your crime.

Before he can answer, an old monk with a twig-broom appears in the temple doorway. I hide beneath the incense table as Athens relieves him of the broom and sends him, smiling, down the stairs toward the dining hall without so much as a backward glance.

We make our way to the garden shed. The interior is musty and full of cobwebs. The first moonlight peeks tentatively in through window glass so old it has run down in its frame. A little red spider watches from a high rafter. Athens gathers some old hay together.

"Your bed," he says.

The prospect of being left alone is suddenly unbearable. Panic rises in me. I taste a mixture of garlic and bile.

Don't leave me.

"Stay quiet and rest. I'll be back in the morning."

Wait. You still haven't told me what bad thing you did.

It's too late. He has already gone. The spider makes a leap, trailing silk, and lands on the tip of my nose.

I am grateful for the company.

16

The morning after the ceremony, the line of supplicants at Long Ear's door reached all the way to the banks of the Luoyang River. United by the desire for magic in their own lives and ranging in rank from courtiers to cooks, they bore tributes of stringy stalks, bitter leaves, fragrant flowers, moist fruits, rock-hard seeds, insects with wings, insects with stings, the pungent meat of naked mole rats, and the splintered teeth of forest beasts full of minerals to help the little turtle build her shell. To a one, they sought merely to be in the presence of the magical turtle and perhaps benefit from her special counsel.

"Be patient, and enjoy the food," Long Ears told Yin, where she sat under an eave on the south side of the house.

Eyemnodungry bud eyesmelsumding.

"What you smell is incense made of frankincense, jasmine flowers, tea leaves, pine needles, and the nest twigs of thief-birds."

Eyedondnodatbrd.

"Knowing bird types is not as important as knowing birdness."

Wadizbrdnes?

"Birdness means what it is to be a bird, to have feathers, to live in the air, lay an egg, eat a worm, watch for eagles, and preen your feathers."

Zis iz a terrbl kundry.

Long Ears shook his head. "No, these Central States are a marvelous place with good people. Because they are closer to nature than artisans, merchants, or scholars, farmers are held in the highest regard. Now it's time to enjoy the treats they bring."

So saying, he announced that Yin would take a bite of whatever appealed to her. First in line was a man presenting a head of kale so fresh it still glistened with dew. A woman with a freshwater oyster came next, followed by a thin farmer with a basket of purple eggplants. "They're not really eggs," he explained. "They grow in the ground. Traders brought the seeds from India. Raw, they're bitter; cooked, they're delicious."

Yin took a bite.

Gudfud.

A baker followed with a gooey batch of buns. "The dough is my secret recipe, and I marinated the beans all night for the filler," he said proudly.

Yin struggled to get bits of the sticky dough off her face.

Badfud.

A little girl presented Yin with a forest toad. "I thought you might need a friend," she said.

In one hop, the toad landed in the incense cauldron. Its skin hissed as it burned, and the little girl started to cry. Her mother took her away.

An obese man came next. He wheezed when he kowtowed, and his face turned red, but finally he managed to put a handful of berries in front of Yin. "My feet are so swollen I can hardly walk. Can you help me with your power?"

Eezdoofat.

"Yin suggests you adopt a stricter diet," Long Ears reported.

Next came a starving beggar, bent in half and supported by a gnarled stick not much thinner than he was.

YUN ROU

He iz ungry. Giv him de bunz.

A courtier followed, finely dressed and bearing fish. "Exquisitely spiced and from the palace pond," he announced. "Perhaps, in appreciation of my exceptional taste, she will promote me to duke?"

Eye don't like dis smel.

"She is not too fond of fish," Long Ears explained.

A royal consort unwound her shawl to reveal great beauty. "I bring flowers for the magic turtle," she said, carefully laying out a stunning array of colors and tastes. "I wonder if perhaps I too might not have the gift of a royal child."

If zhe wil stand in line behind egplands she wil do anyding. Zhe wil hav her child sumday.

"Yin grants your wish," Long Ears declared.

The young woman cried tears of joy and hurried away. In an orgy of gustatory pleasure, Yin munched the flowers, churning a phrase over and over as she chewed.

Ze zentral zdates are nod my hom. Ze zentral zdates are nod my hom.

17

Athens brings me breakfast in a slop-bucket while shadows are still long and the monks are exercising loudly in a spot down the hill. While I eat, he cleans me with a hose. I'm increasingly aware of strange feelings in my shell, a new pliability that makes me worry for its ability to protect me from the downward force of the blasting water. I'm thankful that I'm regaining my solidity thanks to the rice gruel, potato grits, and soft tofu he is feeding me.

Slowly becoming formidable again, I feel that the transformation Long Ears kindled within me long ago may have been dormant all these cold, quiet years but is now regaining momentum.

"I can't read these characters any better than the ones on the stele," Athens says, now at work with a stiff-bristled brush to clean up my shell, "but I can say they're beautifully carved."

What else do you notice about them?

"Well, for one thing they're grouped into stanzas."

How many?

I know the answer very well but I want *him* to discover it for himself so I wait patiently for him to make his count, which he does.

"Eighty-one," he says at last. "Do you know what they mean?"

I hope you know that's a ridiculous question. How could I possibly not know precisely what is written on my own shell and why?

"Who knew you could turn your head around that far? Tell me what they say."

Think of them as thoughts to live by.

Footsteps sound on the temple steps, and someone calls Athens' name. He looks around desperately. There's no time to hide me anywhere, so he simply aims the still-trickling hose at the flowers along the wall and acts as if I'm not there at all.

"Abbot Chen," he says, waving to a short man wearing black robes and a thin white beard.

"What are you doing?"

"Gardening clears the mind."

"Do you think your father sent you here to water flowers?"

"No, he sent me here so you would keep me out of prison."

"Such a lost opportunity," the abbot mutters. "Writers, poets, musicians, painters—everyone longs for a retreat, even if it's a forced one. Use your time! Study philosophy, write or draw something. Learn qigong."

"I find my projects," Athens says, still keeping his eyes on the hose.

The abbot finally notices me. I've explored invisibility before. I am so purely elemental that often I am taken for a big black rock, the kind of object the eye does not immediately register. The abbot clutches his hands together in prayer and then prods me with his toe. He jumps back when I move, then circles in again.

"What is this thing?" he asks at last.

"It's not a thing. It's an animal. A giant tortoise."

The abbot wears a string of yellow jade beads around his neck. He takes them off and drops them like a leash over my head. They feel hard and cool against the fragile, weathered folds of my neck.

"Just a big, slow, pet," he says, giving the strand a tug. "Bark like a dog. Go on!"

Through all the odious defilements I have suffered in my years in the world of men, this act is unique. I retreat inside my shell and the beads drop to the ground. I feel the abbot's fingers trace my carvings and hear his breathing quicken.

"These carvings are very old," he says. "Where did he come from?"

"She. Her name is Yin. I found her in Lao Tzu's grave. The real grave, not the fake one you put up for tourists. A piece of the mountain came down after that big storm the other night. I found a stele and dug her out. She was frozen but the sun thawed her. Lao Tzu's powdered bones were beneath her."

That's it. That's the way he puts it. No mystery, no attempt to hide anything, no disavowal of any knowledge of me.

"In addition to being a criminal, you are a compulsive liar," says the abbot.

"Not lying. The carvings are Lao Tzu's book. The most famous book in Chinese history, as you have said. I bet they're original, too. She's got to be a few thousand years old."

I understand what he's doing now. He's taking the truth and making it sound so preposterous that the old man loses interest. It's an interesting plan, but it doesn't seem to work because he hasn't counted on Chen's fascination with pictograms. I put out my head again and find he has put some contraption on his head. It frames his eyes and is made of something disturbingly familiar. When I realize what it is, I bump him hard enough to land him on his rear.

"I wouldn't wear tortoiseshell glasses around her," Athens advises, helping him up.

"There are subtleties of language here," the abbot declares, not registering the reference to my sensibility. "Shades of meaning

YUN ROU

in the roots and radicals. Seriously, Athens, where did she come from? I've only seen carvings like this in a museum."

"I told you. I found her in Lao Tzu's grave."

Abbot Chen waves his hand dismissively. "Enough of your nonsense. Collectors would pay a fortune for these carvings. Are there any more on the creature's underside?"

"I don't know."

"We could sell it and use the money to expand the monastery, restore the old walls, build a Lao Tzu museum and tourist shops like they have at the Shaolin Temple. We'll have to take the meat out, of course."

"The meat?"

"The head, the legs, the viscera."

"I'm keeping her as a pet. I don't want to gut her."

I bite the abbot's foot hard enough to feel the bones crack. He shrieks and hops around like a one-legged crow.

"Here. Let me help you with that," says Athens, shooting me a look that says I've really gone and done it. "She might have rabies."

After they leave, I feel hungry again. I'm not thinking about my impending evisceration, apparently still the inevitable fate of my kind despite the passage of so many years. Instead, I'm thinking about the fact that while the meal seems to have restored the rest of me to my former reptilian glory, my skin seems to be turning paler and more translucent. It is an interesting, perhaps even satisfying, development.

I lower myself to the cool stones and sleep.

18

Rumors of Yin's powers flew through the kingdom like the barbed end of a bronze flail. Sentinels were aloft with signal fires on the ramparts, and drumbeats shook the city like thunder. Spontaneous feasts were served, and everyone from merchants to courtiers wore a smile that said the dynasty, slowly spiraling into unspoken ruin, had been granted an unexpected reprieve by a magic turtle from across the sea.

The king sent for his wizard. "Don't you dare ring that bell of yours around me today. My head is still swollen from a week of wine."

"You desire a hangover cure, Sire?" the wizard inquired from his modest kowtow.

"No, no. That's not why I called you. It's the queen. She's different to the nose."

Peonies and osmanthus. Yum.

"What in the name of the Yellow Emperor is that hissing sound?"

"Yin is asking if she may eat the flowers, Your Highness."

"Seriously? You speak with her?"

"And she with me, though no other ears can hear her."

The king waved his hand. "Tell her to browse the flowerbeds as she pleases. The gardeners will replace whatever she eats. By the way, do you think we'll be able to use her in battle when she grows up?"

"In battle, Your Highness?"

"If she has the power of foretelling she might be useful in planning campaigns. Also, archers can ride her and she can stomp horses to death."

"I don't take her for a fighter, Sire. Hers is a peaceful nature."

"Elephants are peaceful too, but given the right prodding, they can be fierce."

"Elephants have tusks and harems, Your Highness. Territories, too."

"Who is to say these giant turtles do not also fight and mark their lands? And, unlike the elephant, Yin will grow to be immune to the arrows of war if not the arrows of fortune."

"Elephants can run, Sire. A turtle is too slow for war. Now, please tell me what it is about the queen that concerns you. Many husbands find a pregnant woman's energy a fine, balancing tonic."

"Not me. It's disturbing. I can't lie with her."

"Well, your job with her is done for now, Sire."

King Ling pouted as he touched Yin with his toe. "I don't want balance; I want thrills. Nothing is fun anymore. Zhou women are lazy; the court musicians are tone-deaf; the imperial chefs are so afraid of giving me a bellyache that they cook tasteless bland food; and my bodyguards won't allow me so much as a walk in the woods. I'm a prisoner in my own palace, Long Ears. Everyone has more fun than I do."

The wizard had wandered extensively in the countryside. He knew the bitterness, *ku*, which life brought to the farmers and fisherman in the river valley, and how hard and tenuous their very existence could be.

"Not everyone, Your Highness," he said mildly.

"Well, the King of Zheng anyway. The eunuchs disdain him,

but he rises every morning to invigorating music and closes each day with dancing girls in his private chambers. I want such distractions. I want to forget that my dynasty is collapsing, that people don't respect and fear the name Zhou any longer, that there are strongmen sniffing like pigs around my city and foreign soldiers pawing at my borders like wild horses. I want things the old way, the way they used to be."

"Dancing girls may be overrated, Sire. Especially if they cost you sleep."

Yin lifted her head from the flowers to show a beak smeared in fine yellow pollen.

Bud you luv du dance. I've zeen you in de morning in the drizzle, and I've zeen you on the porch ad night.

"Now what does she say?" asked the king, hearing Yin's hisses.

"That proper rest is indeed important, Your Highness."

Eye don't like id wen you change my wurds.

"They say the Zheng king's consorts are naked in the palace," the king went on. "Can you imagine such a wonderful thing?"

"I doubt such rumors, Sire."

"It might amuse me in fair weather," the king said. "But I would not wish to see a single drop of sweat. Nothing repels me more than a woman's sweat."

"Clean perspiration is healthy and natural, Your Highness."

"Do you know the Zheng royals worship their ancestors with carnal parties? They say furthering the royal line honors the dead."

"There is a certain logic to that, Sire. The cycle of birth, death, and rebirth is a pure expression of nature."

"They have parties, and we have earthquakes and floods and enemies on all sides."

And a king who cannod make babies widoud ur help.

"Now what did she say?"

"That you are correct about life being unfair, Sire. That is why a man such as you must be smarter than his subjects, more sensitive to nature's way, and vigilant in all things."

"Persistent and unwavering as you always say," the king waved his hand wearily. "Yes, yes, I know. Still, all I think about these days is dancing girls, and all I hear about is the need for more babies."

"Babies are flexible, and they don't hold onto ideas, Sire. We could all take that lesson from them. Too, they grow into loyal subjects."

"I hear rumblings that the strongmen, those piddling lesser kings, are banding together and even making alliances with the Huns."

"The Huns are drawn to our high culture, Sire. They long for a kingdom like ours with a vibrant and fascinating city at its core."

"They frighten me."

He worries du much and duz too little.

"As always, I strive to keep the dynasty safe, Your Highness," the wizard said, lifting Yin from the flower pile before she ate the last blossom.

Eunuchs appeared with scrolls that needed signing, and the king floated toward them and away. "I leave you to your pet, then," he said over his shoulder. "But do see to more dancing girls for me, won't you?"

19

"We can't stay here now," Athens says.

My sage taught me never to rush.

"Did he teach you to offer yourself as dinner? Because that's what you'll be if we don't move quickly."

I'm a tortoise. The closest I get to moving quickly is to watch an eagle and dream.

"The abbot's tending to his foot now, but he'll be back up here shortly. I'm telling you we have to go."

Can you leave the monastery? Won't that get you sent back to prison?

He doesn't seem to hear me. He's looking around, poking into corners, lifting tarpaulins, and opening temple side doors. At long last he comes out with some kind of cart. It has two wheels and two handles. He tips it downward.

"Climb in," he says.

I humor him by trying, but I'm really too big and all I get is a face full of rusty metal for my efforts to pull myself in. My rear legs stick up in the air. I half teeter, half dangle as he struggles to pick up the cart. He pushes, I pull, and, finally I manage to get in far enough to shift my center of gravity over the wheels. One enormous heave later, we're rolling.

"Whoever would have thought I'd be pushing a giant, treasured tortoise around in a wheelbarrow," he huffs, guiding the cart over the bumpy bricks.

You see me as treasure, too?

"While the other kids were playing shoot-'em-up games, I always preferred treasure hunts. You know, the kind with witches and spells? Axe-wielding dwarves and mysterious sorcerers? Demons spitting fire and ghosts and ghouls casting spells in giant castles with secret doors and perfectly manicured gardens?"

What is a treasure-hunt game?

"Never mind. It's not important."

I don't like the brush off, so I persist.

So you're caught between imaginary worlds and this one?

Athens Li smiles. "I suppose you could say that, yes."

We reach the stairs and he tilts the cart downward. At first, it looks as if we'll make it, since he's leaning back to counter my weight and gravity. The wheels roll over the initial step, but then gravity grabs and Athens cannot stop the cart from upending. In an instant, I am catapulted through the air and land hard on my back. It has been millennia since I was in this position, but it does seem that my landing is gentler than previous times. I know the ground is hard, so I am forced to construe that my carapace has continued to become softer.

Turn me over, please. It's hard to breathe when I'm like this.

Athens gets to me quickly, tugging on my margins to turn me back over. "Forget the cart," he says. "Just walk as fast as you can. I have an idea."

You're a thief, yes? That's your crime?

"Not a thief."

You said something about treasure.

"I never stole anything."

I'm confused. You're stealing me aren't you?

"Walk, will you? There's a van the monks use to go to town

for supplies. It's not fancy, but it will have to do. Seriously. We've gotta be quick. Anyone could see us at any moment."

What is a van?

"You'll see. Now hurry up."

In recent memory, I've avoided suffering by thinking only of my love. Feeling it. Breathing it to augment the lack of oxygen. I'm used to doing what I want with my mind and with my time. I'm not exactly responsive to orders or a schedule. That's what happens when you're buried alive for thousands of years. Now I'm being told what to do and when to do it and what to worry about too.

Nobody's going to have me for dinner.

"You think you have a say in the matter? What are you going to do, bite him again? He'll chop off your head in a heartbeat. He's a businessman in monk's robes, an operator who uses his position for profit. Your life means nothing to him. Looking at you he sees only a valuable carving. He doesn't know or care how long you've lived or how perceptive and smart you are or that you're capable of great love."

You see me as perceptive and smart?

Athens rolls his eyes impatiently. "If the abbot can use your shell to get something he wants, you had better believe he's going to boil the meat out of you. So let's get out of here."

I pick up the pace. We reach a dusty road behind the main building without being seen. We approach one of the rolling bugs, this one long and green. Athens molests it with a piece of metal, and it responds by lifting a rear wing. Athens has me climb up inside. The smell is terrible—rotting food mixed with an acrid, biting smell from deep under the earth.

What do you know about great love?

"Sorry about the gas fumes," he says, as if that answers my question. "There's a leak at the filler cap."

He climbs into some kind of chair in the front. I find myself wondering if this is a unique insect or if perhaps all the other bugs I've seen are identically equipped but at too small a scale for me to have noticed. If this is true, I wonder what else about the world I have been missing. I hear a roaring sound, and we accelerate fiercely, a sensation I know only from plunging down the face of a giant wave, in a boat, in a storm, more years ago than some trees have leaves. I understand now that this is no bug at all but a very fast chariot.

As we pass through the monastery gate, two monks pursue us, yelling at Athens to stop. He doesn't. In fact, he makes the chariot go faster. I cannot see them, but I know somewhere within there must be strong horses.

We descend the mountain and enter some kind of course whereupon other chariots swarm us like bees. Some are small and others gargantuan and laden with chopped trees. I search for some kind of pattern in the way they roll, but I cannot find one. Athens seems very agitated.

"The abbot will call for help," he says. "He won't want to, because it will cost him, and he won't do it right away, but eventually he will. My father's influence only goes so far."

Where are we?

"Not far from the monastery. It's only been a few minutes."

I find the new, fast rhythm of all this movement confusing, all the more as I don't recognize any landmarks. Everything in the valley has changed.

Where are we going?

"I have an idea."

The chariots have stopped at the village. A procession of people wearing white and throwing paper crosses in front of us.

They're making a mess.

"It's a funeral. That's fake money. That box is a coffin. The dead body is inside."

I recognize the instrument, the suona, but not the fake money. Long Ears wouldn't have that box. He wanted to be one with the dirt. He had his own ideas about everything.

"My dad is like that. You can't tell him anything."

I told my sage plenty. I was the only one who did.

There is a magic window to the right of Athens' head, and when he glances through it he can see me even though I am behind him and I can see him, too. I wonder if perhaps this is one of those doors to another world he has been telling me about. Suddenly, he slaps the wheel he is holding and makes a fast turn down a side road.

"They're chasing us!" he cries.

Dust rises behind us. I can no longer see the mourners, but an image of the acolytes gathered during Long Ears' last days floats in. I spend a few marvelous sections in rapture. When I return from dreaming of my loved one, I notice the pursuing chariot is gaining on us.

Athens licks his lips. "They may be faster but I know a place we can hide."

I am suddenly alarmed. I have never been one to trust easily and I barely know this man at all.

What kind of place?

"The kind you can only find with top clearance or the ability to hack into absolutely any network."

What does that mean?

"You'll see."

A moment later, the van goes completely quiet and yet, somehow, keeps moving. I imagine that the horses have broken free, but, in fact, we are coming to a stop, and I don't see them at all. Athens opens the door at the back and urges me out. We move swiftly through the grass until we come to a metal fence.

He climbs over it, pauses, realizes I cannot do the same and climbs back to lift the fence for me.

Ahead of us is a forest of identical metal structures, each bearing a trunk like an elephant's held straight out. We zigzag through them. Angry shouts tell us to stop, but we press on. A loud horn blares. I hear the sound of more cars at the fence. Deep in the maze, Athens gestures for me to climb into a space below one of the buildings.

Where are we?

"Where war tanks go to die."

20

Multi-story construction would come later in China's architectural history, but the pagoda was grand nonetheless. The beams bore the carvings of cranes standing, dancing and flying. The wooden lintels and portico beams were brightly painted with symbols and numbers, and the bronze fittings of the dark, heavy, black wooden doors were intricately engraved with water buffaloes and dragons. Yin paused at the threshold—built tall both to keep out floodwaters and to slow an unwanted entry—until the wizard lifted her up and over.

"This library holds the archives of the entire Zhou dynasty."

It smells like you.

"Ah. You speak more clearly now, and it seems you think more clearly as well. My work is taking hold. And yes, because I spend so much time here, my robes and even my skin have absorbed the aroma of herbs I store here: bark of the cinnamon tree to harmonize the body and mugwort to build power."

Your power comes from a wart?

Long Ears smiled. "Exercise and meditation help me live in obedience to nature."

I see obedience everywhere. I don't like it much.

"Obedience of the wrong kind is painful; obedience of the right kind is a marvelous relief. Tell me, are all tortoises stubborn?"

Stubborn?

"You get an idea in your head, and you keep bumping into it until it falls over."

That is how we eat cactus. That is how we fall on mice.

"You fall on mice?"

Birds, too, although I love mouse meat best.

The wizard straightened in astonishment. "Your kind eats birds?"

Tortoises make a nice cool, shady patch by standing up on all four legs. Birds and mice crawl under us for shade, and then boom, we drop down and smash them. Yummy.

"This is news to me. The Tao works in strange and unexpected ways."

So much you don't know, and yet you use your wart power to make kings. By the way, I smell mice here.

"Kings make each other. You've already learned of the process. I have little to do with it."

Somehow, I think you have a lot to do with it even though you blame it on me.

He just smiled and led her deeper into the pagoda, all the way to a chamber filled with countless bamboo scrolls.

What is all this?

"Knowledge of the ways of men rendered in sixteen different languages."

You can read them all?

"I can write and speak them as well."

Yin examined the tassels on the scrolls, their slats, and some of their inked characters. She pressed her lower jaw against the floor and heard worms roiling in the rich soil below as well as the rumble of carts outside the palace walls and the running footfalls of slaves performing palace business at speed.

The king fears the Huns. Who are they?

Long Ears lowered himself to the floor beside her and rested the back of his head on her shell. "People fear what they don't understand. The Huns are different. They plant no crops and lay down no roots. They live along our borders and move to where the food is. They take shelter under the folded animal skins they carry on their backs, and sometimes under trees. They want access to our rivers and lands. They're fascinated with our buildings and our culture, too, but they prefer taking to making."

Yin followed the wizard to another chamber brimming with artifacts.

And these?

"Treasures from the dynasties before the Zhou, valuable beyond measure because they detail the origins of our culture."

I see bones and shells.

"Detailed prescriptions of rituals inscribed upon the shoulder blades of oxen, the long bones of cow and deer, and yes, the shells of small turtles. This one is by the Yellow Emperor, our first king and best warrior. This bone carving shows his face. Can you see his high forehead, broad brow and fine nose? He was the greatest of all oracles."

Not as great as you. That much I know.

Long Ears smiled. "Far greater. And look. Here are the writings I mentioned to the king. Fu Hsi, who used the pattern on the River Ho to create the divining tool we call the *bagua*. The great shaman, Ancestor Yu's writings are here as well, and here is his portrait in bone as well."

Ah. He looks happier.

"He used Fu Hsi's pattern to create a celestial ladder based on the spirals of galaxies. Diviners like me use it to enhance our vision in much the way we use the Duke of Wen's *Yiqing* to chart the changes in nature."

So, all your fancy speech aside, this is a library full of wizarding tools.

"And look at this. The writings of the sage king, Yao, and in his own hand! Can you imagine anything more precious? Yao lived simply and put hard work and character first. He decreed that kings should be chosen on the basis of merit, not because they were somebody's son. He decreed that kings should serve the people, not the other way around. He was a great engineer and built ditches and dams to save thousands from floods."

Character? Really? What did he say about dancing girls?

"Don't be so hard on King Ling. He is a good man even if he is no Yao. By the way, Yao was not the only great king. Shun and Yu came after him. Shun started his life taking care of pigs and then became a great leader. He chose his ministers wisely and made morals the backbone of our land. Yu believed in transparency and responsibility. He opened the doors of government so that everyone could see what was going on."

If he opened everything, why do I see soldiers and gates everywhere I look?

"Yu's rule was stable, but Ling's is not. There are many small kingdoms in our federation—Qi, Jin, Win, Lu, Zheng, Cao, Chu, Xu, Chen, Song, Yan, Cai, Wei, Wu, Yue and others—and they're always forging alliances and scheming to topple our king. Should his dynasty fall, it will be my job to preserve the contents of this library. It's a heavy responsibility. Wars can be lost, swords rust, kings die, power fades, but knowledge goes on. Culture can be preserved quietly, in scrolls and on bones for thousands of people across many generations to see."

All this is nice, but I just want to go home.

"Perhaps someday you will consider this place your home."

Perhaps not. And by the way, you're just as much a prisoner as I am. You're always busy with the king's business, but I can tell you really just want to live simply in the forest.

Long Ears smiled a bit sadly. "Most of us can't have what we want, Yin, but you're the exception. The magic working within you will soon set you free."

21

Athens' lectures present a whole new scent of man. Smart bombs, cruise missiles, lasers, drones, killer satellites, and atomic and hydrogen bombs help me smell things more clearly. Under my rescuer's tutelage, I discover dark matter and energy, the large hadron collider, and the Higgs boson. I also learn of supercomputers and the digital revolution, epigenetics and the mapping of genomes. Through the use of websites and hyperlinks, videos and more. Athens peels back the fog of centuries until I grasp even quantum physics, a new cosmology that destroys the idea of cause and effect and any necessity of a creator, an odd notion Taoists never embraced.

The more I hear, cowering between the treads of a defunct Chinese tank and suffering drops of dirty oil, the more I realize that humankind has stepped out of the flow of the Tao. Poisoning everything they touch, erasing the delicate energetic essence of so many trees, shrubs, flowers, and herbs, wiping out hundreds of species — a new word I've learned — every day, leaving no habitat unmolested, and demonstrating utter disregard for compassion and harmony, the people population on Earth now resembles nothing so much as a giant two-legged tumor.

I want to say this to Athens, but I sense it will wound him. More, I fear it will lead him to think that I am ignorant of the cycles of things, of the constant flux of agony and redemption.

I don't want him to think poorly of me because I am coming to very much respect how smart he is, how in such a short life he has already apprehended—admittedly on the back of a thousand generations—what it took me millennia to learn. Too, I don't want to deprive him of the optimism of youth.

"We could stay hidden here for days, and they wouldn't find us," he says. "It's like a giant forest of rubber and steel. I've got a map right here, downloaded from a Chinese military site. Not so tough to hack, by the way."

I understand what hacking is.

He grins at this. "Of course you do. Your mind is changing and you're a quick study."

Resurrection will do that. And my mind's not the only thing.

He shoots me a curious look. "No?"

My shell's getting softer.

"I'm not surprised, given how long you slept without anything to eat. A few good meals with the right minerals will square you away."

If a meal would make my shell harder, it would at least be helping a bit by now. No, this is something else. I'm changing. Even my limbs are lengthening, my proportions changing.

"Small wonder after being scrunched up in a hole all that time."

My heart rate is faster.

"Your heart's a muscle. You're lucky it hasn't totally atrophied from disuse."

My heart is as big as ever.

"I don't mean emotionally."

It pumps more strongly, too. I move faster than I ever did.

"The modern world again. It's a pace you're not used to."

Even my senses are different.

"In what way?"

I can't explain it, but it goes along with my thinking, which is also clearer. My vocabulary is bigger and my frame of reference has changed.

"That makes sense. You're in a whole new world. Let me tell you a little bit about the human side of it. I don't know how it was in days past, but today most people are only interested in themselves, in what affects them personally, and in satisfying their urges. The vast majority of humanity is dirt poor, and has no time or opportunity to do anything but scrape out a living and find what little pleasure it can. Many people have so few resources, they can't even afford to dream."

Perhaps that's why the virtual world you've shown me in the computer is so appealing to them. It doesn't cost anything to create a fantasy life there, nor do there seem to be any consequences.

"Actually, there can be consequences in that world and in this one."

Yet you chose to become a criminal. What was your crime, exactly?

Athens "Breaking and entering. Now let's go."

We crawl out from under the tank and leave the graveyard a different way than we came in. A few minutes later, we're on foot on a highway that Athens tells me leads east toward Luoyang, and, if we keep going far enough, to the sea. Athens waves at passing vehicles as we wait for a kind stranger to stop, fervently hoping no one from the monastery spots us.

"You have to understand something about Abbot Chen," he explains as we fend off the rising heat from the macadam. "He won't let this go. He'll track me and he'll track you because there is personal interest at stake, both risk and gain."

I listen, but, in truth, I am as interested in his man-smell as in his words. There is something both compelling and familiar in what I pick up, and it stimulates me in a way that feels both entirely new and entirely familiar. Standing on four legs and watching him shield himself from a flying bit of tire, I find his desire to understand things deeply, to dig beneath the surface of things—and not just mountain dirt—a comforting reminder of Long Ears.

"I've got money, thankfully, and I've got papers," he explains. "I can get you to the port of Shanghai, and we can find a boat there. All we need to do is steer clear of the tens of millions of surveillance cameras the government has installed and of the facial recognition software that is ubiquitous here. It's not going to be easy for a fugitive and a giant tortoise, but we're going to give it a go because it's a damn sight better than sitting still and waiting for a jail cell and a hot pot.."

Athens waves his arm and it isn't long before a bus pulls to the side of the road.

"Must be the sight of you," he says. "They never stop for me alone."

Climbing aboard is no easy feat as the steps are steep and the lowest one is high, and even after we get up, with much pushing and grunting, the entry door is narrow. Inside, the air is cool. I negotiate the alley between the seats with some difficulty. As I pass, there are flashes of light as each and every traveler snaps multiple pictures of me with a digital camera. Some stand on the armrests to get a direct downward view of the characters— which I can feel are distorted by the inward drift of my shell— carved on my back. Others reach out to give the top of my head a tentative pat.

"Japanese tourists," Athens mutters. "So cliché."

We go all the way to the back of the bus. I feel a pressing need to evacuate, but Athens sees my rear parts twitching and gives me a warning look.

"Hold it," he hisses, "or we'll lose our ride."

The fact that he's talking to me has the tourists all atwitter. They want to know if I talk back. Athens lies and says no. He says I understand him as a pet dog might. To mollify me, he adds something about a really, really *smart* pet dog.

The long-forgotten-but-familiar aroma of dried seafood smites me. I can't sit on a seat like Athens can, so I wander up and down the aisle looking for the source of it. Finally, I discover a little girl eating squid out of a plastic bag. I stand there with my neck stretched out in the direction of the treat. She suddenly notices me and lets out a scream. Athens comes running. He looks at me, rubs his eyes, and looks again.

Why are you staring at me like that?

"For a moment there, I could swear you had a nose."

Of course I have a nose.

"Not a beak. A nose. It's gone now."

That's nice. Would you ask the girl to give me a bite of that squid?

He does, but she just hands the bag to him. She's afraid of me now. I open my mouth, and he drops in a few bits.

Apparently, even Athens doesn't want to touch me.

22

A luminous moon squeezed a long shadow out of Long Ears as he prowled the eastern quarter of the city in search of his apprentice. The dirt streets were streaked with splashes of light from tea emporia and marked with animal leavings, puddles from a recent storm, and mounds of household trash.

What would Wang Yi be doing here?

"I've ignored him lately. Sometimes he sulks."

Did you ignore him because of me?

"You needed the attention more than he did."

"Why not dispense your guards to find him?

"I'm not sure where we might find him and I don't want to compromise his reputation."

The streets grew narrower. A man ran past with a mace in his hand. Another man chased him.

What is that stench?

"Rotten food. One of the reasons I don't come here often."

You can block your nose with your fingers, which is more than I can do. And that sound?

"A woman laughing."

Not that.

"Pleasure-house bells."

What's a pleasure house?

"That's not important right now."

You use bells too. You even wear one on your robe sometimes.

"The bells you hear are used to attract attention. I use my own bells to cut through the material world and reach the realm of spirits, gods, and ancestors."

Four men, armed with clubs and knives and swords, suddenly blocked their path. "A fine robe sir," said their leader. "Might you be carrying coins?"

"Your father is ashamed of you," answered Long Ears. "I can hear his bones crunching as he rolls in his grave."

"My father lives in a Western province and believes me a tax collector."

"You never fooled him; he only humored you. He died yesterday. Now he is in the ground. Your mother is all you have left. Since she washes your clothes, she'll know if you spill blood."

Enraged, the bandit tried a stabbing thrust. Long Ears pivoted away, but Yin tumbled out of his grasp and the bandit saw her and pushed her down into the mud with his boot. "Ho! What's this? Might we have the pleasure of addressing the court wizard and his pet, the Great Fertilizer?"

You have no idea how much I hate that name.

"If that's Long Ears, we should run before he turns us into turnips," one of his men said nervously.

"I'm not afraid of him. All he does is give us one fat, stupid king after another."

The bandit chief pressed his attack again. Yin saw her sage duck between the men, brushing them just enough so that one after another lost his footing then groaned as the wizard disarmed them.

You move like a waterspout I saw from my ship.

"Nature teaches and I learn," Long Ears replied.

Leaving their assailants in the mud, they wandered streets

and alleys for another quarter hour before stopping in front of an establishment from which issued the sound of bells and reeds and strings. Long Ears banged on the door with the pommel of the best of the confiscated swords. "Wang Yi favors this place," he explained, wiping Yin's plastron clean against the wooden threshold.

A woman answered the knock. Her bare feet were dirty, but her hair was tied straight up and she wore powder as makeup. "Greatest lord," she said, touching her head on the floor. "Please follow me."

She led them past a host of coarse men to an inner chamber where lantern smoke rose lazily and thick embroidered fabrics hanging on earthen walls muted all sound. At a dividing curtain, the woman stepped aside. Long Ears stepped inside, and Yin heard a woman wail. A moment later the wizard emerged with his half-naked apprentice slung over his shoulder.

What's wrong with him?

"Poisoned with drink."

"Now that you have Yin, you don't need me anymore," Wang Yi mumbled. "I'm useless. I have no purpose."

"Don't be ridiculous. The whole court buzzes with intrigue. I need you now more than ever. Yin is one thing to me, and you are another. Tonight, you are both going to stay close to me."

Tucking Yin under his free arm, the wizard walked the whole distance back to the northern quarter without pause or complaint. Once home, he instructed his house staff to administer herbs to his apprentice and set up a cushion for Yin by the woodstove in his bedroom. Only when everyone was installed and the house was quiet did the wizard himself retire.

Some hours later, Yin dreamed she was swimming in air, gaining altitude free of gravity, floating east like a shelled cloud with purpose. She made short work of the seas that had taken so very long to cross and soon found herself back at her beloved archipelago. She swooped down to the sea coast— where penguins cavorted and marine lizards rasped algae from the surf-battered rocks—and thence to the scrubland, where her beloved *Opuntia* grew.

Rising up the face of a volcanic cliff, she veered around a colony of blue-footed boobies nesting in crags, nearly collided with a waved albatross taking flight off the edge, and then, in midair, was suddenly attacked by a predatory frigate bird by the name of Ding Lok. She worked her legs furiously, but the bird drew close on powerful wings and opened a toothy beak to devour her for what she had done to his nose.

She awakened, limbs out straight in terror, in the hands of a woman with skin so white her veins showed sky blue.

"Be gentle with her," Long Ears advised from his bed. "She belongs on the ground, not in the air."

Who is this?

"Yin, meet my wife, Bao Yu."

You like women with green eyes?

"I like this one, yes."

"I've heard about nothing but you for weeks," interrupted Bao Yu. "Will you do for us what you did for the king and queen and give us a child?"

Tell her I didn't make anyone pregnant. Tell her it was all you.

"When the time is right, I'm sure she will," the wizard told his wife.

"I've been waiting so long," Bao Yu sighed.

As Yin trundled back to her cushion, the wizard covered his wife's mouth with his own and slowly loved her deeply and tenderly. The spectacle should have settled Yin after the terrifying fear of her dream, but she found it oddly disquieting. When she did finally fall asleep it was after all motion had ceased, and all she could hear and feel was the steady beat of her own reptilian heart.

23

The bus does not stop at Luoyang proper but at a tourist attraction called the Longmen Grottoes. The Japanese crowd around me so tightly as we cross the vast, concrete parking area that it is hard for me to find a room for my feet. It's unclear whether they are more interested in me or in the stone representations of the Buddha. The statues come into view as we near a series of caves, themselves carved out of the limestone cliffs along the Yi River. I see the renderings of this master in different sizes and styles, his hands in a variety of positions, wearing varied garb, and with ears nearly as imposing as those of my lost love. The tour guide tells us that statues were once painted, but the colors have long faded.

"Abbot Chen won't stop texting and calling," Athens says, glancing at his phone, and then pulling out the battery. "He's got you under his tongue now, and he likes what he tastes."

You mean money.

"Of course. It's what most of the world is all about these days. The abbot is not the man I expected when I came here. Not the kindly old soul devoted to the spiritual development of the monks in his charge but an operator angling to climb the social ladder. Did you notice his heavy gold wristwatch? He likes luxury. That's why he agreed to hide me. He'll do anything for advantage, and he knows my father's connected."

I marvel at how nothing is as it was, how all the rules of superior living that I learned from my great love seem to have evaporated right along with the clean, fresh world I remember. I hear the tour guide spin a web of history that experience tells me is more fable than fact, and I watch the Japanese devour the details like a sweet dessert.

Buddha was like my wizard, though not as funny.

"His way of looking at things makes life easier for many people," Athens shrugged. "And it requires no belief in the supernatural."

What does that word mean?

"Things beyond our understanding," Athens says. "Out of the ordinary. Amazing."

Everything is supernatural until you understand it better. Then it is just natural, which is super anyway.

We are pushed and swept toward the back of the bus, which makes its way to the city. The sky turns darker and darker.

"This filthy gray-brown is industrial pollution. People here never even see the sun. It just glows more up there during the day. Luoyang kids think that's normal and that Hollywood paints movie skies blue."

I know what Hollywood is now. I know what movies are. I understand the point, and I find it desperately sad. I shudder to think what my wizard, who counted the days at court that kept him from the green embrace of the forest, would think of a world with a hidden sky.

We get out of the bus near the old city walls. I strain to fit my memories with what I see now, to reconcile donkeys and oxen with scooters and cars, to somehow match what Athens tells me is the stench of refineries and mines with the organic smells of the now-ancient city.

"I know you want to reminisce, but there's no time," he says.

"Chen's tracking us, and he'll find us if we stop."

We part company with the Japanese. I feel the urge to stand on three legs and wave goodbye with my fourth but teeter because my balance isn't up to it. Athens urges me to move more quickly. We leave the old city gate area, with its street food and tourist shops and head in the direction of the train station. I can't find a good breath of air and feel an unfamiliar spasm inside my shell and before long it overcomes me. I cannot move another step as it rises toward my throat, pressing me from the inside and shaking me until a strange sound erupts from my beak.

"Weird," says Athens. "I didn't know turtles could cough. Of course, I didn't know they could talk, either."

I have never made that sound before.

"I guess you've never had to breathe air this bad."

We draw attention as we walk, but not so much as I would expect. A few people wave wads of cash at Athens, offering to buy me. He says I am not for sale. A couple of old men with pipes walk slowly beside us, staring at the pictograms on my shell and arguing about them heatedly in a rough dialect. A fearless street urchin jumps up on my shell, striking me with his stringy belt the way I've seen soldiers whip horses. I buck him off as if I have hooves.

This entourage follows us most of the way to the train station. Athens checks the schedule and buys tickets. Waiting by the kiosk, I notice that the place is nearly as old and dirty as I am, but while I feel I am somehow being renewed and transformed by this bright and unexpected cycle of life, the building, with its metal trellis ceilings and cold, concrete floors, seems better suited for demolition than rebirth.

"We're probably on a hundred cameras right now," Athens clucks as we make our way to the platform. "If the abbot calls in a favor, it's hard to say if we'll even make it to Shanghai. We're not exactly a low-profile pair, and China has become a surveillance state."

We wait on the platform. This time, everyone is too engaged with smartphones to pay us much mind.

"It's easy to see how technology is evolving," Athens tells me. "What's not as obvious to most people is how technology is changing us. Take war, for example....

Tanks?

He waves his hand impatiently. "Old school but still useful, I suppose. It's really all about drones now though. In the air, over and under the water, soon on the battlefield. It used to be that the best and the brightest in the military chose special forces and intelligence work. Now they become remote pilots. Instead of going to war in an airplane, they spend twelve hours in a bunker running simulated attacks on Japan, American warships, and Indian border outposts Of course they fly real drones over Taiwan and its holdings. When they're done, they go home to dinner with their kids. But inside each person the consequences are the same as for a fighter pilot who feels the g-forces and pulls a real trigger. Their souls connect to the horror of what they're doing, and they're traumatized. Perhaps the biggest change in the world since you went to sleep is how much better we've become at killing each other, or at least how much more easily it is done. Not only technology's fault, of course. It's just as much about intention."

There have always been violent people, and there have always been kind, gentle ones, too. What I see in this new world of yours is that nobody feels connected to something larger.

Athens nods. "That's why I hack. I like the power of technology but only when it is driven by conscience. My conscience is particular."

We have a compartment that we share. Athens folds up the

lower bunk beds so I have more space to move around, while he climbs to the upper bed and watches me as the train slowly pulls out of the station.

"Something's going on with you," he says. "You haven't mentioned food in hours."

Ideas have been feeding me but now that you mention it, I'm hungry.

Outside the window, we cover as much landscape in a minute as I used to cover in a day.

24

A twisting, writhing, animal mist rolled in off the river that night, carpeting fields, scaling city walls, and growing tentacles as it squeezed between trees. Gutter water, being of like substance, drew the mist down to extinguish street torches and moisten cotton and silk. Mold spread rapaciously in its wake, thirsty plants drank from it, and mushrooms orgiastically opened their gills as it floated past.

The dry timbers under the wizard's roof creaked as they swelled with moisture, the sound masking the noise of a horse on the dirt street. It was a stallion, bigger than most Chinese mounts, black and shiny and sufficiently well-fed to show how highly Ding Lok prized it. Together horse and sea captain had journeyed southwest from the state of Yan and camped out on the outskirts of the city before riding into town under the protection of the fog. In the alley behind Lao Tzu's house, Ding Lok guided the horse past an upended chamber pot, the white bones of a catfish picked clean, and the remains of a shattered porcelain medicine jar. He found four watchmen by the back door and would have slit their throats if they had not been in such heavy, drunken sleep.

Marveling that the wizard's house was simpler than his own, which was decorated with trophies from his many times at sea, Ding Lok slipped by them and into the kitchen. He passed the cook snoring on a wooden plank between a rock stove and a row of bronze cooking utensils, penetrated an inner hallway furnished with milking stools and an apothecary cabinet, and slunk by a room where two sleeping maids lay together, head to toe, sharing a simple bed.

Following the scent of fragrant oils, Ding Lok found Long Ears and his wife on a sleeping platform, pressed together so that her hair cascaded over his great forehead. Using only the moonlight coming through the windows — the crackle and smoke of a torch would have given him away — he found Yin dozing on the floor, her neck flaccid against the base of the bed. He picked her up, and wearing a smug smile and carefully retraced his path.

The moment the captain galloped off, Long Ears sat up from sleep knowing Yin was gone. The sun breaking the darkness about him like pottery into shards, he summoned his guards. Under his baleful eye they soon confessed to having fallen asleep on the job. Rather than punish them and instead of setting off in pursuit, the wizard put out word that he would see Sun Tzu, a mercenary general of high reputation who had recently come to the city. Before long the famous general appeared, bushes for eyebrows, a pair of broadswords strapped to his chest, and leather armor so dense a lesser man would have choked under the weight of it.

"The most senior lord sent for me?" Sun Tzu said, kowtowing.

"I am aware that you assisted the Wu king in conquering Chu, the state of my birth."

Sun Tzu sighed. "And I am aware that you are aware."

"But you have retired from the conflict."

"The King of Wu was greedy."

"So you regret your actions?"

The big general shook his head. "Not my actions. The fact of war."

"You are well to do so. Whether we win or lose, we must

mourn the dead and the failure of our philosophy."

"I gather you called for me because the enlightened turtle has been taken?"

"You've heard of her?"

"I wouldn't be surprised if word of her had not spread as far to the west as the mountains rumored to be stairways to heaven and as far to the east as the whole of the sea coast."

"Excellent guess, then."

"I don't guess; I deduce. The turtle apparently furnishes kings with sons and, since sons are the quickest route to power and every strongman in the federation wants to replace King Ling, I imagine she is quite a marketable item."

"Your reputation is obviously well-deserved. I suspect Ding Lok, the ship captain I sent across the world. His likeness came to me in a vision. He holds a grudge for what he believes was a wasted voyage, and, as an opportunist of high order, it would be just like him to steal her for sale to the highest bidder."

"Such a creature could actually shift the balance of power in the federation," the general mused.

"Will your war wound allow you to fight if need be?"

Sun Tzu peeled back his gauntlet to reveal a stump at the end of his left arm. "I am capable without my hand, although both palm and especially my fingers visit me in dreams."

"In what form, if I may ask?"

"A finger wagging at me in disapproval for my current role at court, which has me training guardsmen rather than fighting, and entertaining maidens rather than rescuing magical turtles."

The wizard leaned in to sniff the stump. "It is wise, this stump of yours, and it speaks to you because it still has room to grow. Now let's be off. We have a very special being to rescue."

25

On the night train, Athens becomes convinced that a man in a green business suit is an agent of Abbot Chen awaiting the opportunity to abduct me. Since everyone else on this train has met my gaze forthrightly with one of their own and only this man can't, I conclude Athens Li is right.

How have you learned to read people so well when you are still so young?

"The Internet. The so-called World Wide Web. That great electronic resource and community I showed you on my laptop. Remember I explained social media? Meeting people only onscreen, you can't smell them or touch them so you learn to find any flies in the ointment by deciphering their expressions and intentions. Of course I have plenty of real-world friends and experiences, too."

Please show me how to use that thing.

As we chug along through the three-dimensional world, he seems delighted to guide me on a whirlwind tour of two-dimensional space, utilizing the limitless boundaries of our minds. We begin with a history of China, browsing through images and articles revealing eras, ages, old pottery, and kings. Things don't look as good as they did back then, which tells me that these Web people have not, for all their formidable feats of imagination and techniques of restoration, taken into account the detrimental effects of what they call progress. I continue to be amazed by the phenomenon of the hyperlink, especially as wish fulfillment. I imagine how much more endurable all those millennia underground might have been if I could simply have warped through time and space with the light touch of a horny claw.

Yes, that's right, I am negotiating the keyboard with my claw. This is something I could never have done before, not merely because I was in the wrong period of history but because my claws, front and rear, were never so sensitive and subtle. Whereas once I was a little worried by being on the edge of lava, I can now feel the edges of each key, and within a few minutes have learned to locate the characters even when my eyes are closed. It occurs to me that surely no other turtle can do this.

While history and psychology do draw me, I continue to gravitate in the direction of science. In doing so, I better understand how Athens can know so very much. All over the world, human beings are connected through such devices as this in unimaginable ways. They share experience and insights, facts, too, at a single keystroke. Even while keeping an eye on Green Suit—no, he has not gotten off the train even though there have already been many stops—I manage to learn a great deal about synthetic biology, which is the science of reinventing nature.

"What makes you interested in this?" Athens asks as I cue up the website of a company in that field. The homepage displays a living organism revealed down to the level of proteins, plasmids, promoters, parasites and bones, fascia and lymph, blood and channels, interstitial spaces, all shown and explained.

How we experience life depends greatly upon our physical characteristics and abilities. That should be obvious, yes? I myself am a chimera of sorts, a deliberate melding of slimy, gritty, violent evolution and ancient energy-transformation technology. It amuses me to see what humans chasing the same goals are up to these days.

"What goals?"

Something new out of something old. Bending nature to human will.

"And yet that kind of bending, which is about control and submission, is somehow exactly the problem."

Something of interest to Long Ears. He thought it was narcissistic. And yet he did it when he made me.

"What was his goal?"

This subject is delicate for me. It makes my heart beat faster to engage it. It takes me a moment to answer.

He wanted a soul mate. He was lonely despite having a wife and concubines.

"He had concubines?" Athens leans forward, a gleam in his eye.

Don't be an infant. He was second only to the king. All the powerful men enjoyed the company of a multitude of women.

"Lao Tzu's girls," Athens mused.

Tell me about your criminal breaking and entering.

"I transgressed in both the virtual world and the physical one."

Tell me more.

My eagerness shuts him down for a bit, so I move out into the corridor again to check on Green Suit. This time, when I peer into his compartment, he looks straight at me. No curiosity there, though. Something else. Something disquieting. As odd as it sounds, it might be hunger.

"I hacked the security system at the Metropolitan Museum of Art," Athens announces when I return. "It's in New York. America. One of the most famous museums in the world. More riches than you can believe. Treasures at every turn. I opened the doors and turned off the sensors and my friends and I had a beer party in the Egyptian Temple. We had time to drink a keg before we were caught."

There were no guards?"

"I diverted museum security by setting off alarms at the opposite end of the building." He smiles. "I had them running in circles."

Just to prove you could.

He grins. "Green Suit is definitely here for you. I saw monastery mala beads on his wrist. He tried to hide them with his cuff when I walked by to the bathroom, but he wasn't quick enough."

We have to get rid of him. I want to go home, not be made into soup.

26

Huddled in the corner of Ding Lok's barge, Yin tried not to think about being alone with the man who had butchered her clan. She watched the traffic on the river go by, first a small ferry headed upriver and then a dinghy carrying a woman and two children.

"He'll be coming after his valuable little stinkpot now," Ding Lok mused, putting his foot down hard on her shell as he pushed his pole into the riverbed. "But I'll have you sold to a king up north before he can stop me."

Pushing up against his boot with a mighty heave, Yin tipped him into the path of an overhanging chestnut branch heavy with blossoms and fruit. Cursing and growling, he grabbed her by the foot and held her high. She tried to pull it in, but he held on until her strength gave way and she exposed the length of her limb.

"I've been looking forward to this," he grinned, producing his sword.

The movement that took her leg was small, quick, and relaxed. She dropped, jerking in agony. He kicked her toward a pile of sawdust. "That'll stop the bleeding," he said. "You have to live so you can bring babies to all those waiting, wanting women with their puffing, primping princes. Dead, you're worth nothing to me at all."

Long Ears is here.

There was movement on the riverbank and the wizard and

his general appeared.

"Go away, wizard!" Ding Lok cried when he noticed them. "She's mine, not yours. I was the one who braved savages and storms to retrieve her while you stood mumbling under a tree."

"Pull to the bank at once!" the great sage roared.

Ding Lok did a dance of denial. Seeing it, Sun Tzu pulled an arrow from his quiver, took aim, and shot the captain's stallion through the heart.

The black horse collapsed sideways, nearly tipping the barge before sliding into the water. Stunned, Ding Lok watched it float away.

"You'll pay for that!" he screamed.

The general and the wizard rode ahead to a bend in the river. Out of sight, they dismounted, shed their armor, which was of leaves of bronze bound together with thick leather, and slipped into the water. When the barge came around, they swam to it and climbed aboard. Sun Tzu engaged the general while Long Ears grabbed Yin and dove into the river once more. "You're wounded," he said, kicking toward the bank while holding her safe and dry but dripping blood.

I know you'll heal me.

It was at that exact moment, not a second sooner or later, that Yin became aware of her strong feeling for the great sage, a sensation that filled her utterly, but for which she had no name.

Back on the barge, Sun Tzu delivered a hard blow to Ding Lok's head. The captain fell off into the water and immediately slipped beneath the surface.

Is he dead? I want him to be dead.

"I don't know."

As they rode back, Long Ears kept a poultice pressed to Yin's stump. As soon as they got to the house, a fierce rain began. The servants put out buckets and used the showers to rinse utensils and clean clothes. Yin found a thick stream of water pouring from the edge of the roof. Tucking in her wounded stump, she stood beneath it, neck stretched out and eyes closed, trying to wash away the events of the day.

"I've never seen your skin look so black," the wizard observed.

For once I'm free of the pale dirt of this foreign land.

"Our loess soil comes from the grinding movements of the earth over vast periods of time and to a great depth. It is old and rich and wise."

You can keep it. I'd give anything for a taste of mouse meat.

Sun Tzu came striding up. Two sopping wet retainers walked with him, holding a bolt of silk over his head to keep him dry.

"Should have just stayed in the river, eh?" he laughed.

"If we were in the river, we could not dance."

"You want to dance in the rain?"

"Of course! Yin's back!"

So saying, Long Ears dragged Sun Tzu around. Where the wizard's movements were agile and light, the general's were comically martial, his elbows flailing back and forth as if at war with each other, his heavy feet sending dirt flying in gobs. At length, he began to laugh at himself, and Long Ears, in the spirit of the moment, took a flying leap into the mud and cavorted there like a schoolboy.

Watching him, Yin experienced that overpowering feeling once more.

27

Early morning sun comes through the train window. Scenery clicks by. One minute I see people living in squalid mud houses hanging laundry out to dry and the next I see a palatial building sitting in the middle of an empty lot, obviously the fruit of some get-rich-quick scheme.

"That's the new China for you," says Athens, fingers hammering the keyboard. "I don't imagine it's much like the old days."

The people of the Middle Kingdom have always been enterprising.

"Listen to you. You're getting smarter by the minute, you know. Absorbing data, understanding strategies, wrapping that unlikely mind of yours around exigencies, possibilities, and angles."

Speaking of all that, have you figured out what you want to do about the man in green?

"I have."

He gets up and goes out of the compartment. In five minutes he's back with a dusty black tarpaulin and a half-filled duffel.

"Found these things in the baggage locker," he says. "We're almost at the next stop, and they're about to come in handy."

As we pass Green Suit's compartment, Athens dons a stolen porter's cap, shakes out the tarp, and puts it over me. The world turns moldy and dark. Within a few minutes, we're rolling into

Fuyang, and he has me following him like a grounded magic carpet with legs. In the corridor, high heels and work boots clatter past. Cuffs too long and cuffs too short rush by a slit in the tarp, along with a couple of kids in pajamas, still sleepy and shuffling. Preparing to exit the train, we're just where Athens wants us, perfectly centered in the middle of the pack.

The mechanical music slows as the train pulls up to the platform. When it stops, we move off the car with the rest of the crowd, then duck suddenly sideways into the baggage holding area. Athens yanks the tarp off me, runs out, and drapes it over a baggage cart that is just about my shape and size. A moment later he's back in. We peek out and watch the rest of the passengers get off. Green Suit is one of them. Through a crack in the accordion between the cars, we see him stealthily tail the baggage cart.

"Keep your claws crossed he doesn't figure us out before the train pulls out," Athens whispers, scrunched as small as he can be against the side of the car and shivering a bit in his t-shirt.

A flood of passengers boards the train. This is the primary local to Shanghai. As we wait, I am aware of Athens' body pressed against me. I notice his firm arm muscles, his wide chest, his strong legs, the small speckle of whiskers on his chin, and his luxurious eyelashes, which he has told me are a gift from his Greek mother.

"Your shell's going soft," he says, poking me with his finger.

Lack of minerals. I need to eat more and better.

We make our way back to our compartment as the train leaves the station. There's a Chinese couple in there. Athens shows our tickets and asks to see theirs. They edge around me and out.

"They were hoping no one was in here," he says. "Enterprising, as you described them. The abbot's connections will give Green Suit access to surveillance camera footage when he doesn't find us. He'll be on the next train."

The abbot has connections?

"I told you that government people rely on his counsel. Lao Tzu's ideas are smart and coercive. They empower the oligarchy."

Long Ears was never coercive. He always told me that the one thing you can never do is control someone else, at least not for very long.

"Nice fantasy," Athens answers, lying back on his bunk and shielding his eyes against the morning with his arm.

I watch him closely. Experimentally, I try folding my spine the way I could when I was first born, first out of the egg. I feel something crack but there is no pain. Athens sits up.

"What was that sound? Are you all right?"

I stand up tall and put a claw on his forehead.

Rest. I'll wake you in Shanghai.

28

The day the long rain stopped, Long Ears took Sun Tzu and Yin for a walk in the forest. After half an hour, the wizard stopped and struck his bell. The sound bounced off wood and stems and rocks and fronds. "Look at that tree," the great sage told Yin. "In autumn it turns beautiful colors. And look at the lovely red of the alpine rhododendron. Notice how the water fills the flower's vault and then spills slowly over in just a dribble. It's a beautiful, delicate process."

"By the ancestors," the general groused, "are you going to keep up this poetic drivel all day?"

I echo the general's sentiment.

"Look at the mole crickets march and the gliding frogs mate on the way down from the trees."

Like you and your wife, Bao Yu.

"Time for a bite," said Sun Tzu, plopping down onto a rock.

I'm surprised not to see pig oil ooze from the man's pores.

"Perhaps while you eat you might devise a military strategy for keeping the provincial strongmen at bay?" Long Ears suggested to the general.

Sun Tzu unwrapped a dumpling. "The king is too nervous to send his soldiers afield to project power. He likes to keep them close. This dynasty you love so much is like a bubble floating downstream and heading for a sharp rock; it's only a matter of time before it pops."

Long Ears sat down beside him while Yin browsed the forest floor for fallen fruit. "The fact that King Ling loves peace more than war is a mark in his favor. It's up to those of us around him to make the proper plans."

"Plans are nice, but what I need is a couple of fat divisions to advance the cause of central government," Sun Tzu said, wiping dumpling juice from his cheek with the back of his one good hand.

On my island there are lizards like him, always squabbling for ground. They're fat too.

"She's complaining about me, isn't she?" Sun Tzu grumbled, giving Yin a little kick. "I still don't know what you see in the beastly ingrate."

A sudden waft of feline musk announced the arrival of a big cat, and a moment later a leopard appeared at the edge of the thicket. Sun Tzu drew his sword, as it eyed Yin with favor, but Long Ears gently moved him aside.

"Allow me. Fighting so soon after eating will give you a bellyache."

Do something before it eats me.

As the leopard pounced, the wizard stretched out his hand. A shimmering purple barrier appeared in the air. Striking it in mid-leap, the cat fell, writhed on the ground screaming in apparent agony, and then ran off.

"What magic was that?" the general whispered.

"The world is energy and nothing else."

"Why talk in riddles when I simply asked what you did?"

"I call it Five Thunder Palm. The vibration burned the cat. He's gone to the stream."

Tell him it was the stink of his dumplings that attracted her in the first place.

Mountain summits known as Immortal Gazing at the Sea, Bird's Nest Rock, and Couple's Peak loomed in the distance as the trio walked on. They came to a stone pool filled with water cascading from a vertical cliff with a tremendous roar.

"Welcome to Dragon Pond," Long Ears announced.

"Wonderful *feng shui!*" General Sun exclaimed.

What is this dragon?

"A giant of rare power. Ages ago, even before the days of the Yellow Emperor, its claws made those striations in the rock."

Is it still here?

"Its descendants remain in the pond. There's no other place like it in these Central States."

Carefully, Yin entered the waterfall, enjoying the same pounding she had received under the wizard's eave, but increased a thousand-fold.

Unnnngggunggg.

"Let's join her," said Sun Tzu. "I haven't had a good scrubbing since I lost my hand."

Yin watched as the men undressed and waded into the pool.

There's something growing below your back.

"The word we use is buttocks," Long Ears said nonchalantly.

Your buttocks are the bulges of your hip muscles. You use them to put one foot in front of the other and walk like a big white bird. I'm looking just above them.

"You mean my tail?"

Hearing those words, Sun Tzu craned for a look at the great sage's backside. "Ah. I've heard rumors. But it's not much of one," he said dryly.

Other men don't have tails.

"Some babies are born with extra bones there. Usually, the shaman or physician cuts them off, but my mother knew I didn't want that. We had many conversations when I was still in her belly."

Sun Tzu slipped back into the cold water with a sigh. "I heard you were born old and with a beard and that you grow younger every day."

Long Ears smiled and massaged his low back. "If only that were so."

Your mother loved you.

"And I loved her."

And now you love Bao Yu.

"Not only Bao Yu."

And without amplifying on the declaration, however oblique, that Yin had waited so long for him to make, Long Ears dropped to his hands and knees and set to prowling the shallows, his pendulous ears flapping and his tiny tail twitching at the sky like a warning finger. After a few minutes he pitched forward and disappeared. The water roiled with mud and bubbles and waves.

A dragon has him! Do something.

Sun Tzu could not hear her, but he knew a battle when he saw one. More than once the oracle of Luoyang came up for air, and every time his eyes were closed, his jaw set. Ravens, magpies and jays, gathered on the branches surrounding the pond, pointed their beaks at the frothing water.

Do something!

At last the wizard shot out of the water with a man-sized creature locked in his arms. It was a giant salamander with stubby limbs, smooth skin, an oversize head, and a mouth wide enough to swallow one of the king's ceremonial bells. He hauled it ashore.

"General. Your knife, if you please."

Sun Tzu tossed him the blade, and holding the salamander between his knees, the wizard took the same leg Ding Lok had taken from Yin, cutting at precisely the same level The beast gaped in agony as the sand turned red.

Stop!

Long Ears made a second careful cut, this time separating the salamander from the toes of its right forelimb.

Violence and more violence. Why, oh why must men be this way?

Tossing the knife aside, Long Ears pulled a bag of herbal powder from the pile of his clothes and sprinkled it on the wounds. The salamander bucked but the bleeding instantly stopped. The wizard eased it back into the water and watched it swim away.

"The dragon will be fine," he said. "The lost limbs will quickly grow back. General, show me your wound."

Reluctantly, the general offered his stump. His flesh was still pink and fresh. Lao Tzu rubbed the salamander toes to it, bloody and wet, touching every inch of his friend's amputated flesh.

"Now the dragon's magic is yours," he said. "In time, your hand will grow back."

Next, he rubbed the salamander's leg over Yin's amputated leg. "Despite what you say about men, we have our reasons for doing things. This will restore the flow of your qi, the energy that runs through the world, and before the month is out, it will return your leg to you, too."

Yin gazed at her sage. Her anger and judgment slowly faded and the now-familiar feeling washed over her and away.

29

The sun warms the compartment as we near Nanjing. Athens is on his laptop when he suddenly lets out a curse.

"Chinese trains!"

What's wrong with them?

"Sometimes great connectivity, sometimes none at all. Right now, there's no WiFi at all. Internet's down. Could be the will of the Party, could just be equipment issues."

He goes out into the corridor as if he's seeking news of a ball game. I hear excited chattering, and he comes back in wearing a huge grin.

"Have you ever considered that God is on your side?"

God?

"The creator."

My creator was a wizard.

"All right, but who created the crawling brute before he changed you? He had to work with something, right? The raw material?"

I was never a crawling brute.

"Tao, then," Athens says, exasperated. "The great process or intelligence behind everything. Whatever you want to call it, you have to admit it likes you."

I don't see such a force as personally interested in any individual or event.

"But you were plucked from your home and taken across the ocean to meet one of the greatest minds of all time, then transformed into this brilliant and amazing being covered in calligraphy."

It's not calligraphy. It's carving, and it's in the hand of the one you call Lao Tzu, who arranged everything.

"So you admit he did it, which makes you totally priceless in yet another way. Anyway, what I was trying to say is that while you flee from our pursuers, a solar flare comes to your aid."

"We have help from the sun?

"Chinese media report a lot of propaganda but they have reported this. Energy from a solar storm has affected digital equipment here on Earth. All the kids on the train are talking about it. Now cellphone networks are offline and sensitive electronics are down."

Why does this make me lucky?

"The abbot's people will be looking for us at Shanghai station. Thanks to the flare, though, we can get off in Nanjing and no camera will see us. Then we can figure out how to get to Shanghai under the radar."

Do you have a girlfriend?

It takes Athens a long moment to close his mouth and answer. "You've never asked about my family — odd for someone steeped in ancient Chinese culture. Nor have you even asked about my father."

I ask about a girlfriend and you offer your father. I find that odd.

"He's an investment banker. Lots of ties to China."

Why won't you answer my simple question?

"I have a crazy idea. I mean really pie in the sky."

I prefer pie in the beak. Used to be mouse pie was my favorite but for some reason I find that revolting now. Fruit works for me. Perhaps mango or banana.

"Mock me as much as you like, but if my plan works, we'll get to Shanghai unseen. And yes, I've had many girlfriends but most of them have been virtual lately, a nurse in Latvia, an office manager in Sao Paolo, even an archery champion in Kyoto, Japan."

You meet them online?

"That's right."

But not in the flesh?

"Not in a while."

I want to go to my island to mate, you know. To lay eggs and then die.

"I've got a feeling that's not how things are going to shake out."

You dismiss my dreams?

Athens shrugs. "I don't think we can predict anything here. We're dancing, you and I, and the steps, music, even the tempo is constantly changing."

A whiff of cigarette smoke comes into the compartment, followed by the asymmetrical face of a conductor. He stares at me a while and finally asks the question that has been burning inside him since we embarked at the old capital.

"This is what?"

"A turtle."

"Where does she poop?"

"She uses the toilet," Athens answers. "And even in the moving train her aim is excellent."

"No doing that unless the train is underway," the conductor cautions.

We sit quietly together until the train pulls into Nanjing station. Unlike the one in Luoyang, it's defined as much by glass as by steel and looks as it might have been designed on another planet, so angular are its surfaces and so alien its proportions.

Thinking about having a girlfriend but not touching her, I watch the passengers disembark. Athens scans the information screens. They remain blank from the solar flare, so he urges us off. We trundle past row after row of planted ferns.

That's a lot of ferns.

"They clean the air," said Athens. "There are many ways to do that, old and new."

I stick out my neck to smell the city and the movement feels odd. I could swear I could reach higher than I could before. We go to the taxi line, but driver after driver passes us by.

People fear what they don't understand.

"In this case I think they fear what they *do* understand."

I try to arrange my features into a question.

"Poop," he says, laughing. "They're afraid what you'll do to the upholstery."

They don't know my true nature.

There's an element of mystery in that last declaration, and I let it hang in the air.

30

Growing increasingly resentful of Yin's presence in her home, Bao Yu fought back by doing small things to make the tortoise's life miserable. She constantly changed the domestic schedule so that Yin could never quite find the great sage. She also had carpenters raise the door thresholds to keep the turtle and the wizard apart. So that she could always find her rival, she installed noisy bamboo mats that made an unmistakable sliding sound when Yin walked on them. Surreptitiously she shoved Yin outside when winter came and it grew cold, leaving her weakly pursuing patches of sunshine to stay warm. On the day of the season's first snowstorm, Long Ears worked late and found Yin nearly frozen solid by the back door. He brought her in, revived her by the woodstove, gave her herbs for her bubbling nose, and issued strict orders to the entire household that she not be put outside until spring.

Bao Yu wants me to freeze to death.

"There's nothing a woman hates more than competition at home."

Competition? I'm just a turtle.

"We both know that's not true."

Yearning for her wizard in his frequent absences and strategizing how best to locate him, Yin took satisfaction in second-guessing Bao Yu's schedule changes. She recognized the patterns in these changes and stayed ahead of them. When she and her wizard were together, he regaled her with the goings-on at court, the conspiring concubines, unctuous eunuchs, and grasping governors of outlying provinces who made illicit pacts with neighboring strongmen for favor and coin. Because he forbade fire at the library—he would never risk the dynasty's greatest treasure—it was months before he could take her with him to that frigid edifice.

On the first warm morning of spring, he did. This was the morning after something propitious appeared in the night sky. At first merely a disturbance in the warp and woof of heaven, it soon began to move, setting the common folks to rumor. Even the king was curious, and he and his guards paid Long Ears a rare visit in his lair.

"The Great Fertilizer grows," he said, pointing his royal scepter in Yin's direction.

"As does the queen's belly," Lao Tzu kowtowed.

I still wish he would not call me Fertilizer. I have recently learned the word has another meaning.

"Is it possible to love a child before he's born?"

"Nothing could be more natural, Your Highness."

My father on my island loved me that way. He would be sad to see how cold I am. The wood stove grows cold by the small hours of morning and I suffer alone in the kitchen. Perhaps, with Bao Yu's permission, I might start sleeping in the winter bed with you so your big feet could keep me warm?

The king's eyes scanned the assembled materials. Long Ears ignored Yin's question.

"You can really read all these old languages?"

"I can, Sire."

"And you know everything that is written here?"

"What I know could be written on a grain of rice, my king,

but the knowledge in the bones and scrolls and shells before you is—your queen aside—the jewel of the dynasty, Sire. We must remember that, and always keep it safe."

"What does this library tell you of the ball of fire in the sky that everyone is watching?"

"Some things about that, Sire, but to know all, I must perform a ritual ceremony."

"Of course you must. By the way, my spies in the state of Yan tell me that Ding Lok carries quite a grudge against you and the Fertilizer and came here to steal her, only to be repelled and forced back to the company of that thieving king who stole my bounty."

He's alive! I knew it!

"He won't trouble us again, Your Highness."

"I wouldn't be so sure. He's Shang. All Shang people burn for revenge at even the slightest offense and always want to be the center of their world."

"Yin is safe, Sire."

"She'd better be, since we both know that bringing her back was the real reason you sent those men across the world."

"Your Highness is too clever for me."

"She's a source of great solace to you, isn't she?"

Yin looked at the king and the wizard looked at Yin and in that triangle of glances a whole world was to be found.

Could it be that you love me and not Bao Yu?

"I knew she would do great things for the kingdom, Sire."

Must you keep up this ridiculous nonsense about me magically impregnating human females? It's degrading. Just tell him you knew you would love me.

"And she has. We will soon have a prince. Please convey my gratitude."

"She hears and understands you, Sire. You may tell her

yourself if you wish."

King Ling massaged his legs for a few moments and then lowered himself into a kowtow to Yin. The guards gasped. Long Ears took his elbow. "The library floor is no place for the knees of heaven."

"Knees of heaven," the king scoffed as a retainer brushed his robe. "What nonsense."

"Not at all, Your Highness. You are king by mandate of heaven. Your reign lifts us all from ignorance to civilization."

"You're the one who does that, not me. You divine the purpose of lights in the heavens, guide us all with your counsel, and send ships across the world for a supernatural turtle. All I can do is worry about the Huns pushing at our borders and the disgruntled princes cracking our bones. Mandate or no, armies or no, what I really need is offspring to consolidate the dynasty."

"Yin will bring them, Sire," Long Ears soothed. "But you must do your part and continue your exercises."

Any fool can see he doesn't exercise as much as he eats.

"Of course," the king said, rising to leave.

"One more thing, Sire."

The king arched an eyebrow.

"Would you consider lowering taxes in this time of intrigue and war?"

"Ha! Sun Tzu suggests I fortify the capital against siege by stocking the granaries. That will cost almost as much as paying the army. I need those taxes."

It doesn't sound like that military dumpling sees things the way you do.

"In times such as these, loyal subjects are a king's greatest assets. A populace lightly taxed is more loyal and productive and willing to serve you."

"You said my greatest asset was the library," countered King

Ling. "Then you mentioned the queen, and heirs, and the turtle. How many assets can a king nurture?"

"It goes without saying that caring for his kingdom is the lot of a king, Sire, and that in return his power and fortune abound."

If it goes without saying, why are you saying it? Everything you say goes without saying and yet I still see your lips moving. You claim to do nothing and yet you do everything.

The king frowned. "It's not just Sun Tzu. All the ministers want more taxes too."

"And because you are so much wiser than they are you must guide them, Sire."

It's shameless the way you work him. I mean it. It's embarrassing.

"I'll think about it. In the meantime, I have a thought about the comet ceremony."

"What thought, Your Highness?"

"Make sure there are plenty of dancing girls."

31

I've spent hours and hours looking at Internet photos of the world, but none of that so-called surfing prepares me for the sheer density of Nanjing, not for the pace of movement there — everyone is running somewhere and nobody seems to walk — nor for the crowds, the architecture, the technologies, and most of all the smells. The town reeks of naked steel, even though Athens tells me there is far, far more new construction in some other cities than there is here.

I have learned that after the Zhou dynasty collapsed, the King of Qin united the warring states in his name. I have learned that there have been several capitals of the empire since Luoyang, and that Nanjing was one. I see the old stone walls of the city as we drive, but since everything has been washed, restored, replaced, and redone. Even the old seems new to me.

Athens is on his phone the whole time we are in the van, variously muttering, cursing, stabbing the glass keyboard, and punching the air.

You're texting with your father, aren't you?

"The abbot told him I ran off. He's threatening me. The museum wants to press charges and he needs to be able to tell them I'm doing penance. The lawyers say that becoming a monk will sound good in court, if things come to that."

So this is all still unresolved. You're just biding time with me until

something breaks, shakes out, changes. Then you're gone.
"I suppose, though it's not clear where I will go."
Sounds as if we should go back to the monastery.
"We go back, you're soup. I can't protect you there."
An excruciating memory floats into my head. There was a time I couldn't protect someone I loved, couldn't rescue him from a terrible fate. In front of me, right here and now, I see a way to do what I could not do before, to feel powerful. To make a difference and be effective in a way I previously could not. I maneuver myself so that I can stretch my neck and raise my head and look him straight in the eye.
I know a way to help you.
He smiles sadly. "I appreciate that, Yin. I really do. But things are not the way they were. It's a new world now."
The more things change, the more they remain the same.
"Maybe that was true a few hundred years ago, but the pace of change, the sheer complexity of the world—we've passed a tipping point. A sea change has occurred. Something qualitative. We're on the way to melding with our machines. We're evolving into something else entirely, an intelligence that will someday be able to understand what's really going on. In some ways we're just tools—manifestations of a universe trying to understand itself."
I have no idea what this sudden, seemingly irrelevant pronouncement has to do with the way humans regard each other and the way debts are repaid. I choose not to engage the point.
You're only seeing half the puzzle.
"What are you talking about?"
Everything is as it was. I know this because I was there; you were not.
He opens his mouth to counter and then closes it again, shut

down by the irrefutable truth of my argument. "You have some kind of plan?"

I do.

"To help me with my troubles."

Precisely so.

"All right. Say for a moment that I agree...."

We will have to make a stop before Shanghai. In fact, we'll have to go in another direction entirely before changing course.

"But we need to get you to the ocean. To your island."

We need to do this first. For you.

"Give me the details then."

As it is, I am fresh and helpless in this world, and entirely dependent upon this man. If I answer the question, I relinquish the one and only position I might hold, the one and only thing he might need from me. Besides, I am entirely sure that what was the greatest of all confidences must, at least for now, remain so.

They're secret.

He looks at me for a long time, a run of variables under analysis in his head.

"You're sure you don't want to tell me?"

You'll find out soon enough.

"And whatever it is you have in mind will change things?"

Completely.

He picks up the phone again. This time instead of texting his father he calls him. Although I can't make out the words, I can I hear the older man's voice come booming through the phone. His qi comes from his belly and his tone is domineering.

"Dad," he says after the tirade is over. "I'm in a bit of a jam. Would you mind arranging a lift?"

The man on the other end yells so loudly Athens has to hold the phone away from his ear. "We're in Nanjing," he says when the yelling stops. "I disabled the GPS on my phone."

More yelling, back and forth this time, but eventually things get quieter and they agree on a plan I don't really understand. Athens hangs up, telling me we have to kill some time. He directs the driver to take us to the Confucian Temple.

When we get there, we find a plaque out front. It explains that the building, an architectural mishmash, was originally erected in 1034 C.E., during the Song Dynasty. I remain unsettled by the sheer number of Chinese dynasties, and by the fact that some brutal, repressive upstart from Qin begat the whole series.

Who is this Confucius?

"China's greatest social thinker. The nation's entire history is based on his ideas. Imperial society was founded on his guidelines for family relationships, loyalty, duty, friendship, and honor. Despite the Communists, he's back in vogue."

The old ways become new again.

"Something like that."

I read some more biographical details, and when I come across his personal name, Kong Qiu, I cough. It is not a turtle sound, and this time I'm not the only one to notice. The surrounding crowd of temple-goers, which has, as a whole, been quite blasé about my presence, is suddenly curious. They ask Athens the usual questions, adding to them the observation that I sound very human when I clear my lungs.

"Something's happening to you," he says when interest subsides. "I think we should talk about it. Your legs are getting longer and your feet are starting to grow toes, not just nails, and..."

I knew him.

"Who?"

Confucius. Back when he was just Kong Qiu. I did not immediately recognize your pronunciation.

"You *knew* him?"

I can't believe that pompous, self-righteous misogynist became more famous than Long Ears.

Athens sits down on a bench near a series of artistic steles, inlaid with gold and silver and jade, that detail Confucius' life. "I'm not sure he did. It depends upon whom you're talking to. The way I understand it, Confucius gave rules about how people should live, whereas Lao Tzu exhorted them to follow nature and maybe their intuition, too. Do I have that right?"

It's a bit of an oversimplification, but I suppose you could say that.

"Well, if there's one thing I've learned, it's that even though they love to bitch about them, people need rules. They even *like* rules."

I'm not quite sure why, but I try a shrugging movement with my shoulders. Doing so, I feel them move freely in my shell in a new and unfamiliar way.

Some do, but only when they're passively asleep the way Kong Qiu wanted them. Long Ears wanted them to wake up. When you really understand what's going on, rules and regulations reveal themselves to be tools for the limitation of freedom and the furthering of someone else's agenda."

Athens grins and shakes his head. "You'd make a great hacker," he says.

The temple is built inside a complex on the banks of the Qinhuai River, a tributary of the Yangtze, according to the tourist signs. I watch the roll of Athens' hips and the left-right swaying of his buttocks as he strolls the grounds, remembering another similar set, so long ago it seems a dream. The growing imbalance between my front and rear legs makes following him a challenge. The nails on my forelimbs suddenly snap off and I stumble and pitch forward. Athens doesn't notice, and, even maimed as I am, I don't mind; having this man to follow pleases me.

He turns down Qinhuai River Street, which is lined with

shops selling paintings, posters, and clothes. "These sculptures," he says. "All fake versions of French boutique glass. Vintage Daum, which doesn't even exist anymore, Baccarat, Lalique. Can't tell the real thing from the copies anymore. That's China for you. A nation looking to be the center of the world again and well on their way."

Colorful awnings drape down to the water. Boats go by and draw small wakes. Athens watches them, then suddenly turns and looks at me.

"What are we doing?" he says.

You have a plan. You spoke with your father.

"That's not what I mean."

An uncomfortable thought arises. *You mean what are we doing together?*

"Not really that. But you have to admit what's happening to your body is stranger than just thawing out after being in frozen ground for 2000 years."

This small sentence he utters pains me. I crumple. When I do, my shell suddenly folds and a large chunk of it falls off. This mortal wound, this terrible, awful, ecdysis, forces me onto my back, from which position I am unable to get right. Shopkeepers gather, pointing, and I feel the ground beneath me as never before, because I'm no longer hard but newly soft there.

Suddenly, I am vulnerable. I am defenseless and unprotected. I am also free.

Athens stares at me for a long moment, then turns me over and covers me with his coat. "Don't worry," he says, his voice strained. "We'll find you something to eat. That will help."

32

On a mountaintop two days walk from Luoyang grew tea plants of the finest variety, strengthened by mountain air, fed by ancient crumbling soil, and caressed by a refreshing rain. Long Ears considered the plants his friends and was grateful for the life-giving brew he steeped from their cooked leaves. One spring day, he took Yin to meet them.

"You're getting so heavy I won't be able to carry you much longer."

Then I'll walk. It's nice being here with you. You really do seem happiest when you're alone in nature.

"I'm not alone; I'm with you."

Turtles don't have lips, but Yin gave her best version of a smile. *Maybe what you love about me is that I am part of nature.*

"We're all a part of nature. That's why we're never really alone. As for you, you're just feminine energy at its purest."

Maybe so, but you are as torn between the forest and the palace as I am between wanting to go home to my island and wanting to be with you.

Long Ears nodded. "That's the draw of heaven above and earth below, an awareness felt by all creatures but perhaps more keenly by human beings."

If it's unique to humans, why do I feel it?

"Perhaps you're more human than you know."

How long will it take for me to look like a woman?

"Ah, Yin. I'm sorry about that but I fear my magic may have failed. What's important now is to pick the choicest leaves so they will strengthen the queen for childbirth."

"What's it like, giving birth?"

The wizard chuckled. "Most women curse about it, but then do it again. Perhaps you'll tell me all about it one day."

In reply, I start munching the base of the bush, which is actually so much a small tree that I have to crane my neck.

It's bitter.

"Please stop that. You mustn't damage the bark. We drink the steeped leaves; we don't eat them."

Scolded, she ambled off in search of flowers while he took the leaves he needed. It was late afternoon before they arrived back at the palace, and Queen Qin Jiang greeted the wizard with a expression that made Yin ache with jealousy.

Bursting with child makes her even more beautiful.

"Rise, great one," said the queen. "Do you have something for me?"

The wizard brushed off his robe and ran his fingers through his beard, then brought forth leaves with a flourish. "Spring shoots fresh from the mountain, Your Highness, for timing is everything."

While a guard took the leaves to the kitchens for roasting, four maids raised a silk curtain on poles and Long Ears went behind it to examine the queen.

"Little Prince Shen only kicks like this for you," the wizard said as he gently probed her swollen belly with his fingers.

"He knows my touch and he can hear my voice."

"I've heard it said you remember your mother's womb."

Long Ears smiles. "Anyone can."

"But no one else does. Is it also true that you speak to your ancestors in meditation?"

"I do," the sage replied, kneeling lower. "Now, may I put my ear to you?"

The maids tittered as the queen bared her belly for him and he knelt.

"It is as I have foretold. The boy will love music. Even now he is singing."

The queen sat up. "It's not fair that you should hear my child's voice before I do."

"You could hear it too, Your Highness, if you would only listen."

"And what of your tortoise? Can I also hear her words if I listen carefully?"

The wizard shook his head. "That would require magic, my queen."

"Then make it so."

Long Ears hesitated. "What purpose would it serve, Majesty? I am happy to relay to you exactly what she says."

The queen graced him with her most radiant smile. "What purpose, Long Ears? Why, it would please me, of course."

Do it for us. No harm can come of it, and I would hear the baby sing.

Yin made her way behind the curtain. The wizard took a few minutes to prepare the required energetic connection. When he was ready, he put one hand on the turtle and another on the queen. The connection was instantaneous.

Ha! I can hear the baby! You're right, he really does sing.

The queen's expression, which had been full of joyful anticipation, suddenly darkened. "Oh, wizard," she said. "What have you done to poor Yin? I feel her mind and she is so sad and full of longing. What happened to her?"

"Hers is not the life she chose, my queen."

The sailors butchered my family and took me away from my island.

The queen started to cry. "I hear you. I feel how badly you want to go home."

He promised me....

Long Ears removed his hands. The queen took him by the shoulder and shook him violently. "Why did you stop it? You should never have brought her here. Her homesickness and loneliness are heartbreaking. And you promised to make her a woman? Do you not realize she loves you desperately?"

"I do."

"And do you love her, too?"

"It's time to prepare for the comet ceremony, Your Highness." The queen fixed him with a sad smile. "I think you'd best go now."

No words passed between wizard and tortoise until they neared the event grounds, at which point Yin paused.

The queen deserves better than the king.

"There is more to him than you know."

Even so.

"Perhaps you're right, Yin, but this is the way things are. The Tao...."

I know, I know. The Tao works in strange and wondrous ways. I can't tell you how tired I am of hearing that. Now where are the dancing girls the king ordered? I'm sure they'll be a great help in your divination.

"Your sarcasm grows more biting every day."

Never mind the girls. Just tell me how you read the sky.

"Do you remember our chat about the *bagua*, the Celestial Ladder, Ancestor Yu, and King Fu Xi?"

I do, but I still think you're just good at guessing what's going to happen.

"What you call a guess I call the voice of intuition—the ability to perceive cycles and extremes of yin and yang. It requires an utterly still mind."

Do you remember when you cultivated my mind and named me for the moon?

"Of course."

You are still the sun to me. We are yin and yang.

"We are."

Do you think I'll ever give you a baby?

"I hope so."

Will you look to my island in your meditation and give me news of my kind? I want to know that no more men have come to kill them and that they are peacefully living the life I remember.

"I'll see what I can do."

Will Wang Yi join us at the party?

"He will."

They entered a large hall where a group of officials was waiting, dragon-festooned robes swishing, ponytails bobbing, a retinue of soldiers stepping in synch, and an entourage of eunuchs scurrying at the rear. Kowtowing to the wizard, they asked what the comet had in store for the kingdom, in particular whether the dynasty would have another heir after Prince Shen. Long Ears assured them they would.

The king arrived on a palanquin, and the show began. Dancing girls were present in force, and commanded the royal eyes with glimpses of their bodies through white silk. Veering as close to the king's throne as his guard would allow, they careened, whooshed, and swayed seductively. Eunuchs clucked, ministers fretted, the grandmasters, *dafu,* kept their eyes to the ground, and the professional servicemen, *shi,* nudged each other with elbows. The girls embraced each other, back to front, in a risqué replication of a comet's head, body and tail. King Ling's grin widened.

I know the king loves all those thrusts and bends, but I find all this rather tiresome. Don't you think you should begin?

In response, the wizard led the crowd out of the hall to a courtyard where a labyrinth, just visible in the starlight, had been intricately worked into the ground. He ordered all torches extinguished and without preamble began walking the maze, his head bowed, muttering unintelligibly.

Wang Yi appeared beside Yin. "Those sounds he's making put him into a trance," he explained.

The crowd watched quietly while the wizard gyrated, circled, and finally made gestures in the air, at which point Wang Yi, ever loyal and devoted to his teacher, rushed to him with a brush and scroll so that he might write for a few minutes before walking again.

"Fragmentation is coming," Wang Yi announced, when his master handed him the still-dripping message. "Danger is present on all borders. Forces will try and tear our dynasty apart."

There were hushed murmurs and a few gasps. Again, Long Ears gestured and again Wang Yi brought him brush and scroll so that he might write furiously, as if possessed.

"Heaven and earth will eventually sweep those forces away," Wang Yi continued. "In time, peace will come to the Central States. Until then, things will be difficult."

Ministers licked their lips, *dafu* exchanged pre-arranged signals indicating their loyalties and intentions, and some eunuchs sank to the ground in dismay. The king, hearing the future thus spoken, felt terrible sadness and worry for his unborn son. Yin thought of her island and imagined that perhaps she and Long Ears could escape the carnage by going there. Closing her eyes under the frigid night sky, she imagined them together.

33

When I eat too much I dream too much. It has always been thus, though of course for the past thousands of years I have dreamed too much of eating. The banquets we enjoy along the Qinhuai River are sensational, for they allow me, a former vegetarian tempted only by mouse meat, to broaden my culinary horizons in ways I never dreamed possible. Together, Athens and I devour river prawns, eels, shark fin soup, chicken prepared in the Szechuan style, beef with Hunan spices, noodles served cold and green and dressed with a silky butter of peanuts.

This new Chinese cuisine titillates me because these are more interesting than the dishes I was allowed to scrounge at court, but it is the Italian food that makes me truly crazy. The smell of the place alone, the garlic, the breadcrumb-laced clams, the pasta made black with squid ink, and most of all the masterpieces created with tomatoes. I eat so much I can look down and see my belly swell. I wash all this down with wine made not from rice but from grapes, and it is smoky and dry and cloud-like on my tongue. Athens tells me I've had enough and pulls me away.

After the Italian food, we try a French pastry place for dessert. Chinese confections are quite simple by comparison, so I've never before experienced a tiramisu, a parfait, a *gâteau au chocolat*, or a passion fruit sorbet. These, in combination with a sip of a wickedly bitter brew called espresso, mellowed by granules of brown sugar that explode on my tongue, leave me first exhilarated and then suddenly and unaccountably exhausted. Now I lie torpid and dreaming in an alley, out of sight of surveillance cameras, which an intricate hack tells have returned to full function.

In my dream I feel pain at the spot where Ding Lok took my leg, and I feel other pain too. That is because some nameless, faceless demon, something large, with snake-like fangs, red eyes, and lips as anatomically unable to smile as my own, is eating me. My wizard always denied the existence of such beings, but now as pieces of my shell are ripped off and swallowed, I know, despite dreaming, that this one is real. Having fought to hold onto life so desperately and for so long, this defeat of my material nature seems both crushing and cruel.

I am engaged in the continuous business of weeping, though I can't say for certain what every species feels when their tears flow. Indeed, how would we really know if they did it, or their equivalent? How can we possibly say that the depths of despair a tortoise feels at the slaughter of her family is less than what a person, elephant, or sea slug might feel at the same? Ever since my sage began my transformation, I have suffered prejudice against my species. Now, ironically, I find myself prejudiced against what I was, what I am becoming, and all the stages in between.

I struggle with the demon, fighting with beak and claws to stop him from taking my flesh as sustenance for his own. His response is to upend me. Upside down, and stuck that way because of the shape of my shell, I wonder if this vulnerability will ever pass. I lash out and find that the armor of my scales has faded like an inked scroll left out in the rain, leaving my skin strangely soft. I feel heat within me, something no turtle can know, and wake to find Athens screaming.

"A nightmare has you! Wake up!"

My eyes blink open, and I find myself in the alley once more, surrounded by multi-colored bits of trashed plastic shaped to echo this new human world in all its frivolous excess. Flies attack the thin river of sewage. The stench is unbearable. I retch, and Athens crouches beside me.

"What happened? Dreams often presage the future, you know."

A demon.

He nods. "Night witches give bad dreams their name."

This was no witch.

"Are you sure? There are so many kinds."

I'm sure. We have to move. It's not safe here.

"It's safe here until tomorrow."

It isn't Besides, the stench is just too much.

He frowns. "You've spent eons in the dirt. Why does street trash bother you so much all of a sudden?"

I draw my claws through the dirt, trying to wipe off the bits of filth clinging to them.

I can't stand it anymore. I need to be clean.

Athens swallows hard. "Look at your nails."

The thick black stumps I've been scratching against the ground have torn off, leaving pink buds.

Grab my shell.

He doesn't move. He is, in fact, frozen staring at my feet.

"You have fingers," he murmurs.

I said grab my shell.

He makes a feeble effort to hold onto the top of my carapace where the scutes make subtle pyramids around the wizard's carvings. I close my eyes.

"Not there. The edges. Good. Now pull up."

The twin forces of suction and stiction define my world. They are all I can hear, all I can sense, all I can think about, and all I can feel. Athens Li peels back all that is left of the formerly solid refuge under which I have lived my entire life, and holds it aloft like a warrior for love. I sob again. More loudly this time.

"You're free," he says quietly.

He waits for me to comment, but I can't manage it. The moment sits atop me like a column of dirt too heavy for me to dislodge.

"And, we have a souvenir for Abbot Chen."

No.

"Why not? He can have the carvings and you can have your life. Deal of the century."

I said no.

"So what do you want me to do with this?"

At one time that glorious carapace could have held off an army, but that time has passed.

It's dust.

As I so declare, it disintegrates in his hands. I watch the particles float downward, unaccountably shiny in the moonlight.

"Your back," he says, staring.

What about it?

"It's beautiful."

34

Prince Shen was born every bit the musician Long Ears had predicted. If he had not so immediately stolen his father's heart, he might have been forced to the tasks expected of a crown prince. Instead, he was leniently permitted to indulge his passion. Years passed and another prince, Gui, was born to Qin Jiang. There was no softness this time, as the king grew more and more worried about the future of his domain. The dangerous forces at work on the kingdom persisted: on the one side the rot in the court and its devious liaisons with agents on foreign borders, on the other the wise, tireless, and judicious wizard desperately trying to hold everything together with just a quiet, influential word here, a deft, energetic touch there.

Gui was forced to memorize scrolls and train in archery and fencing, as his father wanted him to be prepared for anything. Shen, however, continued to practice his music and commune with Yin, whom he loved more than anyone in his world. Under Long Ears' watchful eye, he rode around the palace grounds on her back, oblivious to plots and plans against him and the general unraveling of the dynasty.

One afternoon, Yin found Long Ears meditating under his favorite tree.

Shen doesn't want to be king. Why do some people make other people be and do things they don't wish to be and do? A turtle would never do that. Shen lives for music, not to fight with Huns and rival strongmen.

"He will not have to do so."

You foresee this?

"Yes."

Because Prince Gui will help him?

"Perhaps. Tell me, Yin, how many siblings do you have?"

My mother laid a hundred eggs a year, but the crabs and lizards and birds got most of them. I'm not sure how many are left and because you brought me here, I'll never know.

"You were bound for me from the start. Wang Yi knew that when he saw the constellations in your eyes."

It was his kind heart that drew him to me, not my pupils. He knew I'd end up in the sailor's pot if he didn't rescue me.

"And now you carry a crown prince around on your back."

Holding a bowl of dumplings, and with Shen in tow, Sun Tzu approached from the far side of the garden. "Ho, Long Ears," he cried. "Will you join us on an expedition? Something fell from the sky the other night and landed in the mountains. I want to see if I can find it."

The way he eats he could climb the mountain every day and he'd still be fat.

"Wang Yi needs help in the library," the wizard replied. "The knowledge of the kingdom grows daily, and new scrolls have arrived."

"Let him work on it while we go together. We can take the pale prince along. He could use the fresh air and exercise.

Smiling in acquiescence, Long Ears soon led the party to a mountainside cathedral of overarching trees and songbirds flush with spring. Hanging vines exploded from branches, many of them heavy with spring flowers and dripping caterpillars and beetles in a clicking, chitinous cascade. Shen walked with his hand on Yin's back while the general and the wizard brought up the rear.

"The forest is full of music!" the precocious boy cried in sudden rapture.

The famous general plopped down onto a rock, wiped the sweat off his brow, and offered the prince a dumpling to feed the birds. The boy scampered off to do so, and the general informed the wizard he had bad news to share.

"In so salubrious a setting?" Long Ears protested.

"My spies tell me that Ding Lok has a son, a strapping teen by the name of Ding Fei . He's as greedy as his father and just as obsessed with kidnapping Yin and selling her to the highest bidder."

Another Ding Lok? You have to be joking.

"You believe he will come for her?"

"A declining dynasty emboldens thieves and adventurers. The only question is when and where. In the meantime, look at that furrow in the mountainside. I bet that's where the flaming sky ball hit the ground."

When Shen fed off the last bit of dumpling, they climbed to the swath and followed it until they came to a meteorite protruding from the ground to the height of the general's shoulder. Bits of earth clung to it, along with leaves and branches crisped into twisted black fingers by the retained heat of atmospheric entry.

"Fu Hsi's fingernail, will you look at this," the wizard exclaimed.

A rock falls from the sky and you see the hand of your ancestors.

"Without the ancestors, nothing means anything at all."

Sun Tzu scraped the rock with his sword and put his nose to the scratch.

"There are warriors in Ningxia whose swords smell like this," he mused. "The blades are sharper than bronze ones and ring like bells and bend without snapping. They call it 'iron' and say they take it from the ground."

"A common thing, then."

The general shook his head. "This particular iron is a gift from heaven. Look at the striations in it, and feel how hard it is. Swords of such material will confer an advantage against the Huns and the armies of the east."

"Will you make me an iron flute, general?" asked Shen.

Better a king who thinks of flutes than one who thinks of swords.

The general spied a ginseng root growing beside a tree toppled by the meteorite. He dug it out, broke off a piece, and chewed it thoughtfully. "Today marks a change in the fortunes of the kingdom," he said.

"I'm not so sure," Long Ears replied.

Why do I have a bad feeling about this?

35

We are out of the alley and out of the night, but the air is too dirty for a real sunrise here. What we get instead is a gray glow that gets steadily brighter like a musical note played timidly at first and then with increasing confidence. Athens shuffles when he walks, and he looks over his shoulder and up at the moon, just a light patch of relief in the clouds opposite where the sun would be. I ask about his education.

"Too much of it," he says. "School after school. Year after year. Degree after degree."

It was not difficult for you?

"School? Never."

Not science?

"Math and physics are candy."

Is that right? What about languages?

"I speak eight and understand three more pretty well."

Art?

"In five minutes, and with my eyes closed, I can draw better than the next best students could do with two cups of espresso, a line of coke, and an hour to burn."

Only the course in humility seems to have beaten you.

"You're funny."

What about hacking?

"What about it?"

Another thing you do better than everyone else?

"That's what hacking's all about. It's a competitive enterprise. If you're not better than everyone else, don't hack."

I see. So you hack to be better than everyone else. And how do you decide whom to hack?

"The riskier the more attractive."

What does that mean?

"Well, corporate sites can be a challenge because big companies pay a lot for protection and so they get the best — sometimes even freelancers like me. Still, in the end, I beat most of them."

Which no doubt keeps a bounty on your head.

"That's more likely from government sites. Government computer cops may not be particularly bright but they work in teams, and they just don't give up. Make one mistake, leave one tiny little door somewhere in your program, some trace in your code, and they'll swarm through it like a cloud of bees and sting you to death. The real you. The flesh-and-blood you. Cops. Handcuffs. Jail time. Still, if you plan everything right and you do your homework, you can get into most places. Trouble is, if you really beat the tough firewalls, they won't just post a bounty, they'll be after you for the rest of your life. No hacker wants that. In the end, I looked for a different kind of challenge. Something more nuanced and subtle."

The museum.

"Think of it as a pride point. Guys who protect a place like that work with passion: in this case to protect high art. Feeling like you have a higher calling lends you a certain edge. The firewalls are world-class."

He skirts dangerously close to the river. For a moment I think he's going to jump in, but then he veers back toward me. He reaches into his vest pocket and pulls out a pack of cigarettes and lights one, drawing deeply. The cigarette glows a moment, then calms down. This is the first time I've seen him smoke. He closes his eyes.

"Here," he says, taking off his jacket. "You should put this over your back."

I'm a freak now. I'm going to draw more attention than I did as a turtle.

"We're close to the pickup point."

I shrug my shoulders and the jacket settles down. I'm still on all fours, but I'm not happy about it. My four feet are tender and my front toes have grown and I have to hold them up and back and out of the way because the skin's so thin. I walk on my heels now, front and back.

You just sit in front of your computer and leave the real world.

"I guess you could say that."

You don't really need your body.

"It's a hindrance; I have an avatar."

And gigabytes of information inform your decisions and experiences.

"More. Terabytes. Petabytes. Exabytes, even."

And do all those bytes bring you the feeling of the smell of a rose, the taste of a soufflé, the weight of a lover's leg over yours when you both wake up in the morning, together in the bed?

"What do you know of lovers and legs?"

Assuming you are the one who knows, I'm asking you how the virtual world compares.

"I'm not sure what you're getting at."

I'm trying to say that in avoiding the real world, you avoid yourself. It's like being thirty years old and still wondering who you are.

"Isn't that true of everyone? Aren't we all trying to figure out who we are? Isn't that precisely the point of living? That exploration? That journey? That quest?"

Once you find out who you are, you learn that it isn't.

He throws down his cigarette and with his smelly finger traces the run of flesh where my beak used to be. A nose grows there—not the flat nose of a Chinese woman, because I am from somewhere else entirely—but one with more substance and body.

"Maybe I was trying to figure all that out before, but since I met you, I understand a lot more. Real life is like a run of code I could never predict, a dream unfolding in impossible ways. This face of yours. Your shell turning to dust. The tattoo on your back that shows the same line of characters as the ones on your shell."

You made all this possible. If you hadn't been there when the earth gave way. You and your shovel.

"Still think it's a dream?"

Behind us, even though there should be no one on the street but sweepers, we hear running footsteps draw near.

36

Ding Fei and his men came over the walls wearing black under a black sky. They savaged the parapet guards in an assault all along the palace's northern throw and were soon inside. Avoiding the well-patrolled avenues that led to the royal chamber, they gathered in the wizard's garden, around his favorite maple. Such was their combat expertise that they swayed like saplings in the breeze while conspiring so they wouldn't be noticed among the trees, and used peonies in their armpits to mask the smell of their sweat.

Young Ding Fei was shorter than his father but had the captain's barrel chest, rough hands, and quick reflexes. Leading the silent trek to the library, he kept his eyes down because they were likely to reflect torchlight and attract the attention of palace archers. The men had trained extensively for the campaign. Each carried a map of the building in his head, and after climbing, slithering, and snaking through the collection, assumed a strategic position among the rows of scrolls and shelves of bone and settled down to wait.

His forces in position, Ding Lok made his way to the court wizard's house. The man who answered the door was one of the watchmen who had fallen asleep during the first kidnapping. He had never again dozed off and was now fiercely loyal.

"Your name?" the watchman asked.

"I'm here to see the supreme wizard."

"It's the middle of the night. He's asleep."

"Wake him and tell him of a fire in the library and that the wisdom of the dynasty is on the verge of being lost."

"You say there's a fire? Why don't I hear bells?"

"It hasn't happened yet, but it will if you don't wake him. Tell him my name is Ding Fei."

"Wait here."

The watchman approached the master bedroom with trepidation. Peering in, he saw Bao Yu asleep on her side, her arm draped over Long Ears' back. Beside the bed, the Great Fertilizer abided suspiciously, her pupils reflecting the light from his torch. The watchman was intimidated. Not only had the tortoise grown to impossible proportions but she was powerful enough, through her actions and predictions, to have disturbed the balance of the house, the city, and perhaps the very kingdom.

"Lord," the watchman whispered.

Yin rose up on columnar limbs and looked at him balefully.

"Great lord," the watchman repeated, louder this time.

Lao Tzu gave a single snore. Bao Yu's arm fell off his back and to the floor.

The watchman shuffled closer in a kowtow. "Great lord, someone is threatening to set fire to the library."

The oracle of Luoyang set to quivering like a spear in the hands of a frightened soldier. His pale body stiffened, his fingers and toes grew rigid, and without any additional warning, he began to levitate. He rose a full foot off the bed and hung there, rising and falling with each breath.

So the rumors are true. You only pretend *to be bound to the earth like the rest of us. Are you awake?*

"A young man called Ding Fei is at the door," the watchman went on. "He says the library might be on fire."

Bao Yu stirred as her husband dressed. "What's happening?" The wizard moved her hair from her neck. "Wait for me," he whispered into the white pearl of her ear. "I won't be long at all."

Yin followed him to the door, where Ding Fei was waiting.

"I came for the animal," the boy said without preamble.

"You wear your father's crookedness like a cloak. Why not shed it and be free?"

"My men are in position at your library. If you don't hand over the reptile, they'll destroy it with firebombs. Once that symbol of the dynasty is gone, Luoyang will be just like any other town—a bit more bloated perhaps, but nothing special. Your king's prestige will plummet, and he'll lose his tenuous grip on the federation. I don't think you'll allow all that just for the sake of a dumb animal."

"You don't have to do this," Long Ears replied gently. "There's a better path for a brave boy like you. Send your men away and come study with me. You can apprentice with Wang Yi and learn the Tao."

"Stop dreaming and hand her over."

Long Ears sighed. "Consider the consequences of what you propose. The wisdom of the scrolls…."

"Keep your scrolls and give me a woman flat on her back."

"And what will you share with her? What knowledge will you offer to entertain and enlighten her? The experiences of centuries are stored in the library."

"And you're the author of such a love guide, I suppose—the oracle, a great lover as well as a seer of lands across the sea? I bring plenty to any woman. I don't need scrolls. I've had enough of your delusions and your waxed words, too. Soon it will be the hour of the tiger, and my men will set your precious library to flame. Bring me the animal and be quick about it."

Understanding the situation, Yin trundled off down the hall.

She went through the kitchen and out the back door, passing a guard who assumed she was off to take her toilet.

As she trudged down the alley, rats zoomed by on their way to the fresh leavings of a ministerial banquet. She passed a council of frogs rejoicing around a cistern, their throats pulsing, and sniffed the aroma of torrid lovemaking and the fragrant steaming of fresh bean buns. She heard the high-pitched screams of bats in deadly pursuit of fluttering moths, the stentorian snores of four old men, a child crying for its mother, and a mouse dying in a wet crunch, caught in the claws of a cat.

A cloud flashed across the tiny, almost invisible sliver of the moon. Ding Fei came after her, moving more slowly than had his father, years before, on his ill-fated black steed. She heard Long Ear's footsteps beside him and burrowed into ground softened by the trampling of pigs. As soon as they passed her, she detoured down a side alley to Sun Tzu's house and banged on the door until a retainer answered and ushered her in.

The famous general lumbered out in silk that hung on him like a flag. "You smell awful," he said.

She stared at him wide-eyed.

"Something's wrong or you wouldn't be here. It's Ding Lok's boy, isn't it? Nod your head if I'm right."

She nodded.

"I've been waiting for this. Did he take Long Ears hostage?"

She shook her head.

"His wife?"

Another shake.

"All right. Give me a minute to think."

In all her years in the Central States, Yin had never attempted to draw a character on the ground with her foot, but she did so now, utilizing the dust on the floor and the gleam of torchlight. It was an awkward rendering of the character for library, and it took a moment for the general to understand it.

"The library?" he said at last. "Hostages in the library? Wait. I know. The things most precious to our wizard are those bones and scrolls. That dog, Ding is holding the kingdom's wisdom hostage until you surrender to him."

Yin gave a single nod of her head.

Immediately, the general summoned a retainer, and the two of them lifted Yin into a cart and headed for the palace gates.

37

On the run, we duck into a stand of trees.

"I strolled through this park years ago," Athens huffs, apparently not accustomed to running and certainly not accustomed to half dragging, half carrying the creature I have become. "I'm pretty sure this is the way."

A strong smell of fish is in the air. Behind us, a couple of thickset men materialize out of the crepuscular gloom. Unencumbered by either a smoker's lungs or a dysfunctional anatomy, they close on us. We pass a few elderly people exercising to tinny tunes from a boom box, flapping their arms like cranes. If they notice anything curious about me, they don't stop dancing long enough to show it.

The men chasing us draw closer. We glance back to see one take out something from his pocket and snap it in the wind until it opens like a dark sail.

"A contractor cleanup bag," Athens says. "They want to take you away like trash."

But I'm not just a turtle anymore.

"Even if you were, you don't belong in the trash. As far as they know see you're still crawling, and you've got Lao Tzu's book on your back. You think they care what you're becoming?"

The men break into a run, the bag a black maw stretched between them as if they could just scoop me up. We round a

corner and come to a radiating intersection. Athens throws his
cigarette pack down one path for a ruse, and quickly as we can
we move down another. He throws his jacket over my shoulders
but it slips down and I hear the zipper buzz along the ground.
The asphalt on the path gets rougher, crumbling at the edges
until finally turning to dirt.

Athens huffs and puffs. "This road goes nowhere, damnit."
Ahead is a chain link fence. We don't hear the men behind us
anymore but know it's just a matter of time until we do. Athens
goes over the fence with agility that belies his bulk and strains
to lift the bottom so I can crawl under. It doesn't work. There's
a thick security wire on the bottom that won't give even when I
put my now soft and impressionable shoulder against it.

Athens crouches, pants, and looks at me through the grid.
"You're going to have to climb over."

Tortoises don't climb fences.

"Please. I keep telling you you're not a tortoise anymore.
Stand up and take the fence in your hands."

I reach up as far as I can with my forelimbs.

"Use your fingers," Athens urges. "Hurry!"

My pink stubs fit neatly into the loops near the top of the
fence.

"We don't have time for this. They're going to find us any
minute. Now the same with your feet. Push down there while
you pull up top."

I interlace my feet into the wire below me, and conjure the
mental image of a Galápagos iguana make my way sinuously up
the fence. My movement is more reptilian than human but it gets
the job done.

"Now bend," Athens urges as I teeter atop the wire.

I've spent thousands of years living with a spine that won't
do any such thing. I'm not even sure where to begin. I try, but

tumble off, face forward, into Athens waiting arms.

"You did fine," he says, covering me up with his coat once more. "It takes practice."

We head for the shelter of the building and slip in through a cracked door at the back, away from the main entrance. Immediately, the smell of fish gets stronger. I hear high-pitched cries.

I know that sound.

"This place is called Underwater World. They have a dolphin show."

A dolphin show?

"Highly intelligent and spiritual sea creatures. This is a place where they are abused for profit."

Why am I not surprised? What about Abbot Chen's men?

"If they get this far, there are a thousand places to hide."

We proceed along a walkway through a jungle of humming pumps and bubbling filters, clear plastic tubes, and thick white pipes. The fetid smell reminds me of algae-covered rocks uncovered by the retreating tide on my island. Shouts behind us break my reverie. We redouble our pace and reach the end of the corridor. Ahead is only a ramp to a catwalk. We take it and are soon level with the surface of an enormous tank. The whale song is loud now. and it drums into my brain like a downpour into a barrel.

"Move faster," Athens urges.

How can I explain to him that all my life I have longed to experience music as a human does, to understand the layers, the mathematical relationships, the symmetry of it, and the surprise? How can I explain to him that right at this moment, listening to this oceanic melody, I wonder whether dolphins might not have been brought in from the stars by an alien race and seeded here to lend nuance and texture to the presence of life on Earth? I am as transfixed by it as Athens claims to be by the concertos and fugues of Bach, as lost in the clicks and whistles as was poor Prince Shen in his pipa all those years ago. Who could ever have imagined that it would be a whale that would finally open my soul to music?

I need a quick look in the tank.

I crane my neck over the catwalk, holding on with my fingers, and gaze into the water. This is the first time I've seen myself at this stage of change. What strikes me most is my eyes. I've looked at my face in pools so many times over the millennia. They have become more oval and less round and there are flashes in my pupil like the ones I remember in a certain whale long, long ago, I can still see myself there, the inner me, the part that even the Great Sage could not change. More, the stubs that were my hands have fingers now. Athens has given me a dress. Something athletic and expandable. It's blue and has shorts built in. It was an embarrassing struggle on many levels to try to fit my changing body into it — I'm stranding shakily on my rear legs now. Athens says I have great hips. I'm not exactly sure what he means.

A dolphin rises from the tank and surfaces next to me. I look down her long flank and vaguely remember something larger, blacker, and more menacing rising up to my eye when I was a baby and nothing at all was clear. We stay poised in expectation for a moment, and then I hear her voice in my head. I'm glad for it. There have been far too many human voices, lately, and not enough others.

"I am not a jellyfish, cucumber, damsel, grouper, rockfish, orca, or star," she says. "Knowing all the creatures that I am not helps me to understand the creature that I am, for all life on Earth exists only in relation to other life and only in context of this whole watery globe. I know something else. Even though you have the crouch and wince of a turtle, you are not one any longer, though maybe at one time you were."

Am I a woman, then?

"Nearly so. And if you do become one, you'll have to accept the terrible flaws of humans. You know what people do to each other. You know what a scourge they are on the planet, how your shelled, oceanic cousins choke on their discarded plastic bags and die in their traps."

Not all humans are that way.

"You say so without hearing the moans of a finned shark or the scream of netted tuna or looking a deep angler in the eye as it is brought up and explodes. Why, oh why would you want anything to do with them?"

Love.

"Love as a turtle. Love as a dolphin."

Becoming a dolphin was never an option. Tao flows. I follow it. This is what has happened to me.

She clears her blowhole, sopping me. "Can you get me out of here?"

"Are you alone in this tank?"

She does her best approximation of a blush as I see another torpedo-shaped form heading swimming slowly back and forth beneath the surface. "Us, then."

Ah. Maybe humans are not the only ones who think mostly of themselves.

"Come on," says Athens. "You've had your look. We have an appointment to keep. If we don't show up on time, our ride will leave without us."

"Don't leave me," says the dolphin.

I'm sorry.

"I can see that your head didn't always look human. I can see that you didn't used to be light and quick, that you don't know what to do with agility and speed."

I'm sorry but I have to go.

"I can read your back. I know why you loved him." she whistles as I draw away.

38

To save precious manuscripts from flooding rains and the occasional rise of the Luoyang River, the library pagoda was built up off the ground. At the close of the hour of the ox, with Yin securely strapped to her cart just outside, Sun Tzu ordered his elite soldiers to fan out in the insulating space beneath it. Young and lean, the men did so quickly, but the general's girth made wriggling in the dirt a laborious business. Pausing to catch his breath he put his ear to a floorboard and heard the wizard trying to reason with Ding Fei.

"She's gone. There's nothing I can do," came the master's voice.

"Do you hear how loudly he speaks?" Sun Tzu whispered to his men. "He knows we're here and is giving us clues."

"I'm tired of issuing the same threats while you buy time," said Ding Fei. "If you don't produce her, I swear I'll burn this building to the ground."

"You and your twelve soldiers have better things to do than chase Yin from state to state just to redeem your father's name," Long Ears countered.

"He's clueing us in," hissed Sun Tzu. "They are a dozen plus one."

"My father passed away three weeks ago. I'm not doing this for him. I'm doing it for me."

"My condolences. Now you're free. If you don't want to stay here and study with me then go home and start a life for yourself. Find a wife. Gather men around you who can support you. Contribute your skills to the king of your choice. Educate yourself in the ways of the Tao."

"You sure can spin a web of words. Sorry I have to shred it. You want to save your library, give up your magic tortoise."

"Use the footsteps to place the soldiers," the general whispered, pressing his ear to the floor.

"Yin is able to sniff out infertility from across town," Long Ears explained. "The moment of conception, too. She works her own magic to right what is wrong and make sure babies grow properly. She has a bead on relationships as well. She won't give a child to the wrong mother or the wrong household. She makes her own judgments and follows her own lead. She's wild and powerful and holds her own mind."

"I'm sick of hearing about how great she is!" Ding Fei cried. "I know what she can do, and I know kings who will pay handsomely for her. I also know you can speak to her through silence. Summon her now. Tell her that if she doesn't show up, my men will drop their oil torches and start the blaze we have so carefully planned. Tell her you'll burn with your books. Everyone says she loves you like a slow-moving dog. My bet is she won't want to see you go up in flames."

Outside the library, Yin felt the threat without hearing the words. She struggled against the thick leather straps that the general, the perfect strategist who considered all variables, had used to tie her down. Biting at the one around the forepart of her shell, she discovered that her beak could breach it. Sun Tzu had left two soldiers to guard her, and they immediately threaded a new strap. She bit through that one, too.

Let me go! I won't let him burn for me!

The cart was a stout one, but her nails found crevices between the joints. Pushing outward from her dense, dark core, she splintered the wood. The soldiers pressed the cart to the wall to block her escape. In response, she broke the cart's bottom and fell through. The men grabbed the sides and turned her on her back. *No! Put me right! I'm not worth all this! You have to let me save him!*

She righted herself by pushing her head against the wall and made her way up the front steps of the library. The soldiers tried to stop her but were no match for her combination of muscle and intent.

Under the library floor, Sun Tzu heard an unmistakable combination of bumps and scrapes.

"Yin at last!" cried Ding Fei.

"You shouldn't have come," said Long Ears.

"Attack now!" Sun Tzu hissed at his men, who had positioned themselves one on one under the invaders.

Bronze might bend or crack when resisted by seasoned wood, but iron delivered from heaven by asteroid is another matter. The general's men thrust their blades upward with pinpoint accuracy, pinning the attacker's feet to the floor and, in many cases, delivering mortal wounds. Half of Ding Fei's men died literally rooted to the spot. Others, bleeding at their feet, flung their torches at the scrolls that bore records of the dynasty. The bamboo lit quickly, curling nearby tortoise shells bearing medicinal prescriptions. Long Ears was everywhere at once, using his robes to smother the flames before they could spread.

Seeing his men slaughtered, Ding Fei ran at Yin, his sword extended. "I'll kill you," he shrieked.

Help! He's going to cut me!

Long Ears heard her but was hemmed in by fire; Sun Tzu and his soldiers were deaf to her cries. Seeing no help forthcoming, she shifted from defense to offense, stuck out her neck, and bit through Ding Fei's sword hand, leaving his little finger hanging by a white tendinous thread.

Braggardly, ambitious, and bright, the captain's son was a better planner than a fighter, more self-righteous than seasoned. If he had considered Yin to be anything at all, it was as a slow and helpless animal not a loyal female with a sharp beak and a strong will. The injury broke him at once, and Long Ears found him staring at his maimed hand in chagrin, deflated, covered in smoke and ash, and heavy with defeat.

"What's your escape route?" the wizard demanded.

"A hook and climbing chain hidden behind a pipe along the northern wall," Ding Fei answered quietly.

"We must get you to it at once."

You're going to help him. What's wrong with you? Haven't you learned we'll just meet him again, or worse some sword-happy child of his?

"Sun Tzu!" Long Ears cried.

"Here!" came a bellow from the rear of the library.

"I see men headed for the southern wall!"

Hearing these words, the general gathered his iron force and headed off in pursuit. As soon as they were gone, the wizard bound Ding Fei's finger and ushered him out a side door. He turned and looked at his former captive.

"Why would you help me?"

"Everything turns back on itself. Reversal is the movement of Tao. When you launch a campaign, you should consider more than one possible outcome."

The boy sighed. "Does anybody really understand the things you say?"

"Come quickly. Soon the king will awaken to the smoke and noise, and we'll lose a clear path through the palace."

With that one surprising act of kindness, the senior lord of the Zhou court defused the blood feud so successfully that it would not erupt again until long, long after he had left the earthly plane.

39

Life on two legs is an admixture of fear of falling and elation at the view from up here. Sensing my confusion, Athens interlaces his fingers in mine — a remarkable sensation in and of itself — and half-pulls, half-urges me forward. We leave aquarium property and race through the park. We burst into a large, open area floored in stone and surrounded by lines of manicured trees. Morning has broken, so it is less easy to hide from our pursuers, who are gaining on us. I'm changing faster every day. I'm hoping that my human face, Western nose, proper arms and legs and no trace of a shell will give them pause but their hot pursuit makes me wonder if they don't want Athens more than they want me.

Athens glances at his watch. "Just in time," he pants.

Before us, a park runs north to south and looks about as big as Queen Qin Jiang's private garden. There's a small lake with a pavilion off to the side, but the biggest feature is the mausoleum itself, with many stairs up to it and a big square in front.

Who lies here, in such splendor, while my great sage rots in splintered ground?

"Dr. Sun Yat Sen. Democratic revolutionary. He started the movement that led to the end of Imperial China."

He brought down the last king?

"You could say he inspired those who did."

And people celebrate him for that? People usually bring down a king because they want to be king themselves.

"I already told you that even though the last emperors were despotic, Sun wouldn't be happy with the way things turned out. China still has a long way to go, and as you guessed, the new kings are no better than the old ones."

Athens assures me I'm growing more beautiful every day, but still my uneven gait evokes some human disease. A toddler trundles up to me like a bee to a flower, takes a close look and veers off. I've learned to discern tourists by their dress, and there are plenty of them here. They part around me like water around a stone, edging past me by cleaving to the shrubbery.

"We have a climb, Athens tells me. Can you manage it?"

I think of making my way down the mountain from Long Ears' grave. I was far weaker then, but I had four legs to carry me. I look with trepidation at the long throw of stairs to the top of the mausoleum. There is the physical challenge, of course, but there is also my concern about advancing ever more deeply into this world, a feeling each obstacle generates. I glance back over my newly shorn shoulders. Athens does, too. Chen's men closing in, but we can tell they are confused at the absence of a large turtle, as they keep turning around, looking high, looking low, and conferring with each other.

I'm not so sure about these stairs.

He grins. "I'll help you. I've been planning our escape. I'm a hacker, after all. I evaluate contingencies and always build in a back door."

That grin gives me the lift I need to put my hands on that first step and begin the long climb. As I soldier upward, the profile of the mausoleum evolves from squat and distant to monolithic, its tiered roof of dark tiles jutting out from its retaining walls like a sharp-edged storm cloud.

You're not going to tell me the plan?

"Need to know basis," he laughs, his hand gently on my back as I walk, rubbing. "If you fall into enemy hands, you might give away secrets."

People on the steps move aside to give us a clear aisle. My heart pounds in my neck, which feels as if it's changing shape moment by moment. I feel a buzzing and raise my elbow to scratch my ear. The attempt fails. I am not built that way anymore.

Athens wants to know what's wrong.

A vibration in my head.

Athens smiles and tells me to keep climbing.

I wonder about this sound. I know that the body in the mausoleum is of a powerful man and that powerful men create energy that can transcend death and manifest as ideas, movements, epiphanies, books, music, films, war, and even, as in this case, revolution. Might it be possible that the closer I get to his body, the more the earth beneath my feet takes up his cause? It seems so, because my feet are vibrating just like my ears.

Close to the top now, people no longer avoid me. This is not because they are suddenly comfortable with the glimpses of strange, naked flesh they get when Athens' jacket moves to one side or the other. In fact, they are looking neither at me nor at the remains of the celebrated visionary they have come to see. Instead they are looking at the sky.

40

Oaks and elms were shedding the last of their summer clothes and evergreens were thickening for winter when King Ling summoned his wizard, ostensibly to discuss the education of Prince Shen. Yin trundled along beside him.

"He does nothing but play his flute and read poems in the company of mountain hermits," the regent complained. "It was one thing to let him do what he wanted when he was a child, but he's a man now and he's not prepared to lead either the people or the court."

"We cannot change a person's basic nature, Sire."

"Nonsense. He's just spoiled, and he hasn't yet developed the skills of a warrior."

"There's more to ruling a kingdom than martial prowess, my king."

"Until an assassin gets past your guards."

I'd like to see the king fight someone off, that tub of blubber.

"Sun Tzu tells me he Shen's quite good with the sword," Long Ears answered. "And he has learned much about the flow of nature from the hermits, Your Highness."

"Trees and roots," scoffed the king.

"On the contrary, Your Highness. Sensitivity to the undercurrents of the Tao will allow him to predict events as I do."

"He can hire a wizard for that but you're likely to be around to serve him if what I see of you is any judge. I'm old and gray and you're still fresh as a peony. Truly, Long Ears, there's not a line on your face."

"Shen's music will keep him young, Your Highness. It's no small thing to have such a gift. Still, I don't believe concern for the crown prince's education is the real reason you summoned me today."

"Of course you don't believe that. You see right through us all. Well then, I really wanted to discuss you going to Chu and bringing me back a new concubine."

He doesn't have enough women?

"I would bring no special skills to such a mission, my king."

The king wagged his finger. "You're perfect for the task, Long Ears. Your taste in luscious, young consorts is legend."

What?

"Chu is not a refined kingdom, your Majesty. It's famed for swamps and incantations and magic, which is why it has produced many shamans. A ruler of your taste and refinement would find Chu girls coarse."

"How so?"

The way Long Ears spread his hands suggested it would be coarse to answer the question.

"Well?" the king urged. "You mean in their deportment?"

The wizard gave a nearly imperceptible tilt of his head.

"Their toilet?"

Another miniscule nod.

"Their physical proportions?"

A quiet clearing of the wizardly throat was the only answer.

"Where, then, would you recommend I find a suitable match?"

"Qufu, Sire. Capital of the State of Lu."

"Lu? I thought you would say Zheng?"

"Your Majesty is envious of the Zheng king's parties, I know, but for the ultimate in refinement you must look to Lu."

For the ultimate refinement he should look to his queen! And what scheme has you wanting a trip to the state of Lu? I can't believe you want to go there to procure a woman.

"You have this on good authority?"

"The best, Your Highness."

"So you will go?"

"Your wish is my command, Sire. I should like to take Prince Shen along. We might find him a wife there. Eastern states with seacoasts are always useful allies."

"You're always thinking of the dynasty, Long Ears."

You're up to something. I know you are.

"Thank you, Sire."

"Leave at once. I need you back to keep watch over the river when the winter snows crown the mountains."

The wizard had planned an immediate departure all along and so went straight to the stables, where Wang Yi waited patiently, having gathered horses and soldiers and prepared a cart for Yin. The travelers were out of the palace before the sun, directly overhead, signaled that the hour of the horse had passed and that it was time to head for the barge that would take them east down the Luoyang River.

Even heading in the mere general direction of the ocean makes me wish I could smile.

"Of course you can smile. You're doing it right now."

You can hear the smile, but you can't see it.

Long Ears touched the river with his toe. "You can bend your beak to your will if you wish."

Beaks don't bend.

"Tortoises don't speak, either, but we fixed that."

You fixed it. You wanted a magical companion. It had nothing to do with me.

"It had everything to do with you, particularly with the energy between us. I never managed what I did for you before, and I am certain I will never be able to do so again. I do wonder if perhaps I can only take you so far, and the rest is up to you."

What does that mean?

"You'll know when the time comes."

A red-crowned crane flew overhead, low and just forward of the barge. The motion of its wings pushed down on the surface of the river and brought up the aroma of clean fresh water— the faintest tang of crustacean, the sweet and bitter effluvia of aquatic plants, the pure grit of minerals drawn down from the mountains in sand. The wizard closed his eyes and inhaled deeply, a satisfied look on his face.

That smells nice, but the ocean smells better.

"In longing for your archipelago, you miss the here and now of these Central States. Inside the Tao, it's all the same."

Fine. Now tell me, are the women of Lu really more cultured, refined, and beautiful than the women of Luoyang?

The wizard smiled. "No."

More skilled in bedroom arts?

"I doubt it."

Are you looking to replace Bao Yu?

"Why do you ask that?"

The moon knows things about the sun.

A soft-shell water turtle with beady eyes and a sharp snout surfaced beside the boat.

"He wants you to acknowledge him," Long Ears said, pointing.

Forget him. Why won't you answer my question?

"I don't need a replacement for Bao Yu."

Because you don't want one or because you already have one?
"Yes."
Yin's heart skipped a beat. The silence that followed was excruciating. To break it, she changed the subject.
Why did you bring Shen along for a wife but not Gui? Don't you think he deserves one too?
"Too dangerous to travel with both heirs."
You can't be serious. Gui is a monster. If we were waylaid, he would take out an entire battalion without a bead of sweat on his brow. No one can stand against him. Even Sun Tzu fears his prowess.
"Sun Tzu fears what he is becoming, not what he is. Anyway, stop asking questions and attend the present moment. Someday you'll be happy for detailed memories of today — the sound waves against the hull, the click of crayfish in combat with calcareous claws, Wang Yi and Prince Shen moving *go* pieces on the board, the scratch of my robe on the splinters of the deck, the way the silt on the river bottom drifts like the silk dress of a dancing girl, the patterns beetles make on the surface of the water. The older you get, the more you will find you live in the past."
If that happens to me, I will have to be reborn. I want experience, not memories.
On the third day of the voyage downriver, and tired of a diet of mushrooms and fruits — Long Ears prohibited the consumption of meat on the barge so as to keep congruent the energies of environment and foodstuffs — the sailors poled the craft up onto the bank and made camp. Wang Yi, now a strapping man with broad shoulders, thick muscles, and a beard that favored his master's, readied a fishing net. The prince came to watch.
"I thought the current was too strong for fishing," said.
"We're proceeding overland now and this is the last chance for fish. My master wants me to use my mind to draw them in."
"Can you do that?" Shen pursued.

"I don't know. It's my first time trying."

"Does it make you sad that Yin's taken your place and is always with Long Ears?"

Wang Yi pursed his lips and blew. "My place is with him, too. We mean different things to him, and he to us. I owe him not only my education but my future, my very place in the world. No matter where his journey goes, with his magic and his heart, I will be there to stand in his stead when he is gone. I will never be able to do enough for him."

"It's beautiful how you love him."

"He is a father to me. I love him the way you love the king. Yin loves him too, and he her. It's different between them. Unique. Perhaps it's her compensation for all the suffering she's been through, and his reward for the sacrifices he has made in his relentless pursuit of a pure, natural life."

With that, the apprentice knelt and began swirling the water with his hands. The effort reddened his face but paid off in a whirlpool of current and intention that trapped whatever swam there. The wizard looked on with interest. He had recognized for some time that Wang Yi was an apprentice no more, and it was a source of great satisfaction for him to see the younger man develop his skills, find where his strengths lay, forge his own alliances and relationships, and begin to make a mark in the world. In short, it was fine to see his son grow up.

Yin, however, turned away from the sight of fish gasping on the bank.

Why do you let those poor creatures suffer so? We can't possibly eat them all. What purpose does their agony serve?

In deference to her feelings, Long Ears returned the surplus fish to the water, yet the subject of men abusing animals arose again later that day, when the wheels of Yin's cart broke and she had to be strapped to the back of a horse.

The poor horse suffers so. I weigh much more than a soldier.

"We're only going as far as sacred Song Mountain. You'll see the peak as soon as we're clear of these trees."

Why are beasts everywhere dying for the ambitions of men?

"Everywhere?"

Water buffalo in yokes, horses in saddles, fish on hooks, birds in cages.

"There's no easy answer, Yin. Sometimes such things are the Way, and sometimes they're not. Animals eat each other. That's natural."

But cruelty and exploitation....

"Can be natural too, as difficult as it may be to accept that."

A moment later the wizard raised his hand to bring the procession to a halt. He then directed the soldiers to stretch lines of nearly invisible, finely spun silk between trees.

What is this? What are you doing?

Instead of answering her, Long Ears turned to Prince Shen. "Your Highness," he said. "Please bring down the birds."

Shen produced his flute and began to render a complex array of themes: fast and slow, syncopated and staccato, penetrating and fading. Growing vines chimed in, and unfurling flowers were his whisk and cymbal. Tiny, falling grains of pollen clattered as his castanets, titmice twittered at his tempo, slithering snakes cracked dry leaves to follow his harmonic bidding, an empire of ants chewed soft wood in time with his notes, and cicadas clicked their wings in celebration of his royal rhythm. A red panda flicked its tail in time, a takin trumpeted, too, and even spiders — busy snaring beetles and flies and dewdrops and moths — took time out to sympathetically dance on their webs.

I wish I could respond to this music. I hear it, but not the way others do.

"The music is not his," Long Ears said quietly. "He channels the Tao itself."

Living lives of song, the birds were the first to succumb. Nightingales were first, followed by pheasants, kittiwakes, ibis, tragopans, and crows. All were eventually snared in the silken wires, hanging helplessly, so narcotized by Shen's music that they didn't even care about being caught nor put into bamboo cages. When at last Shen stopped blowing, the silence was so startling it was painful.

You all can't possibly be hungry enough to eat so many souls.

"They're not food, they're offerings."

Offerings to whom?

"The spirits of Song Mountain."

41

Chen's soldiers are only a few yards away. What freezes them in their tracks is not the thing in the sky above but the sight of me. The demands of the chase have accelerated my metabolism and, with it, my transformation. If there is anything that would give me away as not human, it would require a look deep inside me.

"Quick," Athens urges. "We have to get to the roof."

We rush into the mausoleum to find an interior of support columns and crossbeams. A blue rendering of a sun crowns the ceiling. We cast about looking for an access stair and find it guarded by an armed soldier in a hat with a chinstrap. He presents his rifle, replete with bayonet, but when he gets a look at me, he pauses, confused, and we push past him. In the narrow, spiral stairwell I climb on two legs and keep my hands on the rail. We make it to the top and burst through a maintenance door and out onto the roof.

We stand on a sea of dark tiles looking up at something I've never imagined or seen, a flying shark as big as the building upon which we stand. It has a long low nose and an upswept tail, a predator's nose. Four propellers extend backward from its belly, but only two of them are moving. The other two have blades shaped like the wings of swans.

Athens waves up at it wildly and it descends nearly silently, although I can feel the vibration from the engines in my teeth.

Yes. I have teeth. They've just erupted and feel so strange in my mouth I can't stop running my tongue across them. Despite the quiet, the propellers thrash the air so strongly, roof tiles break off. I part my lips and the air rushes into my mouth, flapping my cheeks. When the ship is less than ten feet off the roof, a ladder appears from a hatch in the belly and Athens ushers me towards it.

"Military technology," he yells into my ear. "My father's part owner in the company that makes it. A bigger one is hauling cargo out to some islands that China is squabbling over with the Japanese."

I take hold of the ladder and notice how finely formed my fingers are, how sleek and elegant. I notice my opposable thumb, and I use it with great relish to hold onto the highest rung I can reach as Athens pushes me upward, his hands on my buttocks. What was hidden muscle and sinew strong enough to propel me forward when I was a six-hundred-pound reptile has become buttocks and thighs that are ample yet firm.

I notice too that my arms are pleasingly shaped, and when Athens' coat finally flies off and leaves me naked in the wash of the propeller, I glance down and see three new parts that I have yearned for over more years than I want to think about right now. Where formerly I was uniformly black, I now see an expanse of pale skin and pink highlights. Where formerly my underside was as flat as a battle plain, I now see twin glorious swells. Every part of me tingles in the cool, fast-moving air, but the spot where Athens' palms touch me burns hot enough to warm me through and through.

"We should get you inside and covered," he says.

It is difficult to change so quickly and also learn what I need to learn about propriety and sensibility and the behaviors and patterns of human beings. I'm not uncomfortable, but from

Athens' expression I sense that I should be.

Two crewmembers appear in the hatchway above. They seem simultaneously surprised that I am no longer a tortoise and embarrassed that I am naked. Even so, they stare at my curves and crevices, and at my tattooed back. Athens hands move from my buttocks to my legs as he continues to push me up. Now it is my calves that burn at his touch, narrow but also ripe with muscle. The airship sways and one of my hands loses its grip on the ladder. A crewmember makes a grab for it, catching my wrist. Below on the roof, Abbot Chen's men finally appear in the doorway from the stairs. Athens glances up to see that I am safely held, then charges them like a bull.

His soft and languid body becomes a force of martial intention. Obviously seasoned fighters, his opponents open their arms to his rush. He does the same. They backpedal and he drives forward and there is a moment where the balance of force is in question and then I see his shoulders hunch and I hear his roar and the three of them go sliding over the tiles and down over the edge.

"NO!"

The scream is audible. The sound is coming not from my mind but from my throat. Even as I kick and struggle and try to jump down the crewmembers haul me inside and shout instructions. The giant airship inches downward toward the roof. Peering through the opening I can see that Athens has not fallen but is dangling by both hands, alone, his knapsack hanging from his shoulder. The craft drops closer. Our eyes meet and he smiles. I watch as the larger of the men gingerly descends the ladder and grabs him by the belt, lifting him up until he can take hold of the ladder himself.

He climbs in. We stand there, staring at each other. His shirt is ripped and there are scratch marks on the skin of his shoulders.

His mouth is wide open and he breathes loudly enough for me to hear him above the ship's sounds, which here inside the giant gas bag are softer than they were outside.

"Well," he says, letting out a sigh. "That was exciting."

I cover his mouth with my hand and fall into his arms. I wrap myself around him. Out of the corner of my eyes I see the crew turn away, but then I forget about them because I am about the business of making sure that every inch of me, every craving, patient, long-suffering molecule of my skin touches his. I bring my lips up. He brings his down, but not by much for, in truth, I am not so very much shorter than he is.

The electricity of our kiss shocks me so strongly that I feel my legs give way. He holds me up with one hand at the small of my back and the other behind my head where my thick, dark hair coils tightly at my temples and then grows out so rapidly it pushes through his fingers. I feel his tongue gently touch mine. Inside my own lids I can finally see the stars and galaxies that have always been in my eyes. Pulling him ever more strongly against me, my hand slides down his back.

As far as his tail.

42

The next day's march was through thick mist. That night, a storm brought drops the size of acorns. Soldiers shielded their torches and the horses stirred the soil into mud with their disquieted shuffling. At dawn, the rain was merely a drizzle and Long Ears told Yin he wanted her to play a game.

No games until I breakfast on fresh mushrooms.

"Later. Now is the time to walk between raindrops."

Between them? You mean without getting wet?

"Exactly."

Impossible.

"A skill to master. No more or less."

Give Bao Yu a baby. If you wait much longer, she'll be too old.

"Games of distraction don't work on me. We're not going to talk about this again. Let's get to the exercise."

No game. Your child is your legacy.

"Calculating the trajectory of the drops won't help you; you have to rely on intuition alone."

If I could give her a child as you let others believe I can do, I would. But you and I both know I don't really have that power.

"Enough of this. Of course you do. Now back to work. You and the rain are one. Do it now."

Dry under the bolt of silk the men used to protect Long Ear's from the downpour, she stared out at the drops. A thousand rebellious thoughts passed through her mind. She knew Wang Yi was watching and she tried not to let his expectations distract her. Even after all this time she wanted to please him nearly as much as she wanted to please the great wizard — after all, Wang Yi had crossed the world in order facilitate her destiny. At length she opened her eyes and tried tracking the raindrops. She lost focus but kept going. The blurred world disoriented her but she tried to sense things anyway. After a time, she saw a faint, glowing line on the ground — a slithering snake of pure intuition. She rose up on all limbs.

"She's going to do it," Wang Yi whispered.

Suddenly and blissfully aware of everything, she took one step and then another. Soon she was across the camp, her head and shell still bone dry. Prince Shen clapped in time to her footfalls and when at last she stopped, Long Ears wordlessly served her the requested mushrooms.

Mid-morning, the sky cleared and the curtain of mist lifted to reveal the craggy, complex peaks of Song Mountain.

"Perfection," said Wang Yi.

The wizard spent some time muttering and walking about. Yin watched him intently.

I know what you're doing. You're finding force lines in the earth.

"And you just walked between raindrops."

At length the wizard found a spot he liked and had Wang Yi bring the bamboo cages filled with birds beguiled by Shen's music. He meditated for an hour or so while everyone else looked on, and then released them. The sky filled with a fluttering, twittering cloud that headed for the mountain. When the birds arrived, the mountain seemed to take a deep breath and sigh. The air seemed suddenly clear and vibrant.

"Now that the mountain god is happy, I can warm you with tea," the wizard told Yin.

You've never let me have tea before.

"There's a proper time for everything. This rainwater is perfect, as are these Pu-erh leaves. We still have a good distance to travel to Lu. They will fortify your *qi*."

Preparing the beverage, the wizard's motions were elegant and spare. When the water was hot, he poured it over the leaves, swirled the mixture in the pot, then emptied it onto the ground.

The liquor of life and you throw it away?

"One washing removes bitterness and impurities. Now the leaves are clean and ready."

He soaked the leaves again and put down a small bowl from which Yin could drink. She put her twin nostrils to the surface and inhaled. Tortoises have a sense organ people do not, a sensitive area at the top of the soft palate. Even before her awakening, Yin's nose would have revealed tea to her in a way a human could not possibly imagine. Enhanced as she was, the aroma was positively intoxicating.

Smells like flowers.

"Drink."

She did, and the effect was instantaneous. A hot river ran through her. Layer after layer of flavor ran across her sense organs, overwhelming her with a rapturous sensational play. She thrust her head into the dish and gulped down the contents. Feeling the uncontrollable urge to run, she took off across the camp.

Wheeee!

"It's too strong for her," Wang Yi told his master as Yin entered into the undergrowth at the edge of the camp.

"I have a bad feeling about this," said Shen.

If she had been in her right mind, Yin might have noticed the softness of the ground underneath her feet. As it was, when the earth gave way she plunged down and down until she came to rest on her back, the crown of her carapace indenting a sandy floor. She tried to push herself back over, but the more she wriggled the more deeply buried she became.

Human eyes can detect a single photon if given long enough to acclimate to darkness, but tortoise eyes, even when enhanced by arcane wizard magic, cannot. Yin had never known such inky blackness, not atop her volcanic island, not at the peak of night on the beach, not under the great sage's bed, not inside Wang Yi's robes, and not in the hold of the sailing ship. The longer she lay on her back, the more suffocating the darkness became.

Long Ears! Wang Yi! I've dropped through the ground. Help me!

In concerned pursuit of her, the two shamans quickly found the hole. The soldiers brought torches and everyone peered in. Shen launched some flute notes downward and an analysis of the echoes revealed a long, sloping tunnel. Over vociferous objections, the great wizard gathered his robes, grabbed a pair of torches, and descended into the earth. He found footholds on the sides of the tunnel but, in the end, slid to the sand bottom of what he discovered was a large cavern.

Quickly! Turn me over!

"I'm disappointed to find you in such a panic. You must control your mind. I assume this is overstimulation caused by the tea."

You don't know what it is to be a turtle upside down.

"Slow your breathing. There's dangerous gas here."

I was so alone.

"The limitless pool of intelligent energy we call Tao fills you like a hand fills a glove. You can't be alone because you are part of everything. This system is eternal. It was here before you knew of yourself, and it will be here after you have forgotten yourself and me."

I'll never forget you.

"Perhaps not, but tortoises live longer than man. Someday someone will replace me."

Never.

"A big word," he declared, putting his shoulder to her shell and righting her with a mighty heave.

Let's get out.

"I want to take a look around first."

What about the gas?

"It won't hurt us so long as we don't stay too long."

He began a circuit of the cave, probing, sniffing, running his hands over the walls, kicking the ground.

Well?

"The gas keeps the cave free of insects or any other life. Cracks in the rock tell me the ground is not stable. You did not fall into this place by accident, despite appearances to the contrary. The mountain god wanted us to find it."

But why?

"We'll see."

Your expression says you already know.

Denying any further questions, the great wizard led the tortoise back up the tunnel. Once at the surface, he commanded his men to gather and stack stones in four tall piles.

"You know your music can soothe the hearts of men and beasts," he told Prince Shen. "Now I need you to melt these stones together."

"But why?"

"Because I ask it."

The prince played a low, slow tune, the end of the flute close to the stones. Usually, his face was placid when he played but this time his brow was furrowed in concentration, as if his inhales sucked the rocks together and his notes cemented them. During the last several hours of daylight, the distinctions between the rocks gradually disappeared and they became four vertical needles, each as tall as three men atop each other's shoulders, their surfaces so seamlessly smooth they appeared to have been polished. When he was finished, the prince fell immediately to sleep.

They look like giant needles.

"Because they are."

Yin thought for a minute. *Don't tell me you're going to do acupuncture on the earth.*

"Qi flows through all living things."

But it's a preposterous idea. The sheer scale....

"You say that because you don't understand how little energy is required when the blockages are small and the variance in flow from the true course is minor."

Wizard mumbo jumbo.

Long Ears shook his head without smiling. "Not at all. Think of a giant boulder poised on the side of a mountain, ready to fall. You might think that it unlikely that a person could move such a weight, but sometimes a little nudge is all it takes."

Then why am I not yet a woman?

Rather than answering, the wizard took Wang Yi by the hand and the two of them walked in circles until they identified four major intersections of earth energy beneath their feet. They directed the soldiers to lift and insert the stone needles at these points, and when they did, the loess soil welcomed the intrusion, acting like needy flesh to suck the huge needles down. When the moon finally rose, the shadows they cast pointed right at the cave.

"Now you may close the hole," Long Ears told his men. "The spot is marked and the cave is strong. Not even an earthquake will disturb it."

43

Thousands of years ago, my world was redefined by an act of magic that opened my nostrils to new fragrances, my eyes to new colors, my ears to new sounds, and my thoughts to the thoughts of others. Today, aloft in an airship constructed using unimaginable technology, my flesh is far more electrically alive at the presence of a certain young man named for an ancient city than is my sense of wonder at the ship. Connecting with Athens is a transformative experience. Everything is fresh and new once more, even though my entire past still lives inside me.

Despite the sea of smoggy brown clouds in which we travel, the air inside the ship is as clean as a thunderstorm and as crisp as mountain ice. I equate the spare austerity of the interior of this vessel to the down-to-business construction of the little wooden boat that once took me across the sea.

"I agree it's an oddly beautiful craft," Athens says of the airship as we lie next to each other in two small beds in the belly of the beast. It was conceived by the military for ultra-high-altitude surveillance and satellite monitoring. This particular one was styled for use as an air yacht for Politburo bigwigs and their zillionaire cronies. "

"Why are not all your craft like this one, floating quietly and serenely through the air?" I ask.

"They used to be. A century and a half ago on the other side of the world, ships like this ruled the skies. They were docking stations for fighter planes, suppliers for troops on the ground, even luxury passenger liners. Now they are too slow and vulnerable to attack. And then, of course, a famous one blew up spectacularly upon landing, killing nearly everyone aboard."

"Blew up?" I repeat, nervously shifting my bare leg, which lies casually at what until yesterday would have been an impossible angle.

"Yin?"

"Yes?"

"Do you notice anything right now?"

In point of fact, I notice everything. Especially the fact that I no longer hear Athens in my head but rather with what has become of my ears. Through, rather than with I suppose, as their little fleshy curlicues, which constantly itch and ring faintly, seem to conduct sound to me differently before.

"I hear you through my ears now," I say, reaching up for a scratch there.

"And I no longer hear you inside my head," Athens answers. "I'm a bit sorry about that although your voice is beautiful and I gain much from your intonation and tone."

"I'm confused. There are so many new sensations. Now that we have kissed, I'm afraid to touch you again."

Athens sighs.

"There's no rush for anything now. This ship uses helium to float us. It's an inert gas. No explosions, I promise. The tragedies of the past were because old ships used hydrogen, which just loves to blow up."

"All of a sudden, you're talking to me like a child. Is that just because we're not communicating mind to mind? I still know things. Helium is the number two most common gas in the universe after hydrogen. I remember everything I've learned.

And I do mean *everything*. Even if we *were* floating in a hydrogen bubble, I'd want to be here with you."

He reaches out with his hand. I stare at it for a moment. He wiggles it expectantly. I've seen enough handholding to know what he wants. I give him my hand. He interlaces his fingers with mine. I stare at the mingled flesh. I feel his pulse through the thin skin on the inside surface of each of his fingers, and of mine. This simple act, holding hands, delights me. Thousands of years and thousands of clasped digits have come and gone and I've always been the outsider. Now I'm not. I close my eyes and smile. Smiling with my lips is also new to me.

"You're less afraid."

"I was never afraid."

"Not of the things most people fear, but I *know* you were afraid you would never physically be with your wizard, that another woman would steal his love, or that he would die before you changed."

"These are things you know, huh?" I ask, staying right where I am, fingers in fingers, my eyes still closed tight.

"The important thing is that you're not afraid anymore. You're moving forward into a whole new way of thinking and being. You're on a whole new trajectory. You're done carrying your refuge on your back. You're out in the big, bad world now."

I open my eyes. Everything glows brightly. I keep thinking the world is as detailed and brilliant as it can possibly get, and then the intensity increases again. I raise a hand to ward off thick beams of sunlight filtering in through the porthole, marveling at the way I can turn my thumbs in and then out.

"I don't think the world is so bad," I say. "And I'm not trying to steer the ship. I let Wang Yi do it, and he brought me to Long Ears. I let Long Ears do it, and I became who I am. I let love do it, and I persisted long enough to meet you. I'm along for the ride."

"You mean destiny? Fate?"

"I mean just what I say."

"I wasn't raised that way," Athens says stubbornly.

"To believe in fate and destiny?"

"To believe in belief. It's all about logic and reason for me. Belief is like intuition. It can't be trusted. It's primitive and unreliable."

I disengage my hand. "I get it. You think you're a computer man. A hacker extraordinaire. All thinking, no feeling. And yet here we are, no logic and no reason anywhere in sight."

"We'll be in Shanghai in a few hours. We'd be there faster if this was a plane."

I sit up. "I don't want to go to Shanghai."

"That's where the ocean is, Yin. That's how we get you back to your island."

"Later maybe. Not now."

He rises to stand over me, self-conscious in his underwear, his hand draped in casual embarrassment over the piece of flesh behind him that no man is supposed to have.

"I thought you wanted to go home to Galápagos. That's what this whole thing is about, isn't it?"

"We both know it has become about more than that, but anyway something else comes first. Tell them to turn around and fly west."

"West?"

"Toward the mountains."

"Why?"

"It's important."

"You didn't think of it before?"

"Is it not obvious to you that circumstances have changed?"

He studies me for a moment, then nods. "I'll submit a request to the captain, but I'm not sure he'll listen to me. This is a working ship limo. It came for us because my dad called in a chit, but nothing says they have to ferry us where we want to go. Others may be waiting."

"I'm counting on you to make it happen," I say. "I've trusted you, now you have to trust me. It's very important."

Nodding, he slowly gets dressed. I can't take my eyes off him, can't stop thinking about how I know I can help him, something I could never before manage for the man I love. I rise from my bed wrapped in the sheet. Nudity is another thing I'm confused about. I don't know when it's okay and when it isn't. I'm confused by my own confusion, and to cover my discomfort take a pen and paper from the little table between the beds.

"Write your name for me," I say.

He gives me a funny look, but does as I ask.

"Not in English. The Chinese character. Family name only."

I can see he's not skilled at calligraphy, but he tries. I puzzle over what I see. There are elements I recognize, others I don't. I hold up the paper, turn it, and then see the root I'm looking for.

"How long has your dad been in the United States?"

"Twenty years. He's a citizen now."

"What part of China did he come from?"

"Hubei Province, down south."

"Grandparents?"

"Same place."

"Great grandparents?"

He frowns. "Family's been there forever, as far as I know. Why are you asking?"

"The tail a family thing?"

He blushes. "Everyone cuts them off. They did mine too, but they didn't get all the cells and it grew back. I've gone in twice to have it removed and then chickened out at the last minute. Somehow it seems I should leave it alone. Doesn't hurt or anything, and nobody cares if I wear baggy clothes."

A crewman knocks on the door. I feel the urge for better cover so I swap the sheet for a blue crew uniform I find in a bureau drawer. It's so big the pants make paddles under my feet and my breasts sway inside the shirt. The feeling that I must do something about my hair and nails seizes me.

Athens opens the door.

"Breakfast is ready," the crewman says, avoiding my eyes.

We follow him out. Walking down the narrow corridor, Athens whispers in my ear.

"You're something to see."

"Always have been," I whisper back. "A curiosity."

"Not that. You're beautiful. Vibrant. You radiate something. You have the men under your spell."

"But not you, huh?"

He smiles.

When we get to the bridge, the captain—he looks younger than Athens—launches into what seems like a canned monologue about the ship's special technology. The airframe is titanium, he tells us, and the gas bag is a double-layered Kevlar matrix formed by nanotechnology. The portholes are crystal to augment receptivity to radio waves.

"Basically, the whole ship's an antenna," he says.

I ask him if he knows of Song Mountain.

He punches the air and grunts. "Tourist trap. Shaolin Temple. Near Zhengzhou."

"We need you to take us there," I say.

He stares at me. "We were told to take you to Shanghai."

I clear my throat.

"Plans have changed," Athens interjects. "My authority."

There is a moment when my entire plan hangs in the balance. The captain and first mate look at each other. I start to wish for

Wang Yi, as he would know how to handle this, but a moment later I am ashamed for doubting this man I've kissed, this direct descendant of my sage.

"Your decision, of course," Athens tells the captain. "It's just that I would hate to report to my father, a major stakeholder in this vessel, that you are not the kind of commander who cannot come about in a changeable wind."

The captain takes a deep breath and then circles his index finger in the air. The navigator, who has been watching, presses a button on his console and holds it down.

The giant ship slowly comes about.

44

After two more days of traveling toward the State of Lu, Long Ears commanded a sudden stop at the edge of a clearing in the dense bamboo forest. "Bearcats," he hissed, putting his finger to his lips.

A moment later, a procession of the giant, black-and-white beasts passed through the underbrush. I knew them from previous encounters to be solitary and shy but this group was garrulous, mewing in incongruously high-pitched voices.

"It's a mating council," Long Ears whispered. "Few men ever see one."

The cats began to couple, the males rolling over on their backs to first be tended by the females and then, when the urge was upon them, rising to their full height to take charge. During breaks they contentedly munched stalks of the giant grass and watched each other as Yin had watched farm animals, alley dogs, and finally, painfully, Long Ears and Bao Yu.

A man with a pinched face, a long nose, and a scholarly mien appeared in the stalks on the other side of the clearing. He was attended by a handful of other scholarly-looking men.

What's he doing?

"Watching the cats, apparently."

Yes, but he has a quill in his hand.

"I believe he is taking notes."

On the mating of bearcats?

A sliver of awareness seemed to spread through the clowder. Bears that had been mating ceased to do so, and those who had been spectating on the periphery drew in. The largest cat assumed a central position and immediately articulated a complex string of grunts and clicks.

I don't usually understand animals but I have a sense that one is trying to organize the others, to get them to act together instead of spending so much time alone. There's something special about him.

"He senses Tao," said Long Ears.

The giant tried gathering the other cats together, but after forty minutes of effort finally gave up and shambled off into the bamboo forest. There was one last burst of fevered copulation after his departure, and then the group disbanded too, some individuals, already in the very first stages of pregnancy, passing so close that Long Ears' men could feel their heat and smell their musk. When they had gone, the wizard approached the man on the other side of the clearing and bowed low to him.

"Kong Qiu of Lu?"

"The same."

"I am Long Ears of Luoyang."

Kong Qiu, a knife-faced man, returned the bow, slightly lower, with military precision. While the soldiers made camp and dinner, the two men drank tea by the fire.

"Fortuitous that we should meet this way," Kong Qiu said, his eyes twinkling a bit.

"A magical coincidence," Long Ears agreed, grinning.

It's obviously no coincidence at all. You made up the whole thing about Lu girls just to meet this person, didn't you? Who is he?

"You're lucky to have steady work."

"Archives do need tending," Long Ears nodded, "as do princes. In fact, we are on our way to Lu to find a wife for Shen over there."

"Well, you're lucky to see the bearcats. They're usually confined to the Qinling Mountains. I follow them to learn of nature. You, of course, have your tortoise to teach you. A creature as unique as that big male bearcat."

That's all he has to say?

"An interesting comparison," Long Ears replied dryly.

Kong Qiu rubbed his hands together in excitement. "Interesting because the thread is sentience, which isn't limited to humans. It was clear just by watching that the big male was trying to establish a code of social conduct for the greater good of the group."

Long Ears demurred. "I'd rather see him cultivate himself than control others."

"It's not control he's after, but order and harmony for all."

The barge captain, who had taken over as the expedition's chief cook, interrupted the exchange with mushroom and pheasant soup. Kong Qiu drained the bowl in seconds.

Look at the way he eats. He's trying so hard to be polite, but you can tell he's starving.

"I've read your discourse on relationships and can see why an organizing bearcat would appeal to you," said Long Ears, "but I find categories, rules, and regulations unnecessarily rigid and limiting. We may be one thing one moment and another the next, and if we are not allowed to adapt, we become inflexible and lose our way. Besides, sometimes relationships are difficult to define. How, for example, would you characterize my relationship with Yin?"

Kong Qiu wiped his face. "May I speak directly?"

"Of course."

"She is your first wife."

Lao Tzu smiled. "She's a tortoise, Kong Qiu. I have a first wife at home in Luoyang."

"And you have many other wives scattered about the city, I warrant. Yet the tortoise, Yin, is your first."

Long Ears took Kong Qiu by the elbow and led him back to the soup tureen. "One must define things by looking inward, not outward."

"Exactly why I said what I did about you and Yin. Living with her the way you do takes the courage of a true dragon. I salute you."

"And I your insight and your grace."

45

Drifting west, I feel uneasy in the air. Tortoises are never comfortable with flying — the experience evokes being carried off by a raptor — and even though I am no shelled reptile anymore, certain fears remain.

"Helicopters want to fall and planes rely on speed for lift but airships are naturally, effortlessly, and happily aloft," Athens assures me. "It's a question of coefficients of lift and drag, but this really is the safest way to fly."

"I'm not sure what you're talking about."

"Perhaps another Internet session on flight dynamics?"

"I've had enough of the computer for now."

"Do I sense resistance to learning?"

"You must be joking. All I've been doing is learning. You've complimented me on how well I do it. One thing I've learned is that resistance to change is the most natural biological response of all. It helps with homeostasis. Resisting change, I stayed with my wizard all those years…."

"And now you're trying to preserve this precarious balance between us. Has it occurred to you that your whole life is about change? Have you thought about the fact that when Lao Tzu changed you, he defined you, and that perhaps the reason the process slowed down was that you worried that the outcome might not be the one you hoped for?"

I stare at him.

"Don't be mad. Life is change. To learn is to change. I was only suggesting you might enjoy knowing more about the process of flying, about the terms we use to describe the physics...."

"That wasn't all you were suggesting."

"You said you didn't want to steer things. Didn't your wizard teach you to flow like water? Go with it now. Everything is unfolding. Once you hit your stride, you're gonna love what happens."

"You're talking down to me."

He puts his arm around my new shoulders and guides me to one of the airship's many computer terminals. "I'm not," he says. "I just want you to understand that you're not the only one who's evolving. Here. Just have a look at this page. It's happening all over the planet."

I expect to see images of bees and fish and birds, but what he calls up are images of robots. Round ones that vacuum the floor, giant, arachnoid designs that use their arms to assemble cars and trucks, humanoid ones that help damaged people in and out of chairs, disembodied arms that hold razor knives that go in and out of ailing hearts leaving the barest wisp of a trail beyond a miracle cure.

"Organic life and inorganic life are melding," he says. "That's the big picture. Environmental activists mourn the loss of owls and rain forest trees, but big thinkers see the long throw of history as a story about evolution, which inexorably moves towards manifesting an intelligence great enough to understand the universe and everything in it."

"Tao," I interrupt.

"Lao Tzu would have said that, yes. I'm not concerned with the label...."

"Neither was he," I interrupt. "But where is compassion in all this? Where is love?"

"If the universe becomes aware of itself, love will be all there is."

I read the blurbs under these pictures of robots. Many of them are made in China, some in Japan, some in America. "This romance with technology seems to me to miss the point. It seems like one big weapon of mass distraction."

"Technology makes life and saves it too. The list of advantages is so long I don't even know where to start. More and more, technology and society are a blend."

"Are the Chinese leading this evolution?"

He shakes his head. "They were a great culture when you were a turtle, perhaps even as great as ancient Greece or Egypt, but the depth and scale of evolution transcends any group, country, or even species. China been an imperial nation for thousands of years. Hard to say if that will ever change."

"I have faith in the Middle Kingdom," I say.

I move until our sides are touching. He gently massages my neck. "Funny, because you're so exotic looking with your golden skin and sloping eyes. Almost Mayan. I suppose it makes sense since you come from a South American Island. Regardless of how you look, you're Chinese through and through."

I move to the porthole and look out. "Where are we now?"

"I plotted our route. Those lights are the city of Ma'anshan. The bodies of water are lakes called Yushanhu and Nanhu. Now, will you tell me where we're going and why?"

"You saved me," I say. "I'm going to return the favor."

"You don't owe me anything."

I touch his face. My fingers burn. "It's not about owing, it's about wanting. I *want* to help you."

He rubs my shoulders. My tendons, newly formed, are still finding their place, and the joints pop in and out freely under his

touch. My shoulder blades protrude from my back like swords.
He pauses. "That doesn't hurt?"

"No."

"You're going to be great at yoga."

I look at him blankly. He takes me back to the computer screen and shows me things I haven't seen even peeking through King Ling door to watch him with his pleasure girls. I see men bent backward until their forearms lie flat on their calves behind them, women horizontal in the air supported by only one arm, couples entwined in unimaginable ways.

"The places your mind goes," I say, but he laughs at me because he knows, and I know that he knows, that my mind runs the same way.

The flirtation is delicious, but I feel a knot of fear. Maybe he's right about me holding myself back against the tide of change. It's just too excruciating to think that it was no flaw in the wizard's magic but my own subconscious resistance.

I turn back to look at him. "About us…."

"Yes?"

"I want to be utterly and completely sure."

"You're hungry," he says. "Let me feed you."

46

As the sun gathered its skirt and prepared to step out into the day, forty men clad in loose caftans launched an attack on the royal party. Shooting arrows and throwing spears, the element of surprise alone would have guaranteed victory against any normal force. Long Ears' men, however, were trained by Sun Tzu and equipped with iron weapons. The tide of battle shifted quickly in their favor, and soon the attackers were routed in the very clearing where the bearcats had previously gathered.

Bested, the marauders assumed a tight circle, awaiting their fate with interlocking shields held over their heads.

"We're at your mercy," the bandit leader yelled at Long Ears. "Promise to be quick with us and we will drop our guard."

"You issue orders on your knees?"

"The light of day shows us you are a royal party. We would never have…."

"Who are you?"

"The name is Ma Long. Yours?"

"I am Li Dan, oracle of the king's court."

"Long Ears?" came the surprised response from behind the shield. "What are you doing so far from your capital, great lord? From what I hear, the Zhou king can't make a move without you."

"My king is fully as agile in my absence as he is in my

presence, Ma. Tell me, is it by chance possible that you and your men are hungry?"

The bandit slowly exposed his head. "Hungry?"

"If you were desperate for something to eat, the king's soldiers, being men of character, might look upon your actions with greater compassion."

Ma chewed his lip in consideration. "We *are* hungry," he allowed.

"Starving?" Long Ears suggested.

"So weak with hunger as to be devoid of all judgment," said Ma following the wizard's cues. "From one minute to the next, we know not if our legs will hold us."

"Your accent says Qin. Are you soldiers released from service?"

Ma's expression turned sour. "Deserters, great lord."

"You admit it easily?"

"Our commander was a tyrant who ordered us to murder children and violate women during a border campaign. There was no sense to it and no purpose either, so I refused. I would have been executed had my lieutenant not led half the men you see here to my rescue. The rest of this crew fell in with us during the last year as this same commander continued his cruel and unbridled assignment. We sent word to the regional general for help, but the corruption in the Qin court flows all the way down the chain of command "

"Deserters don't deserve our mercy," Kong Qiu interjected.

"We were farmers and artisans, lord—family men before being conscripted. We've never been afraid to die. We have honor."

"If all soldiers were like you, no war could be won," said Kong Qiu.

"If all soldiers were like them, no war would be fought,"

Long Ears said mildly.

"These brigands will betray us the moment we lower our guard," chafed Kong Qiu.

Yin approached the kneeling soldiers, inhaled deeply, and then returned to Long Ear's side.

Human lies have a certain smell. These men are telling the truth. Feed them and pay them and ask for an oath in return. Alliances and power are shifting. You never know when you might need their help.

"You've shot our cook," said Long Ears.

"We have a talented physician in our crew," Ma ventured. "Arrows in the shoulder are like chicken bones in the teeth to him."

Shields went down and the physician stood. He was blind, his eyelids scarred as if by fire, his pupils white as moons. Long Ears led him to the cook, and he slowly twirled the offending arrow, removing it without starting any bleeding at all. Then he packed the wound with herbs from his satchel. "Let ten days pass and then start gentle stretching," he advised in a quiet voice. "After that you may gradually begin to move the area normally."

The repair of the shoulder, along with a few other, more minor ministrations, convinced Long Ear's soldiers to simply confiscate the marauders' weapons.

Looking on, Kong Qiu clucked distrustfully.

"There is a natural bubbling up of compassion and kinship and wisdom in the Tao," Long Ears told him.

"You're an optimist, I'll give you that. I suppose a man in your position can afford such magnanimity."

I see an issue of tortoise and egg here. Which comes first? Does your good fortune arise from your attitude or does your attitude arise from your good fortune?

"My fortune and my attitude arise as one because I combine rather than divorce them," the wizard replied. "Our minds are better spent writing poems than concocting rumors, and our hands better spent building homes than slicing bellies."

Kong Qiu waved his hand. "Such an idealist."

"Ideals become reality if we make them our priority. Accordingly, I offer you employment in Luoyang. Will you accept?"

"Two kings in a third king's castle?" Kong Qiu smiled. "We both know better, but I appreciate your courtesy."

Ma Long the rogue soldier appeared and kowtowed. "Your wisdom exceeds even its own reputation, Long Ears. You have done a fine thing today and my men and I will remember it always."

Ask if you may call on him some day.

Instead, the wizard clapped the bandit on the shoulder. "We found the Tao amidst the bamboo, didn't we, Ma?"

Just then came a cry from a lookout high up in a tree.

"Signal fire!"

"War," Long Ears declared heavily.

Kong Qiu frowned. "Surely not with Lu? Things were so quiet when I left Qufu, I could hear bearcats conspire a state away."

What a strange fellow he is. One minute he's stuck up and precise, the next he exaggerates like crazy.

"I'm afraid our wedding mission will have to wait," sighed Long Ears. "Whatever war it is, it changes everything."

47

There is too much tension in the little cabin I share with Athens for me to be able to sleep. The tension comes not from the fact that I am a tortoise in transition floating thousands of feet in the air, but from our auras intersecting. If Long Ears were here, he would show me the colors we make and describe the waves of energy flowing back and forth between us. He would tell me to quiet my mind and watch what happens. If that didn't work, he would make me an herbal concoction to relax me. In point of fact, I have been using the only herb available, Chinese oolong tea. Perhaps that is why I am wide awake in the starlight.

It may also be the energy from the computer screen that has me so stimulated. I've learned how to use the keyboard and I've mastered browser commands so as to effortlessly do what Athens calls "surf the Web". While he snores softly, I explore the topics of genetic plasticity and epigenetics. The former gives me a better understanding of how I relate to my environment on a genetic level and can change my "phenotype", while the latter has me believing that affecting my emotions can affect the direction and rate of my own evolution. Together, they paint a picture of how my new circumstances and strong feelings — so long as I can ditch my doubts and gain confidence — might actually enhance and speed up the process of change boiling within me. If my emotions turn negative, though I may end up a fearsome chimera shunned by Athens and every other living thing in this world.

I fear the latter so much—exactly what I'm not supposed to do—that I sob uncontrollably. So as not to wake Athens, I bury my face against the flesh inside my elbow. This particular position, while not yoga, is a new one for me, and it allows me a whiff of my new self. I wake him anyway.

"You're pretty sensitive to caffeine," he says, placing his hands on my shoulders and whispering in my ear.

I shiver from his touch. "I'm pretty sensitive in general, but remember, turtles are born both vulnerable and competent. Our shell protects us and we're not nurtured the way human babies are. We come out of abandoned eggs buried in the ground. When the time comes, we use a tiny tooth on the front of our beaks to break the shell. For the first week or so we rely for food on a sac of yolk. When it shrinks and dries up we're on our own and have to find food to fill our bellies. I do have just a few memories after climbing out of the nest. They're terrible scenes. Blood. Swords. Fire. Soup. My parents taken away for food by whalers. Most of us, unprotected, eaten by iguanas and birds. Perhaps one or two of us out of a hundred survive to produce eggs of our own. It's a numbers game in a cruel world."

"Yet Lao Tzu saw you in particular. He knew you would survive."

"Yes and maybe his energy from afar helped preserve me. I imagine that might have been possible. Still, he still saw me as no more than raw material for magic at the start. In his day there were legends of the whole world being carried on the back of the turtle. He mentioned that role in one way or another, the pure yin energy thing. The wisdom of the earth thing. Fitting I was buried for so long, I suppose. From an elemental view. I see it now as indentured servitude, as carrying the weight of the world, literally, on my shoulders."

"Atlas does that in Western mythology," he counters. "But I think the quiet, abiding strength of a woman is more suited to that eternal job than the fleeting, flashy strength of a man. A muscled-up bodybuilder like Atlas would be better suited to throwing the Earth around in some cosmic game of planetary basketball than quietly supporting the endeavors of all living creatures on the surface and in the seas."

"Poetic," I say.

He shrugs. "Not my poem."

"Anyway, it doesn't sound like there was a lot of play in your childhood. Maybe not after, either."

"Play?" I repeat.

"You know, fun. Something to help you relax, to stimulate mental growth and creativity, to foster social relationships."

"You're terribly pompous but I think I understand you're referring to the Internet."

Athens laughs. "You're quite right. A lot of playing does go on there. But I have something more traditional in mind. And don't worry. It's never too late to have a happy childhood."

So saying, he opens the door and looks furtively up and down the passageway. There are glowing orange fiber optic cables along the floor, but no other light and no sound save the faint vibration of the propellers far astern.

"What time is it?" he whispers.

I start to tell him it is the Hour of the Rabbit but correct myself. "5:02 in the morning."

"I was looking around when we talked to the captain. This thing has a very advanced autopilot. Weather radar is linked to it, along with proximity detectors, the works. Someone's likely catnapping the cockpit, but the rest of them are all asleep." He takes my hand. "Here, come with me."

We go a few paces, wait for a bit of turbulence to pass, and continue. Halfway to the dining room, he turns and faces the wall.

"Twenty," he says. "Nineteen, eighteen, seventeen...."

"Sixteen," I chime in, not having the slightest idea what he's about. "Fifteen. Fourteen. Thirteen."

He turns to face me. "You're still here."

I look at him blankly.

"It's a form of playing called a game. Human children love it. I'm going to show you what you've been missing."

"What do I do?"

"You go and find somewhere to hide while I cover my eyes and count down to zero. Choose a good hiding place and try to fool me, to beat me, to make me look and look and finally give up. Then I do the same for you."

Hiding is something turtles do well, but I've never tried it without a shell. "Where should I hide?"

"If I tell you, there is no point to the game," he says. "In fact there is no game at all." Then he gives me a reassuring peck on the cheek, shuts his eyes, and starts counting.

I retrace our steps, pass the cabin, and make my way to the briefing room where I've seen the captain address the crew. One wall bears a giant electronic view screen with a toggle lever that allows forward-facing cameras to zoom and pan the sky and the ground below. I know Athens is coming but I can't resist a look outside. I see a strange blue light on the ground and use the control to focus the camera on it. I feel powerful. Godlike. I feel like I can change the scale of the world using only my human fingers.

Zooming in, a small information square appears detailing the "Piano and Violin" building in the city of Huainan. I know these instruments, but I struggle with the notion that anyone would want to walk inside one, to live or work there. Even so, the text that appears on the screen claims that it is one of the most interesting buildings in the world. I am fascinated by this viewing instrument. It changes reality for me, allowing me to blast open the hard edges of things and make them more malleable, and softer.

The patter of approaching footsteps sends me diving behind the wet bar, where I discover—because I am simply not used to such long legs—that I can't quite get my feet out of view. Desperate, I yank open the audio cabinet below the big screen. The bottom section is empty and I fold myself in and pull the doors closed behind me.

Click.

I panic at the terrible sound. My pulse hammers so violently that when I put my hand on my chest. I can feel the skin bounce. I've never been able to touch my heart before, deeply buried as it was beneath my massive keratinous shields. This, I recognize, is a stress response. This is what I felt when I found myself in Long Ear's grave. The association rises up like a poorly digested mushroom meal. I can't be confined this way! I can't be trapped again, unable to move, to free myself, to re-engage the world. I cannot, must not be in a tight, dark prison again.

My panic rises from my feet to my throat and flees my mouth as a desperate keening. Although I have once or twice heard a human sound like this, never in my life have I dreamed I would make one. I hear Athens' footsteps outside the cabinet, and then I hear him shouting. I can't make out the words, as I'm in no state to decipher language, but I don't have to because a moment later he pulls open the doors.

I'm out and in his arms in a second.

"Poor girl," he says, holding me tight and stroking my head. "Poor, poor girl. I'm an idiot. I should have thought of claustrophobia, of your long, dark, frozen sleep. No more hide-and-seek. No more children's games. I'm so sorry. We won't play this again. Not now, not ever. Don't worry. Calm down. Please forgive me."

"You saved me again," I say, the words tumbling out of my mouth, my lips quivering, my body shaking.

"Shh," he says. "It was my fault."

"Again. Again. Again," I say, despising my weakness and at the same time unable to find dignity through my fear.

"You're safe," he whispers in my ear as the crew bursts in and the captain, bleary with sleep, demands to know what's going on.

"I love her, okay? I just love her," Athens cries, as if that explains everything.

And in a way, it does.

48

Signal fires were as plentiful as fears over the next several days, draping the eastern forest in the smell of wolf dung. On retreat inside himself, Long Ears walked quietly, Yin at his side.

Has someone attacked the king?

"Not the king personally, at least not yet, but the city. A force representing the combined forces of Zheng and Wei."

An army?

"More of a skirmish party moving to test Zhou's defenses."

One afternoon in the garden, with Bao Yu watching us through the window, I heard you predict exactly this to the fat general.

The wizard smiled grimly. "A memory like yours can be both a blessing and a curse."

I'm going to go out on a limb here, not the easiest thing for a tortoise because we neither balance well nor climb trees, to say that everything about this trip to Lu — including the nonsense of procuring women — was a ruse to get me and the prince to safety, and to be able to have a talk with Kong Qiu.

"Despite being stuck on some ideas, I predict he will become a great teacher."

And he just thinks you're lucky to have a job.

Wang Yi trotted up and tugged on the wizard's cloak. "Master," he said. "There's something the matter with Shen."

The procession stopped. Long Ears lay Shen on a mattress

taken from one of the palanquins and covered him with a square of silk. Guards surrounded him, facing all directions with stoic, serious faces, blades unsheathed as if they could ward off the source of his illness with iron.

The boy's face was pale and his brow was moist. "We have to keep moving," he said. "We need to help my father."

Long Ears went in search of a healing mushroom. Yin joined him.

It's his time, isn't it?

"It is," Long Ears replied finding the fungus he wanted at the base of a tree, then gently teasing the delicate flesh away from the wood so softly that not one gill was torn.

So right now, with your medicaments, you're just going through the motions.

"I am."

You knew this would happen. You foretold it, in your own way.

"I did."

But not too obviously. Not in a way that would upset anyone who didn't really want to hear it.

"When foretelling has no constructive purpose, it is better omitted or disguised."

Returning, they found the prince vibrating like a palace bell.

When he plays the flute, the whole world comes alive. I can't bear to lose him.

Yin wasn't the only one left at sea by the prince's sudden illness; the soldiers wandered aimlessly and the attendants seemed to have lost their sense of purpose. Wang Yi sat in tears at Shen's side. "His color is bleeding away like a picked flower right in front of our eyes," he whispered to his master. "It must be poison."

Long Ears put the fungus between Shen's lips, and for a moment the prince rallied.

"All tastes of the forest are sublime, are they not, dear wizard? I share that appreciation with you, yes? That and a wish to die among trees?"

"You could reign for a little while, my prince. Just long enough to make your father happy."

"It wouldn't change anything."

"It would fill your mother's heart, too. It's not natural for a parent to outlive her children."

"The Tao works in strange and wondrous ways, dear teacher. I will miss my mother, too, but I will be with her just as surely as I am with her now, as a piece of her in this world and the next, each and every waking day."

"Stay with us a little longer."

"For the war? I'm no fighter. Do tell the men to get going, though."

"Moving you may cause you pain."

"We'll come to a godown sometime tomorrow afternoon. When we reach it, stop again and put me inside."

"As you command, my prince."

"More than war is coming. There will be a drought to suck all water from the world. Peaks will hold their snow and rivers will run dry and fish will twitch in the sun and people will starve. You've seen this too, yes?"

"I have."

"I won't be sorry to miss so much suffering."

"It is the turning of the world," Long Ears sighed.

"My father thinks about young girls because he feels powerless. It's cruel, really, the way nature tempts men by giving them the illusion they can affect things and at the same time teaches, if they listen, that they can affect nothing at all. Making music is better than ruling, don't you agree?"

"Each person has their path."

I don't understand why this is happening right now. He was fine. He was enjoying the trip. Last night he had a strong appetite.

Shen reached out and caressed Yin's head. "In tortoise years, she's younger than I am," he said. "Just a baby, despite those stout legs."

"She's just one of many who'll mourn your passing."

"You'll soothe them all, won't you? Especially father and mother?"

"Not so easy," Long Ears said, taking the boy's hand.

"I'll come back for my father when the time is right."

"You're sure?"

"Absolutely. Tell him to watch for me. When he is ready, I will be there."

"Of course, Your Highness," the wizard bowed.

He gave the prince's order then, and the men packed Shen into his palanquin and resumed their westward trek.

49

The sky through the crystal windows looks black and blue as a bruise. Athens stands beside me, his hand resting gently on my lower back. "The air up here is too thin and dry for clouds," he says. "Only gasbags and rockets thrive here."

"Such relentless sameness," I say, looking for anything that might relieve the monotony of the view.

"Does it make you think of your time underground?"

"That was earth. This is sky."

"What I mean is that time slows down when nothing changes hour after hour. We mark moments by inputs to our brain. I just figure all those years in the dark passed unnoticed."

"Are you serious?" I repeat, unable to keep incredulity and irritation out of my voice. "It was torture. I froze. I ached. I wasted away. Worms crawled up my nose and chewed at the edges of my eyes. Pinned, I couldn't stop them. The moon pulled at me through the dirt and the bedrock below me creaked and groaned. As I settled, my weight cracked my true love's bones. Believe me, I noticed."

He takes his hand from my back. "It was a stupid thing for me to say. I'm really outdoing myself today."

"The way I live now is to just keep going. You understand that, don't you?"

"To Song Mountain, you mean?"

"At this moment, yes."

"I'm told it's a whole mountain range," he says. "Are you sure you'll be able to find what you're looking for after all this time?"

Before I can answer, there a great roaring and the airship rocks as if hit by a rogue wave. Side to side we go, Athens grabbing me and me grabbing the thin edge of the crystal window with poorly practiced fingers not yet strong enough to provide the purchase I need.

"Government fighters," Athens breathes as a dark silhouette slips by the window.

"You said only rockets and gasbags."

"That's a J20. A rocket with wings."

"You recognize it because…"

He waves his hands in agitation. "I made some inroads into a military website last year. It was more an exploration than an attack. I learned a few things. These planes are very advanced. Better hardware than what the Russians have, maybe better than America's best, too."

I get a clearer look as the jets circle down and away, contrails streaming. Black and sleek with tall, twin tails, they swoop into view like the hawk that tried to pluck a tiny, shelled version of me from a narrow boat on a long-dry river so very long ago.

"Chen's behind this," says Athens.

"The abbot has warplanes?"

"He knows people who do."

"Why would he still pursue me? I no longer have meat to boil or a shell to rob."

"Your story is impossible to ignore, forget, or relinquish," he sighs, eyes riveted to the crystal window. "He's curious about where we're going and why. You're a treasure from an invaluable past. He's not going to let you go."

"But jets?"

"All he had to tell government officials is that you're with me. My Chinese visa is as fragile as a raw rice noodle. I don't conform and I don't like rules. According to my father, some folks thought it was too dangerous to have me in the country. Others saw an opportunity to turn me. While I was incarcerated at the monastery, they courted me patiently. I rebuffed them. Even so, they never give up. Now that I'm on the loose they're worried."

"You're both an asset and a threat," I say.

"Exactly."

The captain storms into our cabin. His hat is on crooked and a shaving cut mars his chin. He points at the fighters outside our porthole. "Look at them!" he screams. "Do you have any idea what their weapons can do to my ship? I should have dropped you in Shanghai!"

The moment he's gone, the nose points down. We topple back into the bed. The engines scream. The descent is dizzying. I have never had ears like this and I have never felt such pressure or heard such popping.

"Are we going to crash?" I whimper.

Athens shoves his laptop into its bag and gathers cords together. Lying on his back he looks grimly at my bare feet while tying his shoes.

"No, but we're going to run."

The rumble of the jets grows louder. Down the corridor and through the open door I can hear the crew respond to the captain's orders by issuing orders of their own. I sense that they are working as fast as they can—maybe a little faster. The airframe moans at the strain. The metal skin flutters. I hear the chuffing of valves.

"This is going to require military precision," Athens pants. "A ground force no doubt awaits us precisely at a predetermined landing spot. There will be an opportunity right when we touch down. Not much of one, but all we've got."

Plummeting earthward from the edge of outer space, I am suddenly unclear where my center is, or how to orient in this wild, spinning cocoon of life.

"Oh, Long Ears," I reflexively whisper.

The muscles of Athens spasm. His eyes fill with lead.

"The name is Athens Li," he says evenly. "And I'm here to remind you that Lao Tzu is dead and you're not at war with your future anymore. Not with your past, either."

Out the crystal window, I see we are back in the clouds. Despite what Athens says, my future seems to offer no welcome.

50

Prince Shen died two days later, in the godown he had seen in his mind's eye, a shack a local merchant used to store turnips for sale in winter. Right before the end, his mind clarified by mushroom water, the young prince rose in a trance and walked to the center of the shack. As Long Ears waved his ritual bell in a slow, steady arc, Shen grew progressively more rigid. The tendons in his neck bulged, his chest heaved, and at the last he stretched his maw as if trying to swallow a horse.

He's obviously singing. Why can't we hear him?

"Because this music is not intended for us. He's passing from one realm to the next. He's already said his goodbyes. This is his announcement of arrival."

Shen's final breath hanging in the air, the great wizard of the court of the Zhou kings performed the customary ritual, replete with chanting and circle walking and the invocation of all manner of forest spirits, these last specially selected to match the prince's personal predilections. The ceremony took some time, but when it was over, the men placed his body reverently in his palanquin and the party continued toward Luoyang.

While the invading soldiers represented only a light force, getting safely past them required decoy signal fires, the use of a secret path down the mountain, passwords, scouts, messengers, and a break for the city walls under the cover of darkness. In a remote corner of the western palace perimeter, the wizard guided his party to a secret tunnel. A last-ditch escape route for the royals, it was disguised on the outside by a garbage pit full of decaying fish and was laden with booby traps whose triggers Long Ears had long ago committed to memory.

He threaded a safe path past urns of toxic gas, poison arrows triggered by pressure plates, hidden spikes coated in plant toxins, and beams designed to collapse if even lightly touched. Eventually they reached the king's private chambers, entering through a door disguised as a false wall to find the monarch slouching on pillows, the stench of rice wine wafting from the folds of his robe.

"There you are, Long Ears!" the king enthused, waving his scepter. "I've been expecting you. There's a small war on, you know."

He's drunk.

"The power of Qin is rising and a drought is coming, Sire. These trends complicate things. If the city falls, the people will be killed and the library will be lost."

"Are shells and scrolls all you think about? Your lectures are such a bore."

Whereas his own stuporous royal ramblings are absolutely riveting.

"I'm sorry not to better entertain you, Sire, but I have terrible news."

"Don't tell me you couldn't find me any girls."

"It's about Prince Shen, my king."

"Shen? Where is he? Did he find a wife?"

"I very much regret to inform your Majesty that the crown prince has passed away."

The king froze, his features hardening as all color dropped away. "Passed away?"

"He left this world, Sire, and without seeing battle. The gods,

214

it would seem, grew impatient for his songs,"

Tell him that was always Shen's destiny.

The king's breathing grew frenzied. "It was two days ago, wasn't it?" he whispered. "I woke up and the sound of the world was different and not just because the temple bells were ringing and swords were clanging outside but because the distant, constant notes of that little flute of his was still. I heard that flute every day, Long Ears, even when he was nowhere to be seen. That day it stopped."

He's taking this badly. It's all he needs to simply give up.

"Stay with us, Sire. Your people need you. You will be with Shen soon enough."

Prince Gui burst into the room and immediately grabbed Long Ears by the throat. "My brother is dead? How can this be? You were responsible for him! He was delicate and helpless and it was your job to protect him. I'll have your head for this, you schemer!"

Long Ears carefully freed himself. "Highness," he said. "Your brother departed this plane of his own accord."

"Do you think I want your opinion? It's because of you that upstart dogheads are snapping around my city. Your whispers in my father's ear are the downfall of us all. You're done! You're finished! You have no place here anymore!"

I suppose you're going to tell me that this is just the way he expresses grief.

Gui's rage might have given way to further physical violence had his father not struggled to his feet and embraced his son.

"What happened to Shen is my fault," the king said sadly. "I should never have forced him to study and fight when all he wanted to do was sleep on pine needles and serenade forest nymphs. I should have left him with the monks he loved so much and listened to Long Ears when he told me the king's path was not for him. Our wizard is not at fault, my son. Come grieve with me."

Grieve together they did, not only that day but for the week of Shen's funeral. Long Ears conducted the ceremony as he had after the death of King Ling's father many years earlier. Courtiers and family gathered in the Temple of the Ancestors and for days chanted and carried torches of fragrant wood around a pit that held the remains of all those who had ruled Zhou since the dynasty moved from the original dynastic capital at Haojing.

When tortoises die, birds peck out their eyes and family members feast on cactus flowers. I can't imagine how much longer the queen can survive such screaming and sobbing.

"Each in his own way," the wizard replied.

Yin watched as General Sun placed the prince's asteroid-iron flute atop Shen's casket, which was surrounded by clay renditions of the stuff of the prince's life, including a life-size replica of his favorite horse and weapons and pots.

Why such clutter?

"Ghost vessels, *mingqi*, for use in the afterlife. Shen will know what to do with them."

And those horrible-looking clay beasts the men are bringing now?

"Guardians to protect the tomb."

I bet the king would like to keep the flute. It will provide him solace.

"Perhaps," the wizard sighed.

Prince Gui appeared, followed by a retinue of armed guards. "We'll close the tomb tonight," he said.

"Better tomorrow, my prince," countered Long Ears. "Tonight's stars are not quite right for Shen's voyage to the ancestors."

Gui scowled. "There's a war on, wizard. The longer we draw out the funeral process, the clearer it will be to the enemy that a royal has fallen. Losing a prince in the ancestral line is a sign of weakness we can ill afford at this time. The tomb closes tonight. The king and queen will join us shortly."

"Your forces are working hard," Long Ears replied. "Yesterday you dumped flaming oil from the ramparts. This morning I sent spies to meet with our allies. Just a few hours ago our troops, hidden underground, surprised and destroyed a band of attackers. Nobody has neglected any military duties, my prince. I protract this ceremony not only to benefit your brother's spirit but also to allow your parents to grieve for a child who was a blessing to all who knew him. Without ample time to mourn, your father in particular will be ill equipped to handle the challenges of war. Please allow the traditional ceremony to continue."

Prince Gui's face grew red. "You're always working some secret angle, you and your allies, supporters, spies, and magical beasts. I don't know what you're up to here and I don't care. We face an existential threat. Grieving makes us weak."

He knows the ways in which Shen was his better and doesn't want the court reminded.

"One more day, please, Highness," Long Ears said mildly.

"I said no."

Bowing in acquiescence the wizard drew a *bagua* symbol in the ground. Assistants positioned bronze cups of clear water at each of the diagrams eight corners, then raised polished metal shields to properly direct light and sound and the rising earth energy.

Can you do something to intimidate Gui now? Perhaps make it rain?

Eyes still closed as the royals assembled, Long Ears merely smiled. When everyone was in his designated place, he began to speak. "Time is an illusion," he said. "It does not travel in one direction but in all directions at once. Shen is with us now just as he was last month. All that matters is how much we love him."

"He's *not* with us, wizard!" cried Gui. "Will you try to delude us even at a time like this?"

Long Ears looked sadly at the young prince and held up his finger. "With us he is. All you need do is listen carefully now."

Such was the oracle's power that even Gui fell silent. A moment passed, and then another. Finally the silence broke.

The queen was the first to hear the faint but distinctive strains of the kingdom's one-and-only iron flute issuing from where it lay atop the dead prince's remains. Bewitched, she drifted toward the burial pit.

"Can't you hear the music?" she asked Gui when he moved to intercept her.

Slowly, gradually, the music grew louder. Shen's chief bodyguard leapt into the pit and emerged with the flute held aloft. When he put his hand over the end of the shaft, the volume of the music diminished, proving it as the source of the sound.

"Look!" he cried. "Prince Shen truly blows notes from beyond the grave!"

Perfect.

Weeping, the queen fell into her husband's arms. Gui, momentarily shaken, joined their embrace. Flute melodies of increasing beauty and complexity continued to entrance the court all night, until daybreak, when a single flaming arrow, a reminder of the forces gathered outside, came flying over the palace walls and landed, shuddering, in the wood of the royal coffin.

51

Song Mountain bares its teeth at the night as we drop in from above. The angle of descent is gentler now, and the bridge is awash with plans and commands. Athens knows better than to ask any favors of the captain at this point, and I see him working the GPS on his phone.

"Get ready to bolt," he says, zipping his pack around his shoulders.

I hear the word bolt and I think of stormy skies and lightning. Too, I envision a piece of hardware I saw on a schematic diagram rendering the construction of airplane wings, something Athens wanted me to understand, perhaps forgetting that I had been a tortoise, not an eagle, and had therefore no affair with air.

The jets still follow, streaking back and forth across the sky like comets and setting the airframe aquiver. "They're tracking us," Athens tells me as the belly hatch begins to slide open. "But I have a little surprise for them once we are on the ground."

Escape has a new dimension for him now. Previously, I've felt that attachment to both my agenda and my transformation drove him. Now he's obviously also worried about his own fate. I understand, but am slightly saddened by the feeling that our impossible fairytale, sewn together by ancient and ethereal threads, might be unraveling in the face of circumstance. I so want this not to be true of love, but our communication has become formal. Speaking my wizard's name has cut a rift valley in the continent we've been birthing together. It's my fault, I know it is. Such landmasses of the heart are made of shifting rock and soil as light and fine as duck down. How can I tell him that even when a new love grows, the old one is always there, another continent with its own borders and ranges always just over the horizon, no matter the distance, no matter the fog.

"You're going to use your phone to throw them off the scent?"

He looks at me with great surprise. "What makes you ask that?"

"You did it to your father."

He nods. "Not just the phone, but the laptop too. I've installed some specialized software in both devices."

"I can't find where we're going at night," I say. "I need sunlight for direction."

"8,000 feet," the navigator intones.

The captain adjusts the controls. Our angle of descent eases and the roar of the engines subsides.

"Do you have parachutes?" Athens asks suddenly.

"You have to be joking." the captain snorts.

"Does this seem a time for comedy?"

"You have jump experience?"

"None."

The captain shakes his head. "I can't do one more thing for you. I'm being forced down by military craft. What happens to you two is no longer my concern."

"I have a plan in mind. We could say we overpowered the crew and took two of your escape chutes. You have them, yes?"

Through his stress and fatigue I see how very young the aviator is. If this country works the same way it did when I was afield on four legs, he is the son, grandson, or nephew of someone very important. Perhaps competent, but more importantly, connected.

Certainly not very experienced.

"Who would believe such a preposterous story," he says. "They'll interrogate us."

"We are legendary outlaws already. Our powers are untested and unknown. Such a turn of events would surprise precisely no one."

The captain closes his eyes and rubs his chin. His thoughts are running, and perhaps not in our favor.

"You were watching when Yin changed," Athens says. "You saw the whole thing on the belly cam as you came down. She's a supernatural being. You can't imagine her strength. Just say so when you're asked. You don't have guns on board, do you?"

"Of course not. One hole in the wrong place...."

"Every passenger needs to know that we keep emergency chutes in the storage bin near the main hatch release," the navigator interrupts, speaking with exaggerated and false significance. "It's the first thing we tell *anyone* who comes aboard."

The captain exhales with enough relief to fill the gasbag. Athens takes my hand, his grip all business. We descend into the hatch. By the time I am all the way down, he has my parachute ready.

"Wear it just like I wear my backpack," he instructs.

I turn around and slip my arms through. He cinches everything—shoulder harness, waistband, chest strap—a bit more tightly than he needs to. I sense the disturbance in his force.

"This is the release," he says, putting a thick tab of red plastic in my hand. "I'll go first. You follow. Keep your eyelids tight against the wind and watch me. The moment you see my chute, pull your cord. You'll feel a strong jerk and then you'll start floating."

"I thought you said you've never done this before."

"I watch movies."

"It's dark," I say quietly. "I'm accustomed to solid ground. Air is not my medium."

He is suddenly loud and fierce, his breath hot on my face. "You were earthbound. Now you are free. I know everything is happening quickly, but if you don't let go of the ties that bind you, you'll never be free."

He shrugs on his pack, opens the hatch, and drops into the night. I stand frozen at the edge of my life, blackness roaring past. I think of the abbot. I think of the fighter jets. I am terrified of falling and terrified of being left behind. I think of the abbot's agenda, and I think of the freedom Athens has promised.

I jump.

52

Despite the best efforts of the great wizard's staff, his house remained redolent of both wolf dung from the persistent signal fires smoldering in the ongoing campaign against the king, and from the odor of inhabitants forbidden to bathe during the drought.

Humans have a stronger smell than tortoises.

"To your nose, perhaps."

You mean I stink?

"I mean you smell like a tortoise, all the more since the garden pool dried up and you can no longer soak in it."

And you, of late, reek of the juices of your young consorts.

Lao Tzu put down the peach he was eating and looked at Yin with amusement. "What makes you say that?"

Do I not have a nose?

"Such women require comfort and solace in these stressful times."

The way you say 'such women' makes it sound as if they are needy and weak. They're not. The only reason they put up with you and with their sad lot is that they must. Don't you think they want a loyal, devoted person to love and who loves them?

"Some may dream of such a thing," Long Ears allowed.

What you call 'such a thing' is everything. You may know rivers and you may know stars, but I'm not impressed by what you know of women. Why did you make Bao Yu wait so long for a child? All the powerful men in court have more children than your treasured maple tree has leaves. Do you even know she is pregnant?

The wizard pursed his lips. "Scholarship and divination fill my days, Yin. It has always been thus. A man like me must avoid attachments and dance only with the Tao."

Why marry, then?

"There are certain conventions. I used to pay more attention to her."

But you stopped when I arrived in Luoyang.

"She's been very patient. Had I waited much longer, she would have been too old to bear a child."

I wish I could give....

Bao Yu chose that moment to enter the room. "I must speak with you, husband," she said, staring balefully at Yin.

"Of course."

"Alone."

You'd think that since she is soon to give you what I never can, grace and compassion would find her tongue.

Banished, Yin lumbered out into the cool courtyard and stared at the sun setting over the city wall, its rays beautifully refracted by the smoke of war. Such moments usually made her homesick for her island, for the shining black sand, the sweet crunch of Opuntia cactus, the feeling of sea air in her lungs, the floating motes of seabird dander, and the reassuring clack of Sally Lightfoot crab claws. This time, she felt a different kind of longing, and said to herself what she had not been able to say to her man.

I feel I am still changing for you, but I worry the process is too slow. I would give anything and everything to feel you, to touch you the way a woman can, to accept your seed and give you a child.

The clatter of running feet interrupted her yearning. For a

moment she feared that some foreign interloper had managed to breach the city walls but soon saw a soldier clad in the official yellow of the king's guard.

"Where's the great lord?" he huffed, looking straight at her.

It happened sometimes that members of the palace staff addressed her directly. Yin pointed with her foot.

"The bedroom?"

Yin nodded encouragingly. The soldier hesitated. "Is it a bad time?"

Yin shook her head.

A moment later, Long Ears emerged. "Come with me quickly," he commanded her. "Prince Shen's shade has paid a visit to the king."

53

Never before have I been able to lick the sky with my tongue or reach out and touch a star. All that links me to the life I had is the cold. Everything else is new. Where once I feared birds, now I am one. Where once I was weighted and heavy and constrained by hard limits, now I am a winged bag of water able to flap my wings. Before I was manacled at four points to the ground, now I am weightless and at speed and free to spiral and spin without encumbrance. I am lost in my sensations, and lost in revelation too. Tears freeze hard on my cheeks and I pry them away with my nails, grateful for the simple ability to touch my own face.

It is Athens Li who has brought me to this moment, Athens Li who has released me from bonds within and bonds without. There are smells of summer in the sky to link me to earthly nature below, and gravity to guide me, but in the darkness I cannot see Athens and therefore cannot follow his cue to pull the cord that dangles before me. Still, in all, I do not worry. If this is how it ends, in a stunning, killing congress with my old nemesis the ground, then so be it. I won't see it coming and I won't feel a thing. What a way to go this will be! What a way to end my journey and get back home.

Despite my acceptance, I feel a tingle of remorse. Whatever had been growing in me has become a romance waiting to pierce me. Athens' touch and his kindness and his bravery and his gaze are no longer merely a seed but a tree whose roots wrap up my heart and whose branches extend to my curling hair and my fingers and my toes. There is something about him that completes me, something that gives me strength and structure, too. Just as I begin to remember that he needs the gifts I have for him as much as I need those he has for me, I see the white flash of his parachute below me.

I drop past him and when we are on one level, I see the panic on his features, his open, shouting mouth, his hands wildly miming the pulling of a cord, the adoration in his eyes. I yank the cord and am jerked suddenly up just as he said I would be, from what he learned watching movies. Now the umbrella of fabric above me obscures him, but I feel him anyway. I only wish I could gaze at him all the way down.

When the ground finally does reclaim me, the contact is rough, and perhaps because I have had my eyes trained upward or perhaps because I am so unwilling to relinquish the remarkable lightness of my new being, I am unprepared for it. My ankles give way and my knees buckle and I roll against slanted ground, experiencing the still-new sensation of shrubs and stones against my softness. I find my feet and explore myself but find nothing broken. I brush off leaves and dirt and watch the sky for Athens.

Fiddling with his straps, he loses vertical alignment when he touches down and swings sideways into a pile of rocks. It is too dark for detail, but I hear a soft thud and instinctively know something has gone wrong. I cry out to him, but he doesn't answer. Slowly his chute collapses over him, covering him like a shroud. My stomach rises in my throat as I run to him, tearing off the harness as I go. I rake away at the fabric and find him lying motionless, his eyes open yet staring with a terrible lack of focus.

"Athens," I whisper, shaking him gently.

He slumps down against the rock.

"Athens," I say more urgently and loudly. "Get up. We have to go."

His throat gurgles. His eyes flicker and close. For the vast preponderance of my life, my voice resonated only inside a great wizard's head. In recent days, however, it has gained the capacity to cross chasms and fields, and I have not had time to learn to control it.

"Athens!" I scream.

Sand around the rock pile adjusts to the noise. Athens twitches and then grows completely still. I bend down and put him over my shoulder in the way I watched soldiers do with their fallen comrades, from the ramparts, so very long ago. I head toward a cluster of lights flickering off in the distance. With each step, the boulders in my path become pebbles and the burden on my back becomes lighter. I smell meat cooking in the distance and I redouble my pace. My toes find their purchase and I use it to steady and strengthen me. Athens' electronics somehow work to obscure us because even though the jet planes strafe loudly and low and even though the airship drifts overhead like a small and sensitive moon listening for sparrows, my love and I remain blended with the land in just the way of a turtle and her load.

54

"Shen played music for me at the window of my bedchamber," the king told his wizard that morning in his private chambers. "He was surrounded by light and beckoned with his finger. He wanted me to come to him but I wasn't ready, so we just talked."

I think he's more ready than he knows.

Long Ears nodded, crushing a potion of calming herbs with a mortar and pestle. "Perhaps now you can tell him what you couldn't when he was with us in the flesh, Sire."

The king closed his eyes and ran his fingers up and down the fine silk hem of his robe. "I told him I appreciate his music and not to worry that he failed me. He told me to show more love to Gui."

"Gui will reign during hard times, Your Highness. War and drought are hard on any king."

"He can't make rain, old friend, but he is a soldier. Trying to keep him from his sword is like trying to keep Shen from his flute."

"Gui has General Sun to teach him about battle, Sire."

"Good, because I no more understand what these warlords want than I understand why that huge tortoise follows you around like a cow. What has she done for you lately? I don't see any of your many women swelling, Long Ears."

"Actually, Bao Yu is with child, my king."

The king opened his eyes at this, and his face brightened. "Yes? Wonderful news. Perhaps you will have a son who plays the flute!"

"I would be honored to have a child half so talented as Shen, Sire."

"There's a light around him when he comes to me, did I mention that?"

"You did, Your Highness."

"It's human nature to have a leader, Long Ears, even if heaven's mandate can shift with the wind. I try to spread peace and the rule of law, but the cycles of man will replace me with a tyrant and that tyrant with a good man and on and on."

Long Ears smiled. "You have learned more than you know."

"I'm sick of it all. My queen's beauty fades and despite the best efforts of my most beautiful courtesans, I can no longer perform."

"I could send you more beautiful girls."

The king brightens momentarily. "Really? I could use another son. If Gui falls in battle, the dynasty is truly lost."

"I will tend to it at once."

"Make it soon, Long Ears. Shen awaits me in the forest."

Promising to do so, the wizard left the king to his ruminations and went to consult with General Sun about the state of the war. He found him in the palace armory.

"The king should have listened to me about conscripting a larger standing army," the general reported glumly. "Sadly, Gui is no better a strategist than his father. He takes bait too quickly and commits in the wrong direction. Word of his impulsiveness and the king's sadness has spread. The state of Wei grows bold, Chu may send troops against us, too, and Yan has created a supply chain stretching north and east almost to the sea. We'll have a real siege on our hands soon and with our cisterns so low, we won't hold out long."

He won't say it, but he's worried he won't be able to save the royal family.

Long Ears tiptoed to the door and yanked it open. Two eunuchs collapsed over the threshold. Sun leapt for them with shocking speed, bringing a sword to each of their necks before they could even bumble through an explanation.

"If your ministerial masters have questions, they can come ask me themselves," Sun thundered. "Now go before I take your heads."

Long Ears appeared suddenly exhausted. Yin presented her shell as a perch. "The dynasty is attacked from outside with arrows and by termites from within," he said once the door was closed again. "If the city falls into enemy hands, the library will be lost and the Middle Kingdom will sink back into the Dark Ages."

Perhaps you need to move it.

Sun chewed his fingernail. "We could secret away the most important texts. The question is where?"

"I have a place in mind."

"Such plotting reeks of defeat," said the general. "I preferred the days when Wang Yi was a lad and we worried about women and peonies, back when we still had Shen and his music and I ate more dumplings than I should."

I have to admit he has slimmed down.

"Nobody must know we have this plan," said Long Ears. "One stray word could change the course of history forever."

Sun Tzu gave his pledge, and Yin and her wizard departed the palace. On the way home, they passed the very market where years before, Wang Yi bought himself a dragon robe to wear when presenting a certain baby tortoise to his teacher. A customer was complaining to the proprietor.

"The bird died the moment I brought him home," the man groused.

"He was the picture of health when I sold him to you," said the seller, glancing at Yin with an acquisitive glimmer in his eye.

"A dead bird in the house is a terrible omen with all the talk of surrender, rape, and plunder. My mother saw it and fainted straight away."

"No bird's going to change the war," the seller said. "It's just a matter of time until all we have and know is lost."

Long Ears intervened. "You sold this young man a dying bird?"

In earlier days, the man would have dropped and knocked his head on the ground at the sight of so august a personage. Now he merely inclined his head. "A merchant has to make a living, sir."

"One minute after your birth and one minute before your death your actions have only the value you give them, and that value can only be measured by your adherence to the Tao."

"If you say so, sir."

He rolled his eyes at you.

Long Ears turned to the buyer. "Your mother is unwell?"

"She suffers from delicate nerves, lord."

"And your father is still among the living?"

"He lost his leg in battle, lord, and now spends his days at calligraphy."

"Do you have a brother in the army?"

"I am an only child. Because I doctor the poor, I have not yet been called to service."

Long Ears selected two fine larks for the young man. "You are right to think birdsong would calm your parents. It's a shame they can no longer leave town and walk in the forest to quiet their souls. Take these as a gift from the court."

YUN ROU

As soon as the man left, the vendor put out his hand for payment. The wizard fixed him with a stare. "Count yourself lucky I don't send constables for you," he said.

Save the time and cut off his head.

"This lesson is sufficient. No need for another."

When they arrived home, Bao Yu was waiting. She pointed at an incense clock whose ashen remnants formed a spiral on the table.

"I lit it to freshen the house for your arrival, my husband. Now it has almost burned out."

"Things are developing quickly on the outside. Affairs of the court pressed me."

"When you left, I heard you tell the houseman to prepare your travel kit."

"Ah."

"You don't think I know you're leaving? After all these years, don't you think I know your little signs?"

"I know you see a great deal."

"Don't patronize me. I noticed the way you turned around and looked over your shoulder at the house this morning. You never did that before. Go ahead and admit you won't be coming back. You're not just leaving, you're going for good."

The great wizard sat down quietly beside his wife. "We have had many good years together. Soon you will be occupied with raising our child."

"Our son," she said, shifting away from him. "We both know he's a boy. If he survives the war, it will be as a slave to the court of Wei."

"You'll both be safe. I've made arrangements."

Bao Yu began to cry. "You made me wait twenty years for a child and now that I'm pregnant you tell me you're leaving as coolly as if you were delivering a crop prediction to the king.

Well, I won't let you go without me. I'm your wife and I belong at your side."

"I can't protect you where I'm going."

Bao Yu convulsed with rage. "The first thing I'll do when you leave is chop the head off that disgusting animal of yours...."

Suddenly she stopped talking and reached out for the support of a nearby table. "You're taking her with you," she said dully. "I can see it in your face. That's what this is about. You gave me a baby as compensation for the fact that you want to be alone with her."

"Why do you talk this way, Bao Yu? She's a tortoise."

"I know better than you do what she is!"

So saying, she ran from the room. A moment later she returned with a cauldron from the kitchen. The bottom was glowed red from the cooking fire and the top frothed with a stew of autumn vegetables and pork.

"Die!" she screamed, hurling the boiling liquid.

Yin withdrew her head and limbs as the stew cascaded over the margins of her shell, trickling to the floor in a curtain of carrots and onions and pig fat and greens.

Two housemen ran in and helped Long Ears restrain his wife from her fit of kicking and punching.

"Calm yourself," Long Ears begged. "Your tantrum will hurt the baby."

"Don't you dare pretend you care about the baby!"

In response, Lao Tzu withdrew his mortar and pestle for the second time that day and selected herbs for a burn poultice. Passive and beaten, Bao Yu wept as he applied it to her palms.

I'm sorry she hates me. I understand why.

"Don't be silly."

There's nothing silly about it. Her pain is real. Is my shell cracked?

"There is only a small dent at the crown. Are you burned?"

Only on the tops of my toes. But know this, Bao Yu has no shell to protect her, and soon she won't even have you.

55

Curled about me like a boa made of anything but feathers, Athens' ribs and hipbones dig into the hollows of my shoulders. My shoulders, newly free of the support of a shell, take a while to figure out how to support his weight. I find a stride, and with it, advance in the direction of a complex of buildings set into the side of Song Mountain. I feel his hearbeat in his neck, which is braced in my arms, perhaps the only way I know he's alive. I can see a grand arch of flying multi-colored flags, a forest of tiered, stone steles, and a sterile sea of concrete that renders petite even Sun Yat Sen's mausoleum from which we were so recently pulled up and away.

I am drawn to a rhythmic, throbbing sound. Following it, I arrive at a dusty field covered by monks in orange robes. They move in unison to a beat issued on giant kettledrums. The pace of their practice matches Athens' heartbeat, which I feel in his neck. The presence of a line of vendors offering souvenir trinkets suggest I have come to the temple the airship captain called Shaolin. If so, it is too early for the tourist trade he derided, as the light is still low and a slight mist covers the ground.

A lone, older monk in wire-rimmed glasses walks towards me. The creases in his jowls are thick enough for secrets. The closer he gets, the more worried he looks.

"I need help," I say. "My friend hit his head."

"Perhaps you could put him down?"

I shake my head. "Not on the ground."

"May I help you carry him, then?"

"No."

He looks at me closely and nods. "I understand. Please come with me."

He leads me to an infirmary, a room with four tables and scrolls on the wall and acupuncture charts and a wooden wall of apothecary drawers each half the size of a shoebox. I recognize the aroma of mugwort and other dried herbs. I lay Athens on a treatment table. I want to switch places with him so his suffering will stop. His stupor does not put me off; I know what it is to be trapped in my head.

The monk disappears for a few minutes and comes back with a younger associate he introduces as a doctor.

"I'm sorry, but I need you to release his hands," the doctor tells me.

"I can't."

"I need to feel his pulses."

"Touch his neck. I felt it there."

"Different pulses," the older monk explains. "The neck reveals the heart, but the wrists reveal all systems."

"He hit his head. His systems are fine."

"We're doctors. Please let us help. It's what we do."

Reluctantly, I let go. My flesh burns with loneliness at the spots that have touched him. His expression grave, the doctor's hands move up and down Athens' forearms while the old monk dresses his head wound. I close my eyes and try to reach him through the ether. I call to him, I cry to him, but nobody answers in just the cruel and hopeless way nobody answered when I called out from below ground. I feel the tears on my cheek. I grab the doctor by the shoulders and shake him violently.

"You have to save him!"

The old monk takes me by the shoulders in turn. "Head injuries are complicated. He may need a hospital. Fluid can build up in the brain and the pressure may need to be relieved before it damages the brain."

"There is no pressure and there is no head injury! There is no damage to his brain. He's not swollen. He's going to wake up any minute. It was just the wrong angle for parachute landings. The movies taught him wrong."

I know what those monks are thinking, and not just from the looks on their faces.

"I'm not crazy and I didn't hit or shove him. We fell from an airship in the night. Look at the insignia here above my breast. This is the ship uniform."

The doctor glances at Athens, obviously torn between the need to heal and the need to deal with my outburst. He shrugs out of my grip and mouths the word police. The old monk grabs me more tightly. I struggle in his grip, my face red and my muscles tight. I want the whole thing to stop. I want them attending Athens, not me, but the old monk uses some fancy move and sweeps my feet. The former turtle in me knows how to handle myself down on the ground, but in the end they pin me top and bottom.

"I didn't hurt him! I love him!"

Even as they press my head to the floor and trap my feet, I recognize the luminosity of those last three words. So enlightened, I cannot tolerate confinement. Not anymore. I can fall through the sky but I cannot suffocate under the weight of men. They feel too much like dirt. There is only one thing I can do and I do it. I slip out of my clothes like one of my snake cousins leaving its skin behind. In the lamplight of the temple clinic, witnessed through the hollow eyes of dried beetles and geckos and frogs, I am naked once more, and free.

My tattoo glows. Monk eyes grow wide.

56

Winter weather slowed the war, but when word leaked out that King Ling had finally stolen away to the forest to join his eldest son, the attacking forces rallied fiercely in hopes of disrupting the transfer of power to Prince Gui, now King Jing. Catapulted stones fell on the city, one of them demolishing a storage shed adjacent to the great sage's beloved library. An hour later, the court wizard sent a runner to Ma Long, leader of the Western Forest bandit brigade, to announce that a secret party was coming to the forest and to be on the lookout for signal fires. As soon as the runner had left, the wizard went to ask a favor of General Sun.

"I hear the new king has replaced you with another advisor."

The general chewed his lip. "A lesson in acceptance."

"Not everyone is able to master their impulses and ambitions. Those who cannot may not be able to see the brilliance of your strategies clearly. My cousin is king of my home state of Chu. The southern flank of the federation is expanding and I believe he would benefit from your superior counsel and service. Would you accept a post with him?"

The old general's face twitched with emotion. "Gladly, great lord. And thank you."

"I hate to burden you, but might I ask you and your men to take Bao Yu with you? She is with child and must be kept safe."

I knew you would ask him.

"I am honored you trust me so completely, though your request makes me wonder if I will ever see you again."

"My role is shifting," Long Ears allowed. "I have always been better at sensing trends in nature than in men."

Don't think you fool the general with that nonsense. You knew Shen would never rule, you knew the king would leave, you knew Gui would bring down the dynasty, and you knew Sun Tzu would look out for your wife.

"I'm sure you'll continue to influence the course of events in the Middle Kingdom," Sun Tzu said. "Though perhaps more in the way of Fu Hsi, Ancestor Yu, the Yellow Emperor, or the Duke of Wen."

Long Ears inclined his head. "Those men are legends, old friend. My only connection to them is to preserve their lessons so that future generations will not have to learn them all over again. I've hidden the most important works under rice in two carts on their way to feed the troops running missions outside the city walls. We leave tonight and I ask that you and your men accompany us. We can part company at the Eastern Wall. Please be there at the hour of the ox."

The friends stayed together as long as they dared, reminiscing of old opportunities and joys. Finally, as night fell, Long Ears and Yin went to take their leave of Qin Jiang, their last, best ally in the court.

"Where will you go?" inquired the queen.

"Best if I not say, Your Highness."

"Ah. I understand. Would you be headed north?"

"As I said,, Your Highness, it is best if you don't know."

"If you're leaving, it means you think the city will fall."

"Whether it will or not, I cannot stay. The king doesn't trust me. He has replaced the guard with his own men and tucked the powerful eunuchs under his wing. He's looking for a reason to have me executed."

"I would never allow that."

"And I would never, for any reason, pit you against your own son."

"I hear that the Huns are likely to take advantage of the struggle here and attack the borders of the federation."

"That may happen," Long Ears agreed. "If it does, the strongmen will withdraw their forces to protect their own lands and the city may thereby be spared."

"It sounds as if you think that would only delay the inevitable."

"There are larger forces at work, my queen. Spirals of fate upon spirals of greed producing, overall, a trend toward replacement and renewal."

"Leaving me just an old queen."

"Hardly old, Highness, and wiser every day. Your son will need that wisdom in the days ahead."

"Wisdom is what you point to after a woman's charms are gone," the queen sighed bitterly. "Next you'll compliment my gown, my jewelry, perhaps even my hair. This is how it goes. Tell Yin she should count herself lucky she's not a woman. Instead of fading and bending and drying up, she gets bigger and stronger and more impressive every day."

Tell her I would give anything to be half as human and half as beautiful as she is.

The wizard complied and the queen touched the great tortoise's head. "Our great history may be coming to a close, but it all started with you," she murmured, her eyes filling with tears. "You'll remember me, won't you, when I'm just dust in the Tao?"

I don't know why but I am certain you will be remembered for far longer than you could ever imagine.

At that moment, the great wizard did something that no member of the court, indeed no member of the kingdom save a king would ever have dreamed of doing—he took the queen in his arms and tenderly kissed the top of her head. She clung to him, sobbing silently until, inevitably, it was time for the wizard to take his leave of another woman far less inclined to forgive him for departing.

It could have been a great moment for the sage and his wife an hour later, outside the city, in the presence of decoy rice. Tenderness might have flowed and words of forgiveness, held back for decades, might finally have been uttered. Under the threat of crossbow bolts and the prying eyes of spies and agents, a last loving embrace might have been stolen, and sweet promises with references to a reunion in the realm of the ancestors might have been whispered.

Instead, as an icy wind blew and the men unpacked the dynasty's wisdom and transferred it to packs and satchels, Long Ears and his wife parted in quick, quiet fashion. Sun Tzu gave a final kowtow as his men led Bao Yu away, then trotted off to join them. The wizard lingered a moment, watching them recede to the south, feet crunching on frozen ground, until they finally turned a corner. He would forever carry a final image of his pregnant, broken-hearted wife encircled by a group of protectors and bent against her lot.

In the future she'll realize that you were gone long before this night, and that your parting was not the beginning of her pain but the beginning of her freedom.

"Even before you came to the Middle Kingdom, she always gave more than she got." Long Ears answered as the troop moved quickly toward a steep and rarely used forest path.

No. She got as much as she gave, but in a currency other than passion.

"A quality it saddens me to be taken for lacking," said the wizard, "especially since I feel such a sense of wonder and appreciation at the marvel of the ever-changing Tao, in all its wigs and guises."

You keep those feelings on the inside.

"I do what I must to play the role I've been given."

What are you feeling now?

"I miss the music and wistful smile of Prince Shen. I regret that I will likely never know my son. I am comforted that he and Bao Yu will swim free of the tides of war."

What else?

"It is time to signal Ma Long."

As his men lit a fire, Long Ears prepared tea for Yin, whose difficulty moving in the cold had been slowing the party's progress. The smoke rose thick and dark.

I had no idea this hard cake was tea.

"It is *Mangzhi* from the southern mountains. It travels well and will warm us for our task."

Yin resolved to savor the earthy brew slowly, but her willpower vanished at the first sip and she gulped it down until it came out her nostrils. She felt her mind clear and her heart pound and she began to gallop. The men extinguished the fire and took advantage of her energy by resuming their trek.

Once again, they walked through the night. In the morning, Yin watched the wizard studying the clouds.

"Gravid with storms," he murmured, gesturing aloft.

They are speaking to you of Bao Yu.

"They will deliver before she does. We must hurry."

You think Gui has sent men after us?

"He will discover what I've done by now. Even though he will no doubt be glad to be free of me, his ego will not allow him to ignore a perceived insult."

Ma Long's men will come to our aid before he can find us. They know these woods better than anyone.

"I was expecting to see them by now."

Why don't you just leave me behind? I'm not worth losing the library.

"I ask only that you move faster."

I'm sorry, but my feet have frozen.

A tortoise ankle cannot be turned upward, so in order to conduct a proper examination of the problem, the wizard had to lie on the ground. When he did, he saw that the icy ground had deeply damaged Yin's footpads. He directed the men to pitch camp. As they worked, he applied a poultice, and Wang Yi, always handy with a needle, fashioned protective hemp slippers.

A copper moon rose to reveal the night tracks of rabbits, foxes, bears, and wolves. Secure in their tents, the men slept heavily. In the morning, they awakened refreshed and were off again quickly.

I smell Song Mountain.

"You smell well. If not for the low clouds, you would see the peaks."

I know where we're going.

"I assumed you knew all along."

That afternoon, they arrived at their destination and finally delivered the wisdom of the Zhou kings to the mouth of the very secret cavern that had been stabilized by the rock needles the prince had melted with his song. As they all descended into the tunnel, the snow that had been dogging them finally began to fall. The wizard gave instructions that no one was to spend more than a few minutes in the cave because of the gas.

You think the library will be safe here?

"I'm sure of it."

And the gas won't hurt the scrolls and bones.

"On the contrary, it will preserve it."

When do you think we'll be able to retrieve it?

"I don't know. The greatest treasure of the dynasty may have to stay here for a while."

57

They are down on the ground for some time, these monks, or more precisely they are up and down in a type of ritual bow that reminds me of ones I have not seen in thousands of years. I put my clothes back on, but not before they have inspected my back with great interest, and, with my permission, photographed it with a smartphone. Through all this nonsense, I want only doctoring for Athens and am furious at their interest in my wizard's Taoism when a life is hanging in the balance.

"You can study my back later," I say, shrugging into a tunic. "Would you look after my friend now?"

"What happened to him?" the young doctor inquires.

"He fell and hit his head and went unconscious. Can't you see the wound?"

"You say he fell?"

I realize they don't believe me. Perhaps they think Athens is playacting.

"From the sky," I say. "When he wakes up you can ask him. Please. I'm worried about him."

"Amnesia sometimes follow a knock on the head," the doctor explains casually, breaking little needles out of paper wraps and inserting them with the suddenness of a striking cobra into points down the centerline of Athens' chest, the side of his neck, and also on the inside of his leg. "Most of the time it's transient."

"The characters are Taoist," the old monk tells me as if it is news. "Very ancient. They look like the *Tao Te Ching*, except for the turtle characters."

"Lao Tzu liked turtles," I snap. "And why are you Buddhists so interested in him anyway?"

The doctor rows the needles in Athens' neck like little oars. "Chan Buddhism, our sect, has a strong Taoist core," he says. He shows me a point halfway down the web between Athens' thumb and forefinger. "Massage this point. It will ease his headache when he wakes up."

I squeeze as energetically as possible.

"Not so hard."

"Why do you have such a tattoo, anyway?" the old monk wants to know.

"Just one of those things."

"It looks like it was done in a museum. Do you happen to know what the tattoo artist copied when he did the work?"

"It was freehand. Original."

Athens coughs, bringing up a tiny bit of blood. It perches on the crease of his lips.

"Not to worry," the doctor reassures me. "It's not from his lungs. You see how bright and thin it is? He must have bit his cheek at the time of impact."

I kiss the blood away. The doctor looks unnerved. He points at the stain on my lips. I lick it rather than wipe. He winces. The old monk comes close to my back and tries to peer down my top for another glimpse of the tattoo.

"What I mean to ask is not about the tattoo technique per se, but about the source of the characters, the way in which the stanzas are grouped, the particular sequence of the pictographs within each one."

Athens stirs. For a moment I think he's going to wake up,

but then he goes still again. One more time, the doctor makes the rounds of the needles, starting at the feet and continuing upward, rowing each one. I feel certain that if he were awake, Athens would find this quite painful.

"Do you understand my question?" the old monk pursues.

He's the one who doesn't understand, not me. He's the one who can't seem to grasp that while I am profoundly fascinated by the limitless possibilities of my future with Athens Li, I give not a whit for this man's academic preoccupations. After an entire life lived with every possibility continually squelched, then an eternity reliving my frustrations, I cannot possibly focus on or care about anything other than where Athens and I might live together, what it would be like to go out to dinner and hold hands under a table, how it might feel to have kisses available, spontaneously, at any moment. How happy I will be to see my island again in his company, what it could be like—would be like, will be like—to see his child issue from between my thighs and look up at me with the Long Ears' family expression.

"She's preoccupied with the young man," the doctor tells his companion.

Athens body vibrates. His abdominal muscles contract, lifting his torso off the table. I wait for him to awaken—and indeed there does seem to be a moment during which he is hovering between two worlds—but then he slumps back down. I look at the doctor expectantly.

"We really should get him to a hospital," he says.

The irrepressible old monk continues to try for a look down the back of my neck. I stymie his efforts by shrugging my airship uniform higher. He sighs and lights up his phone to look at the photos he snapped, but I can see that engaging a facsimile is not going to satisfy him.

I release Athens' hands and make my way to his poor,

bandaged head. I avoid one particularly long, thick needle protruding from his neck and put my tongue in his ear, but gently, slightly. I nibble on his earlobe to taste him.

"It's time to come back," I whisper. "I want to be with you, joined to you. I want us to be one."

58

Yin and the men huddled in tents outside the cave, unable to light warming fires for fear of giving away their location to the pursuers they knew had to be close behind.

Oh, that gas. Soon I won't be able to think or speak to you. Already, I cannot move. Everything is growing so dark and quiet I'm afraid that when I die, I won't even notice.

The wizard moistened a clump of dried herbs and put them in front of her beak. "You're not going to die. Here. Chew on these."

I'm not sure I have the energy.

"Try."

What's in it?

"A yin and yang balance to draw in your energy and preserve it. Huang Qi is the chief, Bai Zhu the deputy, and Fung Fung an addition to support your digestion.

Yin took in the herbs and crushed them with the plates of her beak. The men prepared a breakfast of cold rabbit and rice. Long Ears went back down into the cave to sort and wrap the library, applying a seal stamped with his personal chop as he completed each wrap. When he had been down as long as he safely dared, he asked Wang Yi to continue the work, directing that his apprentice organize the material as it had been in the palace library.

He's so happy you asked him. It makes him feel useful, especially as the task is so special.

As Wang Yi went back down to work, Long Ears, in a jovial mood, began to sing and dance. The men grinned and clapped as he pirouetted, bobbed, ducked, and swayed.

You're thinking of King Ling, aren't you?

"He's finally with his dancing girls."

You've done the last of your formal duty by protecting the library. You're free now, and happier than I've ever seen you. Would you also like to relinquish me?

Instead of answering, Long Ears suddenly stopped dancing and stood still. The men stared. He raised his finger to his lips, then made a gesture to the surrounding trees.

"Palace soldiers are here," he whispered. "Cover the entrance to the cave."

But Wang Yi is working down there.

"Do it now. They will appear any moment."

The men disguised the opening thoroughly, then grabbed swords and stood uncertainly in a circle.

Let Wang Yi come up.

"He hears us. He knows what's happening. He's patient."

But the gas....

"There's nothing I can do. They're here and they cannot know of the cave."

I don't see anyone.

"Many will die before you do."

Can't you stop it? What about your magic?

"I wish I were as powerful as you think I am. I cannot defend against so many men, especially at such a distance. I must save what I have until our attackers reveal themselves."

An instant later, a rain of arrows began. Terrified, birds screeched and flew. Yin withdrew into her shell, but the men had nowhere to hide and were slaughtered in minutes, taking shafts through their hearts and heads and necks. They died where they fell, in pools of blood, twitching and crying and gasping. Time stretched. In the silence, the distant peaks pondered their bulk, and melting icicles clicked and snapped a symphony of their own composing. Insects at industry buzzed. Bushes newly free of the burden of snow undulated in the breeze, and, far off, deer locked antlers in play.

Long Ears rose slowly and circled the field. He closed the eyes of his fallen men and arranged them in natural positions. Covered with the blood of his comrades, he waited for the new general of Gui's killing corps to descend from his perch in a tree.

"Our new king, Jing requires your return to the capital," he announced rudely, without a kowtow.

"Of course he does," the wizard answered. "Tea?"

"Not from your hand."

"I see. Tell me, how did you find us?"

"You and your band of traitors are clumsy in the bush. We would have been here sooner had the queen mother not led us to believe you had headed north."

"The men you call traitors were more loyal to the dynasty than you can ever hope to be."

"Why, because they followed you? You're the biggest traitor of all. After you're ripped to pieces, I will personally feed your skull to rats."

Please tell me this isn't happening. After all I have lost, I can't stand to lose you, too.

"You won't be feeding anything to anybody," Long Ears said sadly.

"You're deluded."

"No."

"Where's the library?

"What library?"

"Answer my question."

"I don't know what you're talking about."

The general laughed, but it was a hollow laugh and there was a tiny note of worry at its base. "In case you haven't noticed, the battle's over."

Long Ears shook his head. "Actually, it's about to start."

What are you talking about? You know what? I don't care. Save Wang Yi. Bring him up now before he dies from the gas.

59

The doctor selects a chopstick-sized needle from a stainless-steel sterilizing oven on a table in the corner.

"What are you going to do with *that*?" I ask nervously.

"I'm going to make a stab at something."

"Very funny. You're not seriously going to stick that thing into him are you?"

"It's important we revive him. Prolonged unconsciousness has serious consequences."

I bite my lip. "Where are you going to put it?"

He points at the bottom of his foot. "*Yong quan*," he says. "First point in the kidney meridian. It can be helpful in seizures."

"He didn't have a seizure. He hit his head."

He avoids my gaze. "Sometimes one follows the other."

He can't insert this monster with the same flick he used with the small needles. Rather, the process appears as excruciating for him as it must be for the somnolent Athens. He stares at the spot, touches it with his finger, weighs the needle in his hand, mentally calculates it against the top-to-bottom thickness of Athens' foot, and then in an act that strikes me as more about blind faith than skill, rams it home.

The effect is immediate. Athens rolls off the table. On the floor, his trousers slip, exposing his tail. The old monk has been perusing his photos of my tattoo but the commotion commands him and he turns and sees the pink protrusion. His preoccupation with my tattoo vanishes and he drops his phone. His mouth falls open and he looks at me as if I've been keeping some vital bit of health information from him.

"You knew about this?"

Athens comes up on all fours like a tortoise, shakes his head, wipes his face, plucks the needle from his foot, and stands up. When he does, his pants slip down further. I fix them for him, tucking in his tail and cinching the drawstrings on his pants.

"This is the reason I keep away from medical men," he says, touching his head.

"Welcome back," says the doctor.

"We're at Shaolin," I say. "You've been unconscious and this monk has been treating you."

Athens leans against the table and raises his pierced foot. He rubs it ruefully.

"Needles," he says.

"They worked," I tell him.

"What's the last thing you remember?" asks the doctor, keeping his suspicious eyes on me.

"Falling," he says.

"Perhaps shoved?" asks the doctor.

"They think I pushed you," I say.

"What? No. We parachuted in."

"You hit a rock," I say.

He rubs his foot, then his forehead.

"How did I get here?

"She carried you," said the doctor. "Tell me, why would you parachute into Shaolin?"

The older monk's phone is lying on the shelf and Athens catches a glimpse of the photo of my back on the screen. Nothing if not quick of mind, he leans in conspiratorially.

"We're members of an ancient Taoist sect," he whispers. "Very secret."

"Why secret?" the old monk whispers back. I find this funny. There's no one around but us. Whispers, I seem to remember, beget more whispers.

"Powerful knowledge. Mystical ways. People who want it are after us."

"What did you do?" asked the doctor.

"And who's chasing you?" the old monk chimed in. "The tattoo artist?"

"Lao Tzu did the tattoo himself," I tell him. "He carved it into my shell back when I was a tortoise."

The silence in the little treatment room is suddenly so loud I can hear the rush of blood in my ears. Finally, the doctor beckons to Athens. "She is a mental health patient, yes?"

Athens shakes his head. "She may not look it, but in all the important ways she's more Chinese than you are."

"I didn't ask you about her genetics."

"It's complicated, but she's anything but crazy. She sees the world in a way the rest of us can't possibly understand. Extraordinary. Penetrating. Experienced in ways impossible to explain. I can tell you she means no harm to any living soul."

"I see. Tell me, are you experiencing any headache?"

"None," says Athens.

"Dizziness?"

"Not that either."

"We have to go," I say. "We're on an important mission."

"We should eat something," adds Athens. "If it's not too much trouble."

"You need to rest," the doctor says. "At least for a day. Complications from head injury are common."

I can see Athens weighing his recovery against the prospect

of pursuit.

"We can offer *rice gruel* and tea," says the older monk.

My heart sings at that last word.

Athens spreads his hands. "I know you don't believe us, but people really are after us. They'll be coming soon. They may already be here. I need to know you won't give us up."

"Police?"

"No."

"Tea sounds good," I interject. "Do you perhaps have any dumplings?"

The older monk, who has gone back to looking at the pictures on his phone, laughs out loud at this.

"If you make us dumplings," I say, my hand poised over my buttons, "I will take off my top again."

"Considering you've only been a woman for a few days, you're sure mastering the finer points quickly," Athens mutters.

"You have no idea," I say.

60

In their years on the lam, Ma Long's vagabond deserters had lost none of their military conditioning or skills. Having found a home in the forest, they were able to traverse it as stealthily — regardless of sun, moon or season — as a spider with eyes for a fly. Delayed by the storm, they arrived too late to stop the massacre of Long Ears' men but not too late to see the wizard raise his hands when the young king's men came to take him, nor to see the air before the wizard vibrate and the general and soldiers crumple to the ground screaming, steam coming off them like freshly baked buns.

Stunned, Ma Long's forces paused at the edge of the clearing. Yin, however, was not surprised at all.

Five Thunder Palm at last. Such a force of nature. Woe that it could not save more of us.

"Yes. Regrettably, it takes time to for the energy to intensify and the purple cloud to gather. It was never intended for sudden combat."

The purple cloud rises again. Don't you worry that will mark our position?

"There's nothing for it. It is both the source and expression of my energy."

All this blood....

"We live in a wonderful cocoon, you and I, dear Yin. Rivers

of blood run the world over. The world of men is a red-stained canvas of struggles and scrapes, even though it need not be so."

They started this fight, not you.

"Win or lose, going to war means we have lost touch with the Tao," Long Ears said sadly.

The library is safe. Nobody but you and I know it lies beneath us. You can bring up Wang Yi.

"To do so means to uncover the carefully disguised opening and reveal the cave to Ma Long's men."

But they're our friends.

"They are also poor, hunted bandits trying to stay alive in a harsh world. To tempt such men with great treasure is not only unwise but cruel."

But he's been down there for hours. He'll die of the gas!

"He won't reveal himself. He knows that to do so would be to risk the library."

Did you not hear me say he will die of the gas?

"Did you not hear me say that he must not reveal the cave?"

How much longer does he have?

"He may already be gone."

What? No! Dig him out right now.

"I'm sorry."

You won't? You would sacrifice him to save the library! A living person? Your apprentice? The person most loyal to you in this world? I wouldn't be here if it weren't for him. I wouldn't even be alive!

Long Ears looked infinitely sad. "Larger forces than our personal cares are at work here, Yin, larger even than our lives. We are subject to the ebb and flow of history, of knowledge, of energy, and now, here, right now, the preservation of a great secret."

You drone on about ideas while our friend dies. Forget your philosophy and your scrolls and bones! Tell him to come out!

"My entire life has led to this moment. Saving the library has been my purpose. I must not reveal the cave."

It's not all about you.

He sat down beside her and touched her head. For the first time in her life, she recoiled from him. "I never said it was. It's all about the future."

If you won't save him, I'll dig him out myself.

She tried to move but once again the wizard raised his hands, turning the ground below her into a liquid in such a way that a terrestrial undertow took her.

Let me go!

"When the Tao seems cruel, it is because we don't understand it."

Yin let loose the chelonian version of a scream—a protracted hiss that sounded like a volcanic geyser. Forest animals scattered, and the bandits dropped to their knees in fear. Ma Long approached. "What ails her, lord?"

"Terrible sorrow at all she has to leave behind."

"A feeling with which we are all familiar," Ma Long sighed as, above them, the purple cloud floated away to the west. "Come. We must make it to the observatory at Hangu Pass before nightfall. We'll take shelter and find rations there."

Yin kicked and snapped, but on Long Ears' orders Ma Long's men trussed and subdued her and set off toward the state of Qin.

Wang Yi....

61

Framed by mountain vistas and creative landscaping, energetically alive, engaging, and architecturally beautiful, the Shaolin temple strikes even my jaded eyes as a place of wonder. I consider it quite young, as it was erected for the first time in the fifth century, but as we walk the grounds, the old monk, who turns out to be a senior teacher, explains that due to the shifting allegiances between the impressively athletic warrior monks and the emperors of successive dynasties, the temple has been repeatedly razed and rebuilt through the years.

"This dance between people of power never changes," I tell Athens.

He nods distractedly, scanning the skies for signs of Chen's forces. "The dance, no; the music, yes. It's a question of matching cadence and tempo to the ever-quickening pace of life. The overall goal of insulating the rich and powerful from the rest of the world by keeping the common man in the dark remains the same."

"At some point, the vibration required to keep up with technology will transform human beings into something else, just as I was transformed."

I question the old monk about his interest in Taoism. He tells me that the first abbot of Shaolin came from India, traveling down and around the bottom of the Himalayas to Guangzhou,

YUN ROU

then up to the monastery. Finding the Taoist monks there weak of body and narrow of mind, he bolstered and educated them with his brand of Buddhism and yoga exercises. I practice rolling my eyes, which makes Athens smile.

"No true followers of my wizard could be weak either of mind or body," I tell the monk.

"Your wizard?" says the old monk.

"Lao Tzu is everybody's, of course, but mine most of all. And, frankly, I would like to see more emphasis on his teachings here. There is so much talk of the Buddha. Strange, given how much he focuses on the downside of life."

"Suffering is unavoidable," says the monk, "unless you follow the Buddha's path."

"That's true of pain," I say. "Suffering is optional."

"Stop bickering," says Athens. "Lao Tzu's work provided a foundation for what you folks do here at Shaolin. Let's leave it at that."

The monk suddenly beams. "That's right. Our perfect Chinese Zen is the offspring of two imperfect parents."

That's about enough for me. "I was there," I say. "Lao Tzu's teachings recognized social responsibility but focused on unfettered joy and freedom. There was nothing imperfect about it. Sounds to me like your traveling Buddhist brainwashed some happy Taoists and now you folks lack passion."

Saying this, I squeeze Athens' hand and he squeezes mine back.

True to my word, in the forest of steles, in a corner and under a pine tree, I take down my uniform again and allow a group of monks to examine my back in detail. They are not only interested in the ways in which my wizard's original characters differ from later versions of his text, but in the way the messages are arranged. They feel that the sequence of characters within the overall work changes the feeling, and they have a lively debate on the subject. As they do, Athens shifts back and forth on his feet, obviously uncomfortable at having me so avidly inspected.

"I remember the conversation that led to the carving," I say.

"You mentioned carving before," says the old monk. "What do you mean?"

"The tattoo," says Athens. "She's from South America. Her Chinese has its holes."

There's so very much to share about Long Ears' intention, but time for such discourse is short, and anyway, not having unearthed me themselves, the monks would doubt my authority. To them, I am merely a walking interpretation of something they have seen before: a piece that fits into the larger puzzle they take as a guidebook for life.

Having repaid them for both shelter and sustenance, I tell Athens we have to move on. I have a memory of a skyline resembling a fork, tine tips pointed up. I will know it when I see it; finding it is another matter. What I remember as a single peak revealed from a forest path I now see as a complex of mountains. I wish I were back in the airship. It would have been so much easier to find it from there.

I take Athens by the elbow and lead him through the clouds of incense and past the tourists and their cameras and past the mess halls and the ticket lines and the shops with plastic monks wielding plastic swords and baseball caps and glass sculptures of the temple. The flags I noticed when I carried him in now appeared faded in the sunlight but even so their snapping in the breeze applauds us as we leave.

Fortified with water bottles, bananas, and dumplings in plastic wrap, we veer off the main road and through a break in the trees. As if by magic, the thrum of monk business drops away, the hiss of tires fades, the smell of roasting chicken and joss

YUN ROU

sticks evanesces, and we are in the forest with only the whisper
of the wind and the faint musk of mushrooms as welcome.

"The forest is so quiet," I say, walking beside him.

"You sound disappointed. Personally, I'm delighted not to
be hearing helicopters. The airship captain will talk eventually,
and if he doesn't someone on the crew will. They'll know
approximately where we are. They have satellites, they have
informants, every cell phone is a spy camera these days. They'll
be here soon."

"The ground feels different through these feet" I say, pointing
down at the thin-soled kung fu sneakers, white and decorated
with a blue and red chevron, given to me by the monks to protect
my toes and soles.

He stops and kisses me gently on the cheek.

"I will help you feel everything you have always wanted to
feel."

Perhaps it is because I am so deliriously happy that when I
see the peaks I am looking for through the gaps in the trees, I feel
a terrible sadness.

"Are you all right?" Athens asks me.

"I'm going to die," I reply.

Athens looks at me with alarm. "What?"

"I have so much to lose now, yet, someday, I'm going to die."

His eyes are a bit bloodshot and he carries his head at an odd
angle, the consequence, no doubt, of his encounter with the rock.

"We all die."

"For so long I longed to, and I just kept living and living and
living. Now I'm desperately afraid that time will speed up and I
will get old and die before I do the things I need to do. Already,
it seems to be passing faster."

"Living fast and dying well is what most people want these
days."

"Long Ears' motto was that anything worth doing was worth doing slowly. He was always careful and deliberate in his movements, yet ready to roar like a swollen river through a tight canyon when the need arose."

"We can go as slowly as you like," he says. "We're both changing quickly. I suppose that's movement enough."

"Fast or slow, I worry," I say.

He embraces me and strokes my hair. "I'm not going anywhere. I'm here with you. Everything will be fine."

"It won't be if they take you away from me. To save you I need to find a certain place. What if I can't?"

"You've already saved me," he says. "My life isn't about me anymore and that's the biggest thing anyone could ever do for me."

"I know where we are, but it's been a long time. Everything looks a bit off," I say, looking around. "The sky's the wrong color, the smells I know are gone, I'm looking at everything from a different height and angle. Even the sun won't help me."

Athens takes his computer from his pack and sits on a stump. "Maybe a satellite view of the area will help."

I snuggle up to him, resting my head on his shoulder.

"Aren't you curious about what I'm after?" I whisper.

"I spend my life cracking codes and solving puzzles," he says. "On this, I prefer just to trust you."

The word trust melts me.

Above and around us, here in this valley, a mechanical noise grows and something unnatural shakes the air.

The trees bow down.

"Our pursuers are here," he says.

62

Hangu Pass runs between two sets of mountains in a valley parallel to the Yellow River. An exposed plain wide enough to accommodate an army. It was a key military gateway to the Middle Kingdom for centuries. In the interest of stealth, Ma Long and his men guided the tortoise and the wizard along the edge of the northern boundary beneath the overarching shadow of the mountains, staying away from open ground. The bandit strove for a jaunty look—hair to his shoulders, a scraggly beard, tunic carelessly thrown over his shoulder, battle-torn shoes—yet he seemed grateful for the opportunity to rest.

"I know that purple cloud is evidence of your powers, lord," he said uncomfortably. "Yet the way it follows you in the sky gives away our location. Can you not disperse it?"

I paid little attention to the exchange. My mind was somewhere else.

Wang Yi might still live. There's a tiny chance.

"Once loosed, the cloud has a will of its own," the wizard answered Ma Long.

Stop pretending you don't hear what I say!

Yin could feel the grass seed straining to sprout against the late winter snow and hear the restless turns of hibernating raccoon dogs in their dens. The shifting wind chilled her first on the side of her shell and then on her front legs. The wizard sensed her discomfort and ordered that the group stop for tea.

"I didn't realize how mightily you had offended the king," he told the wizard as they waited for the pot to boil. "The pass is guarded by a military outpost, but I don't know what force might be stationed there. If they have received word to intercept you, I can't predict the outcome."

"No one is ahead of us," Long Ears said calmly. "Gui will still be waiting for the men he sent to bring me back."

"I expected to see your apprentice with you but didn't notice him among the slain."

"He went to his end with loyalty, acceptance, dignity, and grace."

So he's dead.

"Sorry to hear it," the rebel leader said quietly.

That's all you have to say about him?

The great sage paused. "Gather the men," he told Ma Long. "I would take the time to honor Wang Yi."

And so they stood, hands clasped, in a circle. Lao Tzu rang his bell and Yin tried desperately to reach out into the great unknown, with her mind, for even the tiniest trace of her dearest, dearest friend. Finding none, her tears pooled in the leaf litter at her feet, yet she found some small comfort in Lao Tzu's words of praise for Wang Yi, or, perhaps, in the soothing tones the wizard's voice produced. It would have pleased her to stay longer in that place of grace, and it might have pleased Lao Tzu too, but Ma Long was nervous.

"We must pitch camp," he said. "The sun will soon set and we are still five hours' walk from the outpost."

"We press on," the wizard answered, closing his ritual. "No camping now."

"Even if you lend us all wings, lord, there is still the lumbering turtle."

I don't lumber. I can tell you that I am, without a doubt, the most graceful of my kind.

Long Ears dug into his robe and produced a packet of herbs. "This will be the last of this," he said, "but it will speed our step and get us to the outpost tonight."

So saying, he sprinkled the herbs into the teapot. The steam that arose had so bitter a fragrance that it caused the men's eyes to water. They drank it dutifully, but most retched within minutes.

"No matter," the wizard reassured them. "Even with the stomach emptied, the effect will stand."

And so it was that a crew of men who had labored through tundra and taiga, driven only by a sense of loyalty and what is right moved quickly and without apparent fatigue, leading a grudge-carrying tortoise as if she were straw. They approached the outpost while night was just a hint in the sky and arrived there just before it took hold. They saw that the observatory tower was elegantly decorated with scrollwork around the lintels and the roof tiles were inscribed with ringed planets and comets and clusters of stars. Below that, a high wall surrounded the compound. Yin recognized the type of heavy black wood from which the gate had been crafted.

Someone went to a lot of trouble to bring this wood all the way from the coast.

"Beautiful door," Long Ears said as Ma Long's men formed a protective circle around him. He raised his hand to knock but Yin pushed her way through and struck the door with her shell. Her size and weight and force were such that the stout door quivered.

"You're still angry about Wang Yi."

Still? I always will be. Leaving him was a terrible thing.

She struck the door even harder in her frustration. Her breath came in sharp hisses through her nares. Bubbles formed at the edges of her beak. A voice came from the other side of the door.

"Just a moment please. My goodness. Such impatience. It's nearly dark. I was preparing the observatory."

A moment later, the door slowly swung open. Rather than troops armed with spears and arrows, a thin-featured, rheumy-eyed man greeted them, stooped, trembling, and leaning on a staff. He gazed at Long Ears, then up at the sky, then back to Long Ears, barely acknowledging the raft of ragtag rebels standing at the bush line training weapons upon him. He pointed a bony finger up at the still-coherent purple cloud now dancing with the stars.

"It is a rare cloud that can survive such a piercing moon."

"It was born of a certain combustion to the East," Long Ears said dryly.

"I saw no fire," the man said.

"We simply seek shelter for the night."

"What is the size of your regiment?" Ma Long interrupted.

"My regiment. Goodness. I'm just an old man here to chart the heavens with my lens."

"A lens you turn on the plains in daylight in search of invading forces," said Long Ears.

The man smiled, showing good teeth. "I am bound to do so, but there is more action above than below."

"True," said Long Ears. "I remember reading your reports."

The old man blinked. "My reports?"

"I was the oracle of the court."

"Lord!" hissed Ma Long, aghast at the sharing.

Instantly, the astronomer dropped to his knees. This action caused a puff of air to escape his robe, bringing the fragrance of cooking herbs and incense. He knocked his head on the hard earth, causing three dull thuds.

He feigns age. He's a young man.

Long Ears helped him up. "The ground is no place for a royal astronomer. Tell me, surely you're not alone here?"

The astronomer smiled ruefully. "I do not have so many men with me as you have, great lord. Just servants to help me with my work."

Don't trust him.

"My kind friends escort me west."

"The purple cloud told me you were coming."

"I knew it," Ma Long muttered.

The astronomer smiled in his direction. "Don't worry, friend. That cloud is prophesied to herald the arrival of a great master. I've been waiting to see it for half my life. I had the cooks prepare a banquet in celebration when I saw it. Now tell me, is this turtle the Great Fertilizer? She surely fits the description."

Even out here in the desert, I cannot escape that ridiculous name.

"Yes, she is that legendary creature, though she has not performed that function in some time. These days she prefers to simply be called Yin."

First you leave your most loyal friend to die alone in a cave, then I hear that horrible term, and now you refer to me as a creature. This is not how I had envisioned our release from servitude to the king. I had hoped change and freedom would somehow be different. Do you think we might soon be alone? Do you think my transformation might soon be complete?

The astronomer bent to inspect her more closely. "I see the night sky in her eyes," he said. "The crab cluster in this one and in the other, the cross of the southern land. Has she some connection to that distant, half-legendary part of the world?"

"You see well. Indeed she does."

Is it true she speaks the language of men?"

"She understands it."

"But she communicates with you?"

Tell him he can stop pretending to be crippled. He does it because he never knows who might be at the gate and it gives him an element of surprise. He's actually quite tall, and very capable with the stick he leans on.

Smiling, Long Ears conveyed the message as requested. The astronomer stood up straight, blushing so deeply the color change was obvious in the faint light. He was indeed a tall, well-built man, and the staff was alive and twitching in his hand; no crutch but a weapon at the ready.

"I learned the art of deception from the moon, he said, "the way she sneaks up behind clouds, sometimes hangs low and bright and then an hour later will be small and high and not where you expect her at all."

"Yin is named for that cool mistress," Long Ears replied. "She isn't what she appears to be either."

"She certainly sees things most men don't," the astronomer agreed, standing aside and gesturing for the group to enter the outpost.

"Maybe *she* is the great master you've been expecting," offered Ma Long. "Your prophecy doesn't mention whether the master walks on two legs or four, does it?"

63

Every moment of every day since I entered the ground has been suffused with the wish to have more than I do, to be someone other than who I am, and to find myself in a new and different place. This constant, propulsive yearning has kept me alive, and now I find it reaching a fevered pitch, both because I am close to realizing my dreams and because I sense I don't have much time left.

I am so close to fulfillment. I have survived kidnapping and assassination and the alteration of my innermost core. I have waited and waited to physically become a woman on the outside after achieving womanhood on the inside. Finally, I have been rewarded by complete transformation. I am now more liquid than solid, more sensitive than immune, long limbed, curly haired, smooth on my surfaces, vocal, beautifully scented, and moist. I am now capable of being with the man I love and able to use what I know to buy him freedom and forgiveness. I cannot, must not, fail.

The trouble is, I am completely lost. We have been walking along the base of a steep cliff, amongst trees. It is pouring rain, and a helicopter hovers above us. The sound of the engine is deafening and the wash of its rotors bends big branches just as easily as I have used my breath to blow down blades of grass. We find an outcropping and huddle beneath it because Athens believes the rock above us can mask the heat of our bodies from the chopper's cameras and infrared sensors.

"If I were still a tortoise, I would be invisible," I say. "Cold blood and all."

"I can't imagine your blood ever being cold."

"It's a misnomer. Basking in the sun, tortoises can't sweat, so they get hotter than humans, but on a day like this, in the shade, no heat-seeking chopper could ever have found me."

"I meant it as a compliment."

I kiss him lightly. He shifts and responds. I feel his hands behind me and beneath me. He lifts me up and towards him, pressing us together.

"Not now," I say. "And not here with men right above us."

In the grip of lust, his flesh burns. "If they catch us, this may be our last chance."

"They won't," I say, gently disengaging. "And it isn't."

"It's obvious from the fighter jets that Abbot Chen has upped the ante and made me a government target. No doubt he has them believing I'm plotting against some sensitive site. Manipulating them into finding me, he gets you as a bonus."

"At this point, I can't imagine what he wants with me."

"It's wonderful that you can't. Your innocence is so precious."

"Innocence? Really? After all I've lived and seen."

He wipes his face. "Guilelessness and naiveté then. The world these days is far darker, stranger, and crueler than you know. You will be a curiosity to collectors, a resource, and a great prize. He won't reveal your secret to our pursuers, though. He'll make up some story."

"What kind of story?"

He winces, then shrugs. "It could be anything. Beautiful young women…"

"Not young."

He flashes me one of those rare, conspiratorial smiles of his. "We'll try to keep that special truth a secret, yes? Just know that many beautiful women are commodities in Asia. At the low level there are rings of human traffickers, criminals who steal girls for the sex trade. In more cultured parlors there is the high social reward for walking into a cocktail party with a woman like you on a man's arm."

"On his arm? I don't understand."

"Arms are new to you. I understand. Just believe me when I tell you that your tattoo, the aura of magic about you, your exotic beauty, your unique blend of innocence and wisdom, they all make for an intoxicating combination. You're a prize, Yin, no matter what someone knows or believes about you."

"A prize," I repeat, thinking about the strange coincidence that has an abbot named Chen pursuing me just as two members of a family with almost the same name did so very long ago.

The helicopter descends. Athens furiously hammers his computer keys. "They're zeroing in," he hisses. "Be very quiet now. They must have listening devices."

We sit in silence for a time. I try not to move. This is incredibly difficult for me. Ever since changing, I've been seized by the need to make up for millennia of enforced stillness. My knee bobs up and down like a racecar piston, a tantalizing bit of engineering I came across surfing the Web. I love having knees. I love knowing what the inside of an automobile engine looks like. I love the Internet. For all the disaster I see humankind has wrought upon nature, I still find much to love in the world it has created, especially the wonderful glowing screens of knowledge and the magic of giant flying sharks and the taste of dumplings and the entrancing fragrances I smell in shops and in temples.

And, of course, most of all Athens Li.

As if by low-level magic not worthy of my wizard or his ilk, the end of a rope appears right near us in an open patch between trees. It dances and wriggles like a snake held by the tail.

"Commandos," says Athens.

"There seem to be three choices," I say. "We surrender, we run, or we fight."

Dripping wet, Athens looks utterly defeated. Because I have pulled away, he unconsciously hugs his backpack. "I don't like any of those options," he says.

"Another will present itself," I counter. "When things are moving, new opportunities develop. New choices. If conflict is one door and submission a second, we need a third."

He gestures with his chin at boots that appear on the rope, followed by gloved hands and a contraption that resembles a pulley. "I'm listening. So what, specifically, would you suggest we do?"

I make a decision and step out into the rain while Athens huddles behind some fronds. The man coming down the rope is dressed in the uniform of a policeman. He sees me and stops, dangling at low altitude. The air shakes. I gesture him down. When his feet touch ground, I approach him. He puts a hand on his gun.

"Athens Li is dead," I shout.

His eyes open wider.

"What?"

"Skydiving. Chute failed way back near the temple."

The policeman frowns. "Body?" he shouts back.

This tells me that the monks have not given up any details of our stay with them. I know that I have a chance now, so long as I can just keep the story believable.

"Buried," I shout back. "And please don't take me. I escaped from slavers and they want me back."

"Slavers?"

"Yes. An international ring," I say, only slightly reworking the terms Athens just used.

"I don't know anything about that," the policeman says.

"Unless you're part of it, you'll let me go."

He frowns again. He's so young there is nary a line on his face. "I'm not part of anything," he yells, "but I've got orders."

"I'll end up back with the men paying your bosses," I say. "Following orders won't clean your conscience. I've seen enough to know that. Just ask yourself if chasing girls for rich guys is why you became a policeman."

I can feel Athens' amazed expression right through the underbrush, but I don't dare even dart a glance in his direction. The policeman goes a bit pale. He shakes his head.

"There's something about you," he says.

"Tell them there was only an old hermit down here. I'm no criminal. Nothing bad will happen. Li's dead. There's no threat to national security. Go find his body where we jumped out of the airship. They have the coordinates. Be a hero. Sleep well at night knowing you didn't do something you knew was wrong."

The policeman hesitates.

"Did they accuse me of some crime?"

He shakes his head.

"Because I didn't commit any. You're just sparing an innocent woman a terrible life. Now go."

He bites his lip so hard it bleeds, then presses a button on a control in his hand. A moment later, pulley system begins to lift him up. He watches me all the way up. I worry that he's going to change his mind, but he doesn't.

"I'd never have pegged you for an actress," says Athens as the chopper retreats. "I wouldn't even have thought you capable of lying."

"I told the truth."

"Not about me being dead."

"No? Can you honestly tell me that the Athens you were before you unearthed me isn't dead and gone?"

He takes my hands in his, interlaces his fingers, and closes his eyes. It seems an eternity until he answers.

"No," he says at last. "I can't."

64

Long Ears repeatedly told Yin that following the Tao required an unfettered mind open to constant change. So over the years, despite her nagging homesickness and her ever-deepening love for the man she could never have, Yin grew quite good at detachment. She followed Long Ears from place to place the way one ocean wave follows another, sleeping alone in countless courtyards, enduring bitter cold, and learning not to prize comfort for fear of disappointment and suffering.

Despite all that, she found herself happier and more secure in the remote mountain observatory on the edge of the state of Qin than she had been since she left her island. This might have been because she did not have to share her wizard with Bao Yu, it might have been that the great sage's calm and joy were all the more obvious in such a peaceful place, and it might have been the observatory's marvelous *feng shui*, which was quite apparent to her.

Wang Yi would have noticed the way the earth energies come together here. He would have noticed the wonderful smell of the surrounding pines and the views of the snow peaks and the way the wind carries forest seeds.

"I do find satisfying qi here," Long Ears agreed, standing outside on the observatory's circular stone balcony, stretching his long white arms to the late afternoon sky, relaxing his torso, dropping his tailbone so that his strange appendage pointed downward, and closing his eyes.

That's because you spend all day standing in meditation.

"Making up for lost time," the wizard smiled.

Inside, the young astronomer sat hunched over his viewing lens. Suddenly he straightened. "Soldiers are coming!"

Yin put her front legs up on the balcony wall and stood up on her rear legs until she had a clear view of the pass.

You should have known the king would send them eventually. Why did you send Ma Long away so soon? Now we have nobody to protect us.

"How many?" asked the wizard.

"Five," the astronomer replied. "I recognize their ministerial banners. Their masters disdain astronomy and have their own agendas. They can't be trusted. These men they have sent men will be enforcers or maybe even assassins. They'll say they want to talk and then pull weapons or perhaps poison your tea."

The sun was setting when the soldiers arrived at the outpost gate. They looked up at the tower balcony, where the wind had Long Ears' beard, and each man in turn cried his greeting.

"I bring the great wizard best wishes from the Chancellor of State."

"The Minister of Rites sends the same."

"I carry respects from the Minister of War."

"The Minister of Justice sent me."

"The Minister of Works bids you a good evening."

Pomposity redolent of violence. Perhaps if we wait long enough, they will just go away.

"Open the gate," Long Ears instructed.

The astronomer paled. "But we are safe behind the walls."

"If they were here for battle, they would have a larger force."

"Subterfuge and deception are the highest martial arts.

Perhaps such a force waits at the other edge of the pass or buried, to a one, underground, their mouths dry, their swords dusty."

"Perhaps so, but open it anyway."

Strongly built and tall, the warriors bore the dust of the road and the stench of horses, which the outpost staff took to stable. Talk was light until the men had washed and eaten dinner in the main hall. A light rain began to fall as the royal astronomer lit torches. Yin huddled by the cooking pot as the downpour grew heavier. At last, when the meal was done and the men had unbuttoned their tunics to allow their bellies to swell, Lao Tzu addressed them.

"So. Have you come to take me back to Luoyang?"

The War man was the first to reply. "No, great lord. We have heard that you don't respond well to force."

"So what, then?"

"We are here on behalf of our masters," State's man said.

Long Ears frowned. "Not on behalf of King Jiing?"

I'll never call him that. He's Prince Gui, and that's that.

The man from Works spoke up. "So far from the capital and under the umbrella of your grace and kindness, I wonder if I might speak frankly."

"Please."

This is where he tells you Gui doesn't know what he's doing.

"The king is young and proud," the man from Works continued. "The minister understands the wisdom of protecting the library. The five of us are here to ask a boon of you before you continue your travels beyond the sway of the king."

"A boon?"

"We would like to know where you have hidden the scrolls so that we may retrieve them when the time is right."

"I see."

"And that's not all," Rite's representative interjected. "Bereft of your wisdom, the ministers find the court lacking direction."

"So this is about rituals?"

"If you could, perhaps you might offer some advice as to how the court might proceed," said the man from Justice.

Gui sends soldiers to kill you and now thugs to ask your advice?

"Many people would turn to the very library you have stolen to help them find their way," said the man from Rites. "Now they have no resource. The king is beginning to understand some things that he did not fully grasp before."

I'll bet he is, but not from a scroll or bone, busy as he is always hacking things to bits.

"Perhaps you could pen a distillation," said the man from Works. "You know, a short version without the mumbo jumbo, all we need to know, but nothing more."

"Not a small project," the wizard said dryly.

The man from War stood up. "The king knows you have no fear of pain and no concern for your own well-being, so he wants you to know that everyone you ever cared about back in the capital will suffer an agonizing death if you refuse. Every servant, every concubine, every merchant who ever sold you a plate of noodles or repaired a leak in your roof."

"Torn apart by horses," Work's man added.

"Burned alive in a bonfire," said the representative of Justice.

"Lowered into boiling oil," said the man from State.

"A death of a thousand cuts," said the man from Rites.

"And of course, we will slaughter and eat the turtle," War's man said, as if adding a final flourish to a beautiful performance.

The royal astronomer rose from the table and paced back and forth nervously, a torch flickering in his hand. "There's no need for threats," he said. "I'm sure Long Ears appreciates the young king's growing wisdom and would be happy to jot down some key ideas to help move the dynasty in the right direction."

He looks like he's going to soil his robe.

Long Ear's expression was grim. "I've spent 88 years appeasing rulers and standing in balance with the court," he said. "That time has passed. I have resigned my post."

It's funny how things have shifted since we left the capital. I used to be the one who said no and you used to be the one who said yes. Now it's the reverse. I think you should do this, and I don't say so to save my own skin. I've lived long enough already and the one thing I've always wanted I now know I will never have. I just think this really is a small price to pay for your peaceful exit. You did, after all, abscond with the court library, and even if that was absolutely necessary for the future of the people of the Middle Kingdom, it doesn't benefit Gui much. Enemies surround him inside the city walls and out, his father's gone, his brother's gone, and his mother helped us leave. No matter what you think of him, giving him a little book of instructions might not be such a bad idea.

Even the warriors could see that the tortoise's hisses and grunts were having an effect on the famous wizard. He took a long draught from his teacup, set it down, and cleared his throat.

"I'll do it," he said.

65

We're halfway up a peak. I soak in the silence left in the wake of the departing helicopter. I cannot abide silence. I loathe it. I've had enough of it to last three hundred lifetimes. The entire Song Mountain complex has come to daunt me. It's a maze from which there seems no escape, a last unexpected obstacle to locating my destination. The wind hits me in the face. I breathe it in and expand my chest and tilt back my neck in a way I never could before.

"Anything?" asks Athens.

He still doesn't know what lies beneath. He doesn't know what lies ahead, either.

"There are so many angles," I say, thinking of the peaks and valleys and thinking, too, of how things might change between us when it is I who is doing the saving.

He sits beside me and takes out his computer. "No cell service and no network, but I downloaded the satellite maps so you can zoom in virtually and look at the whole range. Maybe that will help."

Despite his wound, he looks so young, his expression so optimistic, his eyes so bright, his chin jutting out at the world in a way that says go ahead and put it right here, I can take it. The wind tousles his hair. A small trickle of blood oozes out of the bandage on the side of his head and takes a slow, looping ride down his neck. I wipe it away gently

"I'm fine," he says. "That's just seepage."

The maps on his screen are brown and green and even show trees and rocks, but despite their resolution and detail, I see no giant stone acupuncture needles as I roll my finger over the track pad.

"Anything?"

"No."

"You're sure? Look closer."

He tilts the angle of view and I fly over the landscape like an eagle, plummeting down, imagining the joy and the lift and the impact if I don't lift up in time. I start at the edge of the range, circle it, and then move in.

"I'm still amazed by what you call technology," I say.

"You had it back in the sage's time, too. It was just different."

"It certainly was."

I repeat my circle, reducing the circumference of my flight until I am at a still point, a tiny blinking dot on the screen.

"Nothing even a little familiar?"

"No."

He looks chagrined. Even though he doesn't specifically know what he's missing, he knows that we can't move on with our lives and find our destiny until I have what I need. Maybe that's why he suddenly puts his arms around me and lifts me up and carries me to the very edge of the mountain. There is a sheer drop to the abyss below. He dangles me, but I feel no fear.

"I'm reminding you," he says.

"Of death?"

"Of the impermanence of everything. We have to seize every moment."

He turns me around and kisses me. This time I yield. The current is back, and it melds us into one. His hot fingers find their way under my blouse and up and around my breasts to my nipples. I understand these dark parts better now. The muscles in my back weaken and my knees buckle, but it doesn't matter because I'm on *terra firma* again, and a moment later, we are horizontal.

The kiss is the thing. It is as if he is a dragon breathing fire into me. The blaze begins in my teeth and my tongue and goes down my throat and keeps going down. I perspire. I feel his weight on me. I want only to erase every possible space between us. He reaches down to lower his pants and I grab his wrist and stop him.

"Why?" he asks half in a whisper half in a groan.

"The stars don't quite line up," I answer, groaning only a little bit less.

He sits up. "You're kidding, right?"

I blow a wisp of hair out of my face. I love to do that. I straighten my clothes and clamber to my feet, holding onto him through every degree of movement, all the way to vertical.

"Long ago, I learned the importance of having celestial forces behind me," I say. "You light a blaze in me. If it burns now, I'll be consumed. There's something I have to do first."

"Surrender," he answers, still holding me. "Please. We can continue the quest afterward."

I don't know how to explain to him that I'm not sure he's right. I'm not sure myself if my instinct is right, if my intuition is reliable enough to achieve my goal. Cogitating on that question, another kind of answer comes to me.

"It's staring me right in the face," I say.

"What is?"

I point to a beautiful tree not fifty feet away.

"That maple? I don't understand."

"Everything appears right on schedule," I say. "Even you."

He blinks. "Usually, I think I'm a pretty smart guy, but I have absolutely no idea what you're talking about."

I smile at him in the tolerant way Long Ears used to smile at Wang Yi.

"Just be patient," I say.

I go and stand beneath the tree. Remembering the way of Long Ears, I close my eyes and imagine roots growing out of my feet, diving deeper and deeper through the soil and the granite all the way to the bottom of the range and then down lower than that, aimed at the liquid, bubbling, molten center of the earth. I allow the top of my head, in a fashion I never thought I could manage, to connect me to heaven as if by a string. Images and memories pour in, taking me on a wild ride from that first time at sea all the way up the Yellow River to my wizard, then past that to the forest and to the cave and to the outpost and to the State of Qin. I stand and I breathe and I relax my body and I wait for the circle of energy to start flowing up my back and down my front in just the way I know it did for my great love all those years ago.

Eventually, my hands tingle and my thoughts slow down, and as they do, something wondrous begins to happen. The uneasy mental silence arising from my disconnection with the rest of the living world begins to ease. My eardrums tingle and my brain buzzes. Energy—Long Ears would call it qi—radiates from me in waves. Prince Shen comes to mind. My flesh begins to emit a low hum. Vibrating, I am a human tuning fork, an oversize, bipedal version of Long Ears' favorite bell. I ring and I ring as the change takes place within me. I am the missing piece of the jigsaw puzzle of the world, finally set right through completion.

When I open my eyes, Athens is staring not at me, as I expected, but at the tree above me. It is full of crows. Where normally their chattering would be deafening, their beaks are closed and their wings are tight and their feet grip branches and they stare at me in the way crows do, cocking their heads, taking me in with one eye. Despite their silence, I hear them loudly and clearly in my head. I know what they want, which is that I follow them, and I know what they promise.

"Is this somehow about birds?" asks Athens.

"Guides, not birds. All we have to do is follow. They're going to take us where we need to go."

66

You're procrastinating.

"Certainly not. I'm simply making tea."

Your very favorite procrastination method.

"These court people who chased us all the way to this observatory, they won't understand what I write."

How many times have you told me that the only person you can control is yourself? It doesn't matter what they understand. Treat this like one of the thousands of speeches you've made conducting rituals. They'll leave when they have it, and we can too. Already the weather shows signs of warming. Soon trees will sprout green, and I'll be able to walk without freezing. We can head west, find a forest as beautiful as a dream, and stay there forever.

"You don't want to go back to your island anymore?"

I want to be with you.

Long Ears smiled gently. "You can always go back after I've gone to the ancestors."

All this hand wringing and arguing isn't like you at all. It makes me wonder if you're getting sick. Just write the scroll. I'll help you put down some ideas.

"You are a great solace to me, Yin, but your claws are ill-suited for penmanship."

I mean I'll help you organize your thoughts. My first suggestion is to forget rituals and forget divination. Just stick to the big ideas. The details don't matter and if you include them, we'll be stuck here until autumn.

Long Ears sighed and went to the window. They were at the top of the observation tower and the early light was just turning the sky from black to blue. "If only we were birds," he said.

Even if you flew away, Gui would keep sending men after you.

"Writing things is not the same as doing them, reading them is not the same as understanding them."

Think of it as a challenge. Carve it into my shell and sign. That way everyone will know I am forever yours.

Freed from the constraints of court, the great wizard had slowly been relinquishing the tight control under which he had always held his emotions. Yin's words brought him to tears, and he knelt and kissed the top of her head. It was the first time she had felt his lips. They were soft, and they thrilled her.

"Carving your shell would defile you."

Ding Lok defiled me when he butchered my family and sliced off my leg. Even my dear Wang Yi defiled me, oh so many years ago, with the burning poke of prophecy. Your view of the world carved in my hard parts is not defilement but celebration of the great love we share. We do share a great love, don't we?

Long Ears nodded.

Say it.

"We share a great love, but...."

Say it without the "but".

"*And* if what they want is carved into your shell, they will take you back to the capital."

The royal astronomer has a beautiful hand. He can copy whatever you write onto a bronze tablet the soldiers can carry to the king. Royal scribes will copy it again, so it can't be lost. People will ponder your words a thousand years from now when we're dust and gone. Perhaps write it as a poem, or even a song.

YUN ROU

"The clouds are still and the plain is quiet," the wizard said as the sun grew stronger. "I fear a late season storm is coming."

Forget the weather. Get to work. What will you use for carving?

He reached into his robe. "General Sun gave me this asteroid dagger, pounded and folded into layers for strength. I'm sure he never imagined I would use it on you."

Just get started. I keep growing, very slowly, as long as I live, so carve until you see white bone, then pour in the ink.

The wizard furrowed his brow. "It's fine to just write ideas, but there has to be a cohering theme."

The cohering theme behind everything you say and do is living according to the Tao. Start by carving the message that even though that Tao of yours is everywhere; if you try too hard to see it, you'll miss it.

The wizard smiled and set to work. He matched the curves of his script with the curves of her shell. "It suits you," he said. "Are you sure it doesn't hurt?"

I'm sure. Now write that the superior turtle understands that the world is comprised of opposites.

Long Ears laughed but obliged.

Now something for Gui. Write that the superior king keeps his people well fed and encourages them not to think too much.

"All these years you argued with me you were actually listening."

Now this. The Tao gets dirty but still remains pure. It has existed long before the first god or king and will exist long after all are gone. It's like a thin, tasteless broth in which all foods float. It creates the world merely by breathing and never gets tired.

Long Ears blew the bits of tortoise shell off the tip of the iron dagger and got ready for the next stanza. "Perhaps something about water?"

The Tao and the superior turtle both act like water, effortlessly

291

flowing, never getting stuck, nurturing all that thirsts for it, filling what's empty.

"I like this very much."

You always warned Bao Yu about extremes. Write that if you sharpen your knife too much, the edge will break; if you overfill your cup, you will spill your tea.

"I worry about her and the baby."

Sun Tzu will protect them. Now write that we should all be babies, soft and flexible. Also write that emptiness is useful like the space between the spokes of a wheel and between the edges of a window and inside a teapot.

"Good points," the wizard agreed, continuing to carve.

Write that simplicity is best in everything from colors to music.

"Keep going. I'm beginning to believe doing this might satisfy actually satisfy the ministers."

Self-involvement is the cause of great unhappiness.

"Certainly."

The turtles who first discovered the Tao must have been delicate in their touch as if reaching for a flower, and as sensitive in their step as if heading out onto ice. We should go back to those times and be careful. Deliberate. Gentle. Quiet. Soft. The best king is invisible. He satisfies the people yet they don't even know who exactly he is. A less good king has a great reputation. A bad one inspires fear, and the worst is a tyrant.

"And if we ignore the Tao?"

Instead of naturally responding with kindness, compassion, and useful acts, we get caught up in clever labels and shrewd politics, and pretty soon we're judging each other.

"My wrist is tired. Are you ready for some tea?"

Not yet. Carve this: the superior turtle avoids entanglements, keeps her cool, doesn't fill her head with trivia, and meets conflict with emptiness. Drifting outside, she appears to have nothing when in fact she has everything that matters.

"Speaking of what matters, let's eat breakfast. I have a feeling it's going to be a long day."

67

The mountain complex has clefts and rifts and forests and watercourses. We follow the birds, sometimes losing them to the trees and picking them up again in the clearings. Athens worries about surveillance now and is constantly having us duck into streams so as to lower our body temperature and make us less visible to infrared tracking.

"Drones can be any size," he says. "They can even look like birds."

"Don't you think the face-off with the policeman ended this ridiculous chase?"

"You slowed things down, for sure, but unless something else changes, Chen will keep after us. He's lost face now. He's not the kind to let that rest."

"I've met his kind before. Do you think he'll come after us himself?"

"He'd be afraid to dirty his hands. The best way will be to go back to him with something to offer."

"You mean to buy him off."

"Probably."

We still have a bit of food left from Shaolin, but it's tough terrain and my new, ancient body hurts in places I didn't have before. We stop for a snack, and while I eat a banana Athens rubs my feet. As a tortoise, that hard, scaly part of my body was almost immune to sensation. I have a dim memory of my mother's worn claws and the scales on the bottom of her feet smoking from contact with hot volcanic rock, but I can't recall that the burns bothered her. Human feet, however, are a different matter entirely. I may never get used to the constant pressure of shoes, but I could certainly get used to the feeling of Athens kneading my toes and pressing his thumbs into my arches.

"Good?" he asks, bent intently to the task.

"Better than that."

I drift, thinking of my island. I remember the bright red crabs scuttling by, eyeing my tiny young body, and being repelled by the mere presence of my mother's giant limbs. I remember sinking into the hot black sand at the edge of the beach. I remember watching my father rise up high on his front limbs and stretch his neck, mouth gaping, to snatch just one bite of an Opuntia flower. I remember the battle cries of the land iguanas arguing over a hillock or knob. I remember the shifting smell of the trade winds that brought seeds from the mainland and with them, every so often, foreign fruit on flotsam.

Athens senses my reverie. "You must have ten thousand memories," he says.

I don't have the heart to tell him why they are all flooding back to me so insistently just now.

"More than that," I answer.

He pinches the skin on my ankle and points out how it stays pinched a few minutes before flattening. "You're dehydrated."

"Give me a drink."

He hands over a bottle he's filled from the stream and then we set off again. This time the path trends downward and I find the going easier. As we walk, he lays his hand gently on my shoulder. His touch gives me contentment and peace. I consciously try to moderate my stride. If I step with too much ambition, my hips hurt. If I slow my pace too much, I lose momentum and my toes ache from the strain of holding me up on only two legs. We constantly watch the crows. They toy with us, entertaining me by reading my mind and cooperatively recreating shapes they find there: a gun. A teapot. A flute. When they shift or turn, so do I. Yet despite the games, I know they are guiding me.

At one point they scatter as something flies right through them. Athens is looking up when it happens, and he immediately drives me to the shelter of an elm, standing me up against it and forcing me to stay vertical, pressed against the bark, on the side away from its path.

"That was a drone," he hisses. "I told you they wouldn't give up."

"I think it was a vulture."

"Those don't fly alone."

"A hawk, then."

"The wings didn't flap."

"Maybe it was riding a current?"

He shook his head. I wonder if he's getting paranoid, wonder how many drones he's actually seen, wonder if this might be an example of his visiting conspiracy websites just a little too often.

"Do you think it saw us?" I ask cautiously.

"I can't know."

I'm sure that drones can see equally well day or night but, even so, he insists we huddle under the tree until darkness falls. This takes some hours. I haven't seen him so anxious before.

"We're almost there," I say.

He nods.

I try to think of something else to say but sense in him a growing awareness of what's going on. He hugs me gently and strokes my hair.

As the last traces of sunlight thin to shadows, fireflies give us a show, and nearby, under some log, the conductor of a frog chorus drops his baton to set his first violin croaking.

"You're taking me to some kind of treasure, isn't that right?"

"Of course."

"Tell me about it. I can't imagine a treasure greater than you."

"It will solve all your problems," I say.

He appears to consider this for a moment. "Will I be able to carry it?"

I notice he does not say we.

68

The observatory cook prepared a morning meal of *jook* and slices of cold pork meat garnished with winter onion. The sky turned white and flurries danced a rhumba. Long Ears continued to find his gaze irresistibly drawn to the west while Yin pointed her snout eastward, imagining the warm sea and the cold one beyond.

Long Ears lit the wood stove. "The center of the storm is close now."

Imagine how quiet the cave is now under another layer of snow. Imagine Wang Yi's bones.

The sage picked up his knife. "Let's get back to work," he said.

I'm having trouble concentrating now.

"You didn't like the porridge?"

She edged closer to the stove. *When it's cold like this, I crave mouse meat.*

Long Ears leaned out the window and called for mice. A few minutes later, a quizzical stable hand brought up a smashed one. "From the rice bin," he said.

Yin sniffed it, then opened her jaws and swallowed it whole.

Yum. All right. Carve this: Notice the qualities of things and how they reveal underlying patterns. Recognize that there are forces at work bigger than you and your ambitions. Save others from their mistakes without insulting them. Fix broken things so you don't waste them. Tie things so they don't come loose. Don't leave tracks when you travel. Don't speak in a way that leads others to comment on what you've said.

Long Ears cocked his head to make sure his work looked good from a different angle. "You've learned a lot from me. I've used a third of your shell."

Yin folded her forelimbs under her chin like a child. *Write this: Be like an uncarved turtle shell that can be made into whatever is needed. Also, forget about swords. War means losing tranquility, simplicity, and life. If you live violently, you die violently. If you have to fight, grieve whether you lose or win. The turtle who bites others has a sharp beak but a disquieted mind. The same is true of the turtle who bites back. The turtle who is content with what she has is rich, and the turtle who dies but is not forgotten lives forever.*

"You'll never be forgotten."

On the contrary. I'm forgotten already.

Lao Tzu lifted the knife from her shell and bent down to face her.

"Are you happy with me, Yin?"

I only wish I could be with you more completely.

"I did the best I could to make that possible."

I know.

They went to the tower window together and looked out. The snow flurries had turned to flakes, and the ministers' men, in formation, drilled in the courtyard below, stabbing the air with lances and slicing bamboo staves with their swords.

"They're impatient," he said, taking up his dagger.

So carve this: Each phase of the Tao gives birth to the next, so to be strong, first be weak. To be flexible, be rigid at the start. To go up, first go down. To take, first give. Dim your light if you ever hope to shine brightly.

"Speaking of shining brightly, there will be a big moon

tonight. If the snow lets up by then, I believe I can carve by its light."

I'm thinking of the day we met. You were just standing under a tree, yet all around you the kingdom was spinning.

"Spinning apart, I'm afraid."

Carve this: The superior turtle appears to do little but gets everything done. When living creatures realize they are part of everything, all goes well. Returning is an important quality in the world. We start out as nothing, and we go back to nothing. Events and trends repeat themselves.

"I don't remember teaching you this."

Memory fails us sometimes. You have a lot on your mind. Here's some more: if you're cold, move; if you're hot, keep still. Real mastery looks homegrown, and the greatest skill appears unexpectedly clumsy. To be really perfect, things must contain imperfections; therefore, what is truly straight often appears crooked. Once you know the contentment that comes from not wanting, you won't want for anything. Oh yes, and don't clutter the mind with too much studying.

"I'm afraid I haven't followed that last one."

Never too late to change. Carve this: Assume the best of people even when they don't act well. Be a tranquil example to others thereby drawing them behind you like a boat's wake pulls reeds. Take care of your life, but don't become too attached to it.

"If Ding Lok were alive, I don't think he'd be able to hurt you anymore, Yin."

She nodded thoughtfully. *No. I don't believe he would.*

And with that she was asleep.

69

Every day that goes by as a human being, the more convinced I am that Long Ears was right about all the qualities of the world showing the Tao. Fixating on lofty ideas or grand goals only gets in the way. It is indeed the little things that make the magic. Take, for example, the marks Athens' feet make in the ground. There is something so adorable about the way his arch collapses inward to make a deep impression under his left foot and the way his right heel grinds outward to make a smudge in the dirt. I want to snap a mental photograph of those footprints and keep it inside me forever.

I also like the lines of his calves, the way they bulge outward as if he has pears under his skin, stem to the top. I have seen the legs of quite a few men in my short time walking upright and noticed that most of them are sinewy and thin—strong enough, perhaps, but not so pleasing to the eye as those of Athens Li. This heaviness of bone reminds me of my wizard, but there is something else there, for my wizard was more thick than shapely. Perhaps, once again, it is the way his mother's blood meets his father's to create a confluence of east and west that makes this new man of mine please me so.

"Tell me about Greece," I say.

"It's a country."

"I mean the history, the culture. What it smells like."

"I haven't been since I was a teenager."

"Was it there at the time of Long Ears?"

He appears shocked at the question. Sometimes when he gets that look, he stops and we sit down and he educates me on some facet of modern life. This time, he just keeps walking as he talks, and I keep looking at his legs.

"It's the birthplace of Western civilization," he says. "Especially Athens, the city I'm named after. So, at the time you were at the Zhou court, Greece was fighting off the Persians, who actually took over the city for a while but were ultimately thrown out. That's when the great fun began in Athens. There were philosophers there, too, who functioned as both oracles and teachers. Socrates, Plato, Aristotle. They weren't as intuitive as Lao Tzu, not so mystical and perhaps not quite as exquisitely in tune with nature, but they were keenly interested in logic and reason. During their time, Athens was the artistic, intellectual, and political center of the world."

"Maybe on that side of the globe. I'd never heard of the place until I met you."

"It's true that our meeting changed everything."

I've been staring at Athens' legs for so long that when Prince Shen's giant needles of melted stone appear before me I don't immediately recognize them. The forest has grown up around them and so they appear only half as tall as before. The passage of millennia has ravaged the matrix of the stone so that while the needles remain in formation, that formation is no longer symmetrical. Too, my eyes are higher and my perspective is different. I stop walking. Athens does not immediately notice, and so for a moment or two I am left alone in their shadow.

In that moment, I face the first and last physical connection to my long-lost love that I have encountered since I came out of the ground. Seeing those needles proves to me that what I remember really happened. Seeing their condition drives home just how long it has been since they were formed and driven into the ground. I marvel at their specific gravity, their placement, their durable beauty—all signs of Prince Shen's power and my love's sublime mind. Seeing them, I suddenly understand just how penetrating were his insights into the whirls and eddies of the flowing Tao. I comprehend, in that moment, the ineffable, ethereal magnificence of his vision, which could penetrate past, present, and future. I understand now that time and distance were no obstacles to the all-encompassing, galaxy-sized, energetic spirals of his mind. Long Ears, I now realize, foresaw this day. He knew all along what would happen to me one day.

Overcome by emotion, I sink to the ground, lie back, and look at the sky. I deeply appreciate the fact that in a world rich beyond measure, even without any knowledge of muons and quarks, my wizard somehow found the time and the inclination to grow me and to love me.

"What's up? What are you doing? Are you okay?"

"This is my last chance," I say.

"Last time for what?"

"To see the blue, blue sky."

"Will you stop it? There are years of blue skies ahead."

"For you," I say.

He sits down beside me. "I know this is all happening quickly for you," he says. "I can't imagine how overwhelming it must be. You're doing great so far. With everything. You're beautiful. You're magical. You're incredible beyond measure. Please, stop worrying so much. Everything is as it should be and happening right on schedule."

"I know," I say, knowing that in years to come he will look back on this conversation, on having said what he said, and understand it in a fashion he cannot understand it now.

I lie there with him beside me for a few more minutes, watching the branches wave in the breeze and hearing all the rustling sounds beneath me that a person who has not spent millennia underground would never think to listen for or notice. He tucks my head in beside his own so that his chin rests lightly against my hairline and he softly strokes my back.

"I knew a great flute player once," I say. "I wish he was here now. I wish you could hear his music."

"I've got plenty of music to share," says Athens. He reaches for his laptop with the intent of showing me a music video or playing me a sample.

"Stop," I say. "It's enough just to have you lie here quietly with me."

So he leaves his toys alone and instead he sings for me. It's a song I've never heard before. It speaks to a love of silence and a yearning to go where the sun shines through pouring rain.

"*Everybody's Talkin' At Me*," he says.

"They are?"

"That's the name of the song."

"We've found the treasure," I say. "It's right beneath us."

He jumps to his feet and rips open a pocket in his pack, one I haven't seen before, zipped close to the padding that lies against his back.

"Look what I brought with me!" he says, gleefully.

He holds a folding shovel.

If it were not for his penchant for all kinds of digging, I would not be here now. Against the tide of my feelings, against the inevitable course of things I feel is upon us, I give him two thumbs up and a smile.

70

In Yin's dream, Wang Yi spent his last moments sitting on the cold floor of the cave, scrolls and shells and bones on his lap, a small torch flickering as he took in the last wisdom he could manage and dreamed of his master.

Aren't you angry with him?

"He did the right thing," Wang Yi replies. "So did I."

The written word is worth that much?

"It's not the words, dear Yin, but the ideas they carry and what they do for men's souls."

He grieves for you. I grieve for you too.

"So you're free of the king?"

We escaped together to the edge of the Western plain. We await clear weather before pushing on to the state of Qin.

Wang Yi smiled, and despite the darkness she could see the blood on his lips. "I'm sorry for taking you from your home. I should have left you where I found you."

You were acting for him, even way back then.

"Yes, and that's what makes everything all right."

She awoke with a start to the feel of the great sage's hand wiping the snow from the top of her head. "You were talking in your sleep," he said. "Now come away from the window and closer to the stove while I stoke the fire."

I dreamed of Wang Yi. He forgives you.

"I know. Here. Move a little bit. The snow is still blowing on you."

The astronomer appeared at the bottom of the stairs. "Why don't you both come down where it's warm and share dinner?"

"Yin's just awakened, so we will work a while. We have a job to do here. When we're done, you can melt your armillary sphere and use the bronze to make tablets, then copy what I've written for the soldiers."

The astronomer's face blanched. "My armillary sphere?"

"Would you rather melt the swords your men carry?"

The astronomer smiled slyly. "I would."

"Where you get the bronze is not my concern," Long Ears smiled back.

"Do finish soon, lord. The sun is plunging. Soon you won't be able to see to carve cleanly."

"Perhaps the stable boy could bring hot soup and storm torches. We'll come down when we're done."

The astronomer bowed and retreated. When he was gone, Long Ears sharpened his dagger and poured hot tea. "Where were we?" he asked.

Yin sniffed the steam rising off the leaves and sighed, reluctant to release her dream. *Carve this: the Tao is a wide, straight highway, though most people stray from it and get lost in intricate, torturous mountain detours. Just be childlike, as an infant's spirit is pure. Cultivate a mind empty, but pregnant with infinite possibility. Don't commit to any one course until the last moment.*

"So beautifully succinct."

It all comes from you. I've just had a long time to organize it in my head. Here's more: Sometimes we have to embrace the soft, quiet path to accomplish a concrete, obvious goal. Kings should rule their states like frying a small fish, making frequent and careful adjustments so nothing breaks or falls apart. The superior turtle…

"Slow down for me now, so I can catch up with what you've said. I don't want to rush this," he said.

Look. The storm is easing. I can see the moon.

"Good. Now we don't need lanterns."

All right. Where was I? Oh yes. The superior turtle answers hate with love and deals with small problems before they become big. She creates a foundation of great things, and then allows them to naturally arise. Fighting, she uses her opponent's force against him, never underestimates him, and sticks her neck out only when it is safe to do so. Humble, she understands balance.

"Perhaps we should go join the astronomer now."

Squeeze this last bit in, please, because it's the end.

"You mean this is all of it?"

If you agree. I can say it's all I know.

"Go ahead then. After, we'll eat."

Lao Tzu carved as Yin spoke the last stanza. *It's important to serve others and be grateful for all you have and for your place in the world.*

71

As he digs into one of the great tragedies of my life, I watch the dirt fly. Each and every clod transits my firmament as an information comet, showering me with sparks of geologic history. There is the frog layer, holding countless, fragile skeletons—a lower jaw here, an extended, fragile leg there—and telling the tale of a moist era in the forest. Next, there is the flower layer, wherein clouds of pollen free of the dry earth form a cloud above Athens that comes down upon me, coloring my hair blonde and giving me an itchy nose. Below that are several strata of twigs and petrified wood, little shards of which hit me hard enough to make me wish for my shell.

"How much deeper do you think I'll have to go?" Athens asks. It is warmer than it was when he dug Long Ears' grave, but we are in the shade and at altitude, so the air is dry and he's not perspiring much.

"You'll find the entrance soon," I say. "The vegetation we put over it is obviously long dried and gone. Inside, you'll find some things you can use to bribe the museum to drop their claims against you."

He keeps digging. Now and then, he pauses just long enough to look at me with such heartbreaking tenderness I can scarcely bear it.

"I don't know why you had us come all this way," he said. "I would have figured a way to get the museum off my back.."

"Funny choice of words, as it's my back they're after. But anyway, if it were that easy, you wouldn't be on the lam in China."

"I didn't say it would be easy."

"You'd go to jail."

"I've always chosen the experience-driven life."

"No ruminating over consequences for you."

He smiled. "I want nothing more than to get you home to your island. You've been waiting twenty-five hundred years. I'll stay with you. I can work as a guide there or run the research station's computers. Creative tech work at the birthplace of evolutionary theory is a strangely beautiful notion."

As he speculates on our future, I sit on the ground with my hands folded around my knees, something most humans take for granted but which gives me great pleasure. I hear his shovel clang against something.

"Looks like what's left of a sword," he says, reaching up to hand it to me.

Even though it has rusted almost completely away, I know it at once as the patterned, meteoric steel of the Zhou court's elite guards. Gui's stamp is near the hilt.

"You recognize it, don't you?"

"Relic of a slaughter," I say.

"So we're going after a weapons cache?"

"Tools of war won't rescue you now. Just keep digging."

It isn't much longer before rocks in the dirt drop and roll, revealing the long-hidden slanting entrance to the cave. The sound, the revelation, brings my first human friend to mind. My eyes fill with tears. Athens wants to comfort me but I shake him off and begin climbing down. He hands me a palm-size flashlight.

"1800 lumens," he says. "Amazing what they do with LEDs these days. I've kept it charged with the solar panels in my computer pack."

"We can't stay long."

"After what we've been through, you're in a rush?"

"The rocks produce some kind of gas. It's terribly toxic. A short visit is all we get."

"What kind of gas?"

"I don't know."

The cavern is even drier and cooler than I remember it. My footfalls are loud on the granular floor. I keep my eyes cast downward, my flashlight at play before me.

"Are you going to tell me what's down here now?"

Before I can answer, my light reveals the first group of scrolls and bones, all as neatly stacked as they were all those years ago. He gasps and runs over to them. I hand him the flashlight and sink down next to a pile of dust and rotted cloth, hair and bones. I want so badly to be close to Wang Yi that I put my cheek to his. I stroke the dried and twisted bits of skin that are still there, as a mummy's might be, because the gas has kept the chamber sterile all these years. I put my thumbs on Wang Yi's eyebrows and brush them clean.

Athens' attention is torn between my quiet sobs and the incredible treasure before him. His flashlight plays back and forth, first close and bright on a bit of wisdom from the Yellow Emperor, then on the tear tracks on my face.

"A friend?" he asks quietly.

"The very best. Without him, I wouldn't be here."

"What happened to him?"

"Fate. Timing. Service. Devotion. Love. Gas."

"I'm so sorry. Look, this is not just a few scrolls, it's…"

"…the collection of an entire dynasty."

His mouth works like fish gills.

"When you say the collection...."

"The library of the king of the Eastern Zhou. Only the best examples."

His hands are shaking. "This is...."

"My gift to you."

"I can't read all the characters."

"The museum will have people who can. They'll find the work of the early sage kings, the Duke of Wen, the Yellow Emperor, Fu Hsi."

"The Yellow Emperor? But he's a myth."

"A myth with ink and a brush, apparently."

Athens rubs his forehead. "The foundations of Chinese civilization."

"From before China existed. The turtle shells go back to before there were dynasties."

"No museum in the world has anything like this."

"Nothing like this could last outside this cave. Once you take it out it will have to be preserved immediately. Without the gas...."

"....the government won't let me excavate this. They'll want to preserve and protect it just the way it is."

"As well they should. But perhaps a few choice items might find their way into your backpack, and thence into the private collections of some people in New York, some people who could wave a checkbook and make your museum's anger at you go away."

He slides down onto the ground the way I imagine Wang Yi did all those years ago. He stares at the cold, wrapped stacks. He runs his fingers over Long Ears' personal stamp.

"This seal...."

"The mark of my wizard."

"Lao Tzu's chop...."

"They're your bargaining chip," I say. "How it all plays out, how you use it, that's up to you. I offer it in exchange for my life, as an expression of my gratitude and love."

He interlaces his fingers in mine. "But all I really need is you."

Before I can explain to him that I am the one thing he can never have, that it is not my destiny to be with him any more than it was my destiny to be with Long Ears, his lips brush mine. I want to tell him that we must wait, that it isn't safe to stay here for long, that my friend's bones will not make good company, and I should know about lying by bones. I want to tell him that it will be better above ground, in the warmth of the sun and far away from the gas, where we need not rush. Yet I tell him none of these things, because, in truth, no objections matter. Time and space shrink until we are all that's left, just our breathing and his touch.

The flashlight clatters to the floor and rolls so that it illuminates Wang Yi's skull from the far side, casting a projection of my old friend on the wall. It looks as if he is watching us, tall, elongated, giant, and pleased. Because of the way his skin is pulled tight, he seems to be smiling. Dismissing the threat of the gas, I lie back while Athens deliberately, slowly, gratefully takes off my clothes.

72

The journey to the forests of Qin would have taken many weeks if Long Ears had not applied shamanic magic to Yin, shoring up her muscles, tendons, ligaments and bones in a ritual powerful enough to cause surrounding trees to bend inward and a nearby creek to overflow its banks. The changes manifested gradually; each day the tortoise became more and more resistant to fatigue and able to cover increasingly vast distances without so much as a sip of tea. She became nearly as fast as a quarter horse, if not quite so graceful, her forward progress no longer limited by her physiology but by her short, stubby legs.

Her internal shifts matched those in the landscape. In the east, the loess soil was dry and loose, supporting only low scrub — home to nesting birds hiding from snakes, voles that preferred darkness to light, and to mouse pups that fed on sprouting grass. Moving west, the ground became darker, denser, and more stable, and the brush was replaced by thick, intimate, sweet-smelling forestland with a complex topography of berms and ridges. This landscape, and the fact that Long Ears hitched a ride on her shell when he was tired, challenged Yin's balance.

Why do you face backward when I carry you?

"The future will be here soon enough. All my life I work to be present, but on this journey I enjoy reminiscing about the past."

Yin looked at the higher peaks, where juniper trees grew out of what remained of the winter's snow, and around her at the rubber trees, locust, and walnut. A golden-hair monkey dropped from an oak tree in front of her, gnawing on a branch covered with lichens.

If I can think of my island while I move forward, you can think of Shen and King Ling and the queen when you look ahead. Will we see her family when we get to Qin?

"If I never see another court, it will be too soon."

But there might be news there of Bao Yu and your son.

The great sage released a long, silky breath and watched it fog the mountain air. "You're my family now, Yin. I've been waiting all my life to live among trees, and I'm not leaving."

It's cold up here.

"It will be lower and warmer to the west, but we still have some climbing to do."

Tortoises aren't built to climb. The risk of tumbling backward and getting caught upside down is too great.

"Then don't tumble."

They walked deeper and deeper into the vast forest, zigzagging up the sides of mountains, sometimes along precipices so sheer one misstep would have sent Yin hurtling on a trajectory shorter but no less steep than the one a certain meteorite had once followed before blessing the Zhou court with iron. They stopped to drink from icy cold streams, and the great sage collected medicinal roots, mushrooms, fungi, and herbs until his satchel bulged to bursting.

Why take so many? Just more to carry.

"When nature offers, I accept. It may seem excessive now, but if you take a longer, wider view you will see these gifts are rare. We may not encounter them again."

And what, specifically do they offer?

"Ingredients for potions to heal the sick."

I thought you were done with the world of men.

"You never know what life can bring. It's wise to be prepared."

During the next few weeks, Yin noticed the great sage studying the sky more frequently than usual. She said nothing about it, as she had come to trust his ability to predict weather, but she knew his expressions as well as the scales on her own forelimbs and could see and feel something new and different.

What are you waiting for?

"A sign that we've arrived."

They wandered for another few days, and then one morning the great wizard had his sign. At first, he simply began walking in circles while Yin watched him. They were on a slope with a clear view to the south, and the rays of the sun flickering through the trees imbued the space with soft light.

Is this our spot?

"It is."

How do you know?

"My eyes can settle to the horizon and thus my liver *qi* is refined," the wizard answered, settling in to build a lean-to and a fire.

What you stare at affects the energy in your liver?

"Our energy is always a product of what we eat and drink, how we move, and where we put our attention. Knowing this, and being able to control these variables well, is what allowed me to help you become who you are and will be."

That night, the sleeping and waking worlds collided inside Yin's head. In the forest, she was dimly aware of Lao Tzu's snoring, of shapes moving around the camp, causing the rustling of leaves, and of the pulsing energy in the twisted roots of old trees. In her dream, she saw Ding Fei, his gaze reflecting confusion rather than hostility, and Ding Lok, too, his specter floating above in a starless sky, taunting her with a sword stained by the blood of her kin. She saw other snapshots of her life amongst the Zhou, many of them with her beloved Wang Yi. Collectively they gave her a perspective she hadn't had before. She finally understood how the dynasty had collected and cohered the thoughts and passions of so many people over so many millennia into a blossom that might have withered and browned by the time she left but was still a delicate flower of creativity and consciousness well worth celebrating.

"You spoke Wang Yi's name out loud," Long Ears told her when she awoke.

And what if I did?

"I didn't know you could do that."

I didn't either. I don't think I could again.

"The moon is full."

I see that. Look how huge it is, and how close. There are seas on its surface, Long Ears. Can you see them? And river valleys and mountains, too. It's glorious!

"There has always been more to the moon than meets the eye. That's why I named you for it."

73

I hold Athens' head between my hands and half guide half follow his transit across my breasts, my belly, and my thighs. I throw my head back, no shell margin to limit me, open my mouth, and close my eyes. I feel every pore of his tongue and every tiny crease of his lips. My passion, born of thousands of years of patient yearning, explodes so strongly I can scarcely breathe. I wrap my legs around him, my arms too, and draw him into me until I see not merely stars, but entire constellations. I am simultaneously absent and present, here in the moist flesh and shaking bones, yes, but also in every raindrop that has ever fallen to Earth and every tree trunk that has ever reached for the sky. Moaning, I touch Long Ears' ethereal Tao.

"Impossible," Athens gasps.

"What?"

"How amazing you are," he replies. "How stunningly beautiful. How you smell and taste and feel. That we are here together. That this is really happening."

Without breaking our connection, he stands, lifting me with him. One of his big, white hands spreads like a fan across my back while the other holds me up from below. We move together, back and forth, up and down, side to side. I think, briefly, of the little ship in the big storm, Wang Yi guiding us to the still center and beyond. I glance down at my old friend's bones, the dust of his blue dragon cloak curled around them like a snake. I want to cry but instead I smile because he may be gone but he is still here, still with me.

I kiss Athens' neck. "This is about us," I say. "Not about me."

"Us then. We're amazing."

His pace varies, sometimes slow, sometimes fast, prolonging our ecstasy. "I'm out of my mind," I gasp when his tempo drops.

"Never more in it," he answers, his tongue behind my ear.

"No. Yes. That's what I mean."

He laughs. I feel his ribs against my own, gloriously vulnerable, covered only by skin and other soft tissues, entirely free of a shell.

"I'm trying to say I've been trapped."

He pauses and I reach around behind him and pull so he will keep going. "A carapace and a plastron will do that," he says.

"It wasn't my shell that trapped me; it was my mind. Long Ears tried to tell me in so many different ways but I couldn't hear him. I needed you to remove my fears and boundaries, to break my limitations and set me free."

He moves faster. I feel vibration, and pressure building.

"You've waited longer for liberation than any living creature on Earth," he pants. "Now enjoy it."

The distance between us, the air in the microscopic ridges of skin that separate us, each and every one of them vanishes. We are in the thrall of the cosmic bellows that give the universe its eternal, ongoing contraction and release. Up I go. I have no flesh, I have no lungs, I have no heartbeat and I have no breath. Higher and higher I soar, deeper and deeper he plunges.

"I am the flower of Luoyang!" I cry. "The Great Fertilizer! The Queen Mother of the World! I am the moon! I am Yin!"

A blizzard seizes me, each flake a tiny moment, smell, sound, or touch from the past. Together, they create a montage of all the feelings I have had, all the pure and direct emotion that my long, long life has birthed. I grab hold of Athens' tail.

At the moment of his release his voice rises, strangled and high. "I am the wizard you knew and the one you know," he shouts. "I am the past and the present and the future, too!"

I feel his heat and I feel his heart, but most of all I feel two things happen inside me. The first is my own protracted bliss, a feeling unimaginable to any turtle anywhere, ever. The second is that thing I have longed for since the day Long Ears awakened me. I relax. I smile. I understand. Everything is coming to an end, and everything is just beginning.

My whole life is a love story.

74

As spring turned to summer, the refugees built a hut from native timber. When it was done, Yin used both beak and brawn to craft a pleasing garden. She arranged saplings and shrubs, planted flowers, and dropped acorns into a ring of holes around the homestead so that someday giant red oaks would surround it. In the absence of servants and retainers to help with chores, she learned to balance food items such as bird eggs, nuts, fruits, mushrooms, and wildflowers on her shell. Long Ears took what she brought and used it to prepare fresh, vital meals that sharpened their senses, purified their bodies, and cleared their minds for the meditation he held as his first priority.

During the summer she joined him in the practice, learning to focus her mind and quiet her thoughts. Mornings found them greeting the sun together, standing side by side, the wizard with his eyes closed and hands folded over his navel, Yin tall on her columnar limbs. They traveled etheric worlds together, covering lands as an eagle might, gazing at the sights below, even monitoring the progress of the Yellow River as it dragged the silt of the Himalayan plateau down to the sea. Though Yin loved these journeys because they eliminated the physical barrier that stood forever between her and her love, returning from them was always painful.

I feel and see and do so much now. Why can't I have legs and hair and a full human anatomy?

Lao Tzu patted her head gently. "It's best not to focus on what we cannot have, and be happy instead with what we have."

But I'm still changing. I can feel it. I want it to happen faster so I can be with you.

"Physical love pales by comparison to the life we have now. Here on this mountain I call Zhongnan, I am no longer an oracle and you are no longer a curiosity. We are just Li Dan and Yin, tied together by the thread of the Tao."

I want to melt my flesh into yours.

"Perhaps one day that will happen. We still have much time alone here."

As it happened, they did not. Word of Long Ears' plan to travel west had reached Qin Jiang's relatives at the Qin court. When he did not show up, official parties were sent, and the curious made their own private expeditions. It was one of these latter that got lucky less than a week later. They were boys dressed in silk robes and when they stumbled upon the clearing, Yin was alone.

"Look at the size of her. She must be the wizard's pet."

"Do you think we can ride her?"

"I bet she could carry all six of us easily. Her legs are like trees."

"What about these characters carved into her shell?"

A smaller boy climbed her. She violently threw him off. Long Ears appeared from behind a tree.

"You're lucky she didn't bite off your foot," the wizard declared, appearing from the bush with a handful of flowers.

I was going to bite off something else entirely.

So unkempt was the old man's beard and so tattered were his clothes that it took the boys a moment to realize who he must be.

"You are the oracle of Luoyang?" asked the lead boy, dropping into the appropriate kowtow.

"The same."

"Will you teach us spells to control fire and wind?"

"Certainly not."

The boys were crestfallen. "To control minds, then?"

"Control your own, first."

"What about bedroom arts?"

"Such lessons must be conducted in the bedroom."

"Come back with us, then," another boy put in. "We'll take you to court."

"I've had enough of court, thank you."

"What you wrote on the shell? Will you teach us that?"

"Just read it and think about it. That's why I wrote it."

They formed a circle around Yin and did just that. When they were finished, they had a thousand questions. Long Ears began to answer but then stopped himself. "I came here for quiet meditation," he explained gently. "You'll have to leave now."

"But we don't understand," said the small boy who had tried to climb Yin.

"Go now," Long Ears repeated.

Chastened, deflated, and more than a little disappointed, they slunk off into the bush.

That was a bit abrupt.

The wizard sighed. "You know they'll be back."

We could move again.

"And they would find us again."

Sharing the Tao with others is your destiny.

"Sometimes I wish that it were not so."

If it were not so, you would not be you. Just have them build their own huts. I'm not sharing ours when it rains.

75

The roof of the cave reads like a topographical map of my life. Far to the left I see an outcropping that could be taken for a volcanic island. Beside it is a little bump that might as well be Ding Lok's ship, with a tiny calcified protrusion evoking a mast. Next to that I see dark shapes that remind me of the orcas, and off to the right I see a great mass of rock that I just know is China. I trace my journey with the flashlight.

"What are you looking at?" Athens asks quietly.

We lie on the floor looking up, our fingers interlaced, our clothes beneath us as cushions.

"Not looking. Remembering."

"How do you feel?"

"I will never forget this as long as I live."

He puts his hands to my face. I take his fingers in my mouth. He sighs, traces those wet fingertips downward over my throat and then my breasts. He makes circles, heading downward toward my navel. He stops, flattens his palm, and pushes gently, palpating with his fingers.

"Yin?" he says. "What's this?"

"I'm full."

"We haven't eaten a good meal in days."

I have to tell him now. I can't delay it any longer.

"Look at me," I say, aiming the flashlight at my face. "What do you see?"

"The woman I love more than anyone or anything in the world."

I put down the light and take his face in my hands and kiss him, tasting us both on his lips. The kiss goes on and on. He rolls on top of me, but I push him gently away.

"It isn't finished," I say.

He props himself up on an elbow. "What isn't?"

"My process. My transformation."

He gets up and begins to dress. "Can we talk about this outside? I'm a bit worried about the gas."

"We have a little time yet. Why don't you choose what you want from the library?"

"What about the rest of it?"

"You'll have to decide if you think the world is ready for such wisdom. Perhaps it should be trickled out, according to the needs of the age."

"I want your help. This is beyond me."

So I help him. We go through the scrolls carefully. I suggest three small tortoise shells from Chinese prehistory. One is written by the sage king, Yao and describes the flow of watercourses. Another bears the mark of the sage king, Shun, and explains how to read clouds. The last is a short discourse by the great king, Yu. It explains the movements of air and what they mean for crops, rain, and seasons. Athens starts to put them in his backpack, then hesitates.

"They'll rub against each other," he says.

"They're wrapped."

"I don't want to ruin the seals."

I hand him my blouse.

"You'll need that," he says. "I'll use my jacket. You can keep me warm."

"I won't," I say.

"Won't what?"

"Won't need it. Here. Take this last shell, too. It's the Duke of Wen's original writing of the *Yiqing*. Lao Tzu loved it more than anything."

"You called him Lao Tzu," he says, carefully slipping the scroll into his bag.

"Done fighting that. The name I know died with the man."

"Why won't you need your blouse?"

I play the flashlight over my belly. In just the time it has taken us to peruse the library, the swelling has continued to the point that I'm noticeably distended. Athens gives a visible start.

"What's going on?" he gasps. "What is that?"

"I think you know."

"But that's not possible. So quickly!"

"It seems sudden to you but that's just because you're not thinking it through. It's what turtles do and have been doing for tens of millions of years. Maybe longer than that. Besides, a tortoise turns into a woman and you marvel at *this*?"

He gasps. "But why now?"

"I think you know that, too. So many of them have come and gone, but this one, this one is complete."

A tiny smile escapes him. "You're saying I'm…"

"It was the last thing I needed to do. I do it now, with your help."

"When you say the last thing…"

"I'm finished," I say, feeling my own tears and seeing his. "Not too fast, not too slow, not too soon and not too late."

"But you can't. If this means…"

"Yes."

"I don't want it then," says. "Don't do it! You can't leave me. Tell me this is a nightmare, an effect of the gas."

"Not a nightmare but a dream. And the most wonderful dream any turtle could have. The most wonderful journey, the most wonderful life."

I feel my spine curve and my long bones grow brittle. I've held off the end as long as I could, but now, openly acknowledging the end, telling the truth to my love, Long Ears' magic has run its last game. He promised we would be together and we have, though not the way I ever imagined. Slowly, I sink to the floor. I beckon my young man close with a finger already become crooked with age. He takes the dry, brittle, last bit of me in his arms and puts his ear to my lips.

"Take it back," I say.

"What do you mean, take it back?"

The pressure is too fierce to resist any longer. I spread my ancient legs, so glad there are only two, and watch through bleary, fogged eyes as the narrower end of the egg protrudes from me. The pain is excruciatingly wonderful. I bear down as hard as I can, and it slides out. I see Athens take it in his hands in wonder.

"Please let it hatch on my island," I say, knowing they are the last words I will ever speak.

Athens is sobbing now, clutching the egg close to him. His tears wash it clean until it shines so white and brightly I have to shield my eyes.

That egg is the sun to me.

76

The wizard's disciples built not only lodgings but also a platform from which he could address them. The clearing became a village. Healers and musicians trickled in, along with a master chef who put the principle of harmony in ingredients to work cooking night and day for the faithful. Invitations to move to the Qin capital came almost daily, but Long Ears demurred, citing his undying loyalty to the Zhou monarchs of days past.

The pure, unadulterated enthusiasm of his students helped Yin accept the irrepressible teacher in him and lessened her resentment at the loss of their quiet time together. Recognizing that teaching was what Long Ears was on earth to do—even the monkeys sat quietly and listened when he spoke—was a manifestation of the maturity of her love. The wizard noticed this and was grateful.

Decades passed. As he aged, Long Ears suffered some loss of vitality but neither weakness nor pain. Each morning he rang his bell and addressed his disciples, and each evening he spent many hours undisturbed in meditation. In summer, Yin held a broad leaf in her beak and fanned him for hours to deflect mosquitoes and cool his brow. In winter, she made sure his platform was clear of snow and his tea was always hot.

The seekers that came to him hailed from lands far and wide. They were strapping Mongol warriors from the northern steppe, small, dark, agile Southeast Asians, densely muscled, laconic mountain men from the Himalayan highlands—these interested mostly in mastering crops and weather—and courtly scholars who pored over the wisdom originally carved into Yin's shell, but now widely copied. Whatever gifts they brought to Long Ears, he forwarded to Luoyang, to a king he had never even met—a son of Gui—and then a son after that.

During this time, Yin finally grew to the weight of two large men. The wizard's disciples regarded her with awe, both for her proportions and for her close relationship with their teacher.

"They come to see you just as much as they come to see me."

Nonsense. You are the living legend, not I.

"I'm not sure that there's much difference between us anymore."

Every few years a contingent from the other side of the Himalayas arrived, bringing news of another teacher who also gave sermons in the forest. They carried the teachings of their so-called "Awakened One", on scrolls. They shared these with the wizard and he was mightily impressed.

You know you're starting a library again. Scrolls just accumulate around you like moss on a stone.

Long Ears spread his hands and laughed. "This sage from Nepal understands the Tao. His teachings are irresistible, if a bit sad. If I were not so old, I would go find Kong Qiu and take him on a trek across the mountains so that the three of us could drink tea together and talk. What a time that would be!"

I'm sure Kong Qiu has long passed.

The wizard sighed. "I would have liked more time with him."

And Bao Yu? Do you think of her, too?

"I'm sorry that she never felt how much I loved her. I regret never meeting my son."

The next morning Yin found teeth on the wizard's pillow. She scooped them up and clandestinely dug a hole with her claws and buried them. As his end drew near, the great wizard never asked anyone save Yin to attend him. One morning he told her to gather the crowd. She knew at once what he had in mind, and when she did as he asked the word spread so quickly, she knew it had to be magic. Disciples swarmed in from towns and villages across the kingdom, and from the capital too. Each told her that they had awakened from sleeping with an undeniable urge to come.

The forest was in the hard grip of winter. Trees were bare and the wind blew sharply, howling down the mountain and forcing supplicants to bow their heads. Using her beak and her claws, she wrapped the great sage in layers of fine silk from the capital, and wool, too.

"You've become quite dexterous."

My claws obey me in new ways.

They climbed the platform as the crowd watched silently.

All manner of creatures are gathering beneath the platform. Even snakes. How is that possible? It's too cold for their kind to move.

"You're moving and they are no more or less than your cousins."

So you did something to them.

"They're just here to say goodbye."

Tears froze on the scales of Yin's cheeks, dotting her beak with ice.

How can you talk about your own death like it's someone else's?

"You know how."

Because we are all one.

He smiled and turned to address the crowd.

"I appreciate that you're all here to say goodbye," he began, his voice still strong. "I'm sorry to ask you to travel in such cold weather. I'm as grateful for your kind devotion as I am certain I don't deserve it. Please don't mourn my passing. Life and death are two sides of the same coin, and I am sure that my death will be as wondrous as my life has been."

Beside him, Yin teetered. Long Ears steadied her with a hand.

"You see next to me a most magnificent soul. Yin is far the wiser of the two of us and has suffered more than any of you can imagine, not only because she was ripped from an island paradise home but because she has so long endured the indignity of being transformed into a chimera I created for my own fulfillment when I was young and foolish and understood even less than I understand now. I apologize to you, Yin, in front of all these people, for having stolen your dignity and your birthright. I love you more than life itself, and, by way of my apology, I ask those assembled here today to honor us both by doing whatever it takes to return you to your beloved home."

Yin used her armored forelegs to wipe away her frozen tears. They tinkled as they hit the platform.

My home has always been with you.

As she said this, she looked out into the crowd and noticed a man of advanced years staring at her from the south side of the platform. He was thick and tall, with soulful eyes, and a refined, familiar countenance.

Who is that man? Have we met him?

The great wizard did not hear her, for he was already formulating more words for his followers. "When I leave, my body will not decay. I will not soil myself or stiffen, as is so common in death. Nonetheless you may be assured that I have in fact departed for the ancestors. Please bury me, without a casket, deep in the ground so that I may join the Tao by feeding the worms and the trees."

Someone in the crowd began to wail, and then another and then another.

"Mark my grave if you must," he went on. "But please make the stone modest, for I am a modest man, a pilgrim on a path many others have tread and which all of you, I hope, will tread after I am gone."

He bent and kissed Yin on her head. Then he stood straighter than he had when commanding men, wielding a sword, comforting a queen, healing a king, heralding a prince, or transforming a tortoise. "Living the right way changes you," he said. "It reduces your impulses to do things that are destructive, harmful, wasteful, or cruel. One by one, if you all find the path, your actions will have rippling effects, like throwing a stone in a pond. One by one those ripples will change others and inspire humankind. Over time, lives lived the way I have suggested will restore balance to the world."

He waited a moment after that, gazing out at the crowd, touching Yin with only the tips of his fingers. The collected crowd held its breath. Suddenly, the old man cupped his hand to his ear.

"Do you hear that beautiful music?" he asked in wonderment.

The supplicants looked at each other in confusion. Some closed their eyes to listen.

"Shen at last," the great wizard whispered.

He began to dance then, to a sound only he could hear. The dance lasted several minutes. No one who saw it would ever forget it.

At the end of it, the great sage took his leave.

77

Even from here, I can see Athens lying on his belly in Galápagos sand, his hands supporting his chin. Above him, frigate birds eye the nest. Not ten yards away, a pair of waved albatrosses in their mating ritual cross beaks like fencers, breaking combat every few moments to point their long yellow beaks at the sky. A ground iguana crawls over his legs and stops, comfortably draped over Athens' thighs, to nibble an Opuntia flower. Athens locks eyes with a bright orange Sally Lightfoot crab and lifts a finger in warning.

"You're a persistent crustacean, I'll give you that. Every hour of every day for a month you hover here, and every hour I shoo you away. You're not getting a taste of this egg. It's not going to happen. I won't move until it hatches, and when it does, it goes with me."

His beard is long and his body is dirty, but he looks as happy and contented as a man can look. I've been watching him all this time and I know that he feels me, because now and again he gazes up at the sky and tells me how much he misses me, how much he will always love me, how grateful he is to have known me. He has a small tent pitched nearby, and during the night he moves it over the nest, then moves it away again to let the warming sun shine on the egg during the day.

Not far from him, volcanic mud bubbles in a pit. A crowd

of giant tortoises blissfully soaks there as finches pick ticks from their outstretched necks. Dimly, I remember the incredible satisfaction of having someone else scratch an itch I could not reach. Now and again, Athens rises and walks over to them, all the while keeping an eye on the patient marauder and warning him off with a shout if he begins to put claw to sand where my egg is buried. When he reaches the living giants, he scratches their necks and affectionately thumps their shells. He has come to know each and every member of the herd and has even given them nicknames like "Bumpy," "Stretch," "Windbag," and "Tank."

A ranger approaches, a short stumpy man with sweat stains on his shirt and the brim of his hat. "Got another computer glitch," he says.

"I'll fix it tonight."

"Could you make an exception and have a look now? I promise I'll watch the egg."

Athens shakes his head. "No can do. Sorry. Something tells me today's the day."

"You say that every morning. Spending your days in a tent positioned over a nest and only working at night after you zip the tent closed is no way to live, man. You can't be getting any sleep keeping watch like you do."

"When I get drowsy, I lie on top of the nest," he answers. "If she comes out I know I'll wake up."

The ranger rolls his eyes. "That cute new intern keeps asking me about you. You're never going to get anywhere with her if you don't let go of this egg, shave and shower, and talk with her. It's just a turtle, man. They're all over the place."

Athens smiles. "Not like this one."

The ranger gestures in irritation and walks off. Athens goes back to the nest, stopping on the way to pull a music player out of his tent and put the earplugs in. He dials up something classical with piano and violins and settles in again. At length, he falls asleep, his outstretched hand protecting the nest from the crab. It is the tiny sound of the shell splintering that wakes him. He rises slowly to his knees and puts his face down close to watch. He doesn't know what will come up, but I do. I see the nose the same time he does, and the perfect arch of beautiful eyebrows and the lean limbs as they unfold, impossibly long and well-formed despite having been folded so tightly. I see him lift her tenderly, and watch her straighten herself, her spine cracking, her arms straightening. She rubs her nose. What a beautifully human gesture I see in this child, his and mine.

I can hear the glad strong booming of Athens' heart from here, and the subtle, tentative *lub dub* of hers, too. Her eyes flutter open, and there are whirling galaxies there. He lifts her high, so that she is framed against the gigantic blue sky over my island.

"I am yours forever," he tells her. "You never have to worry about anything. I will always take care of you."

There's a hint of beakiness to her smile, but it goes away after she opens her jaw once and closes it.

He holds her close. His tears glisten in her hair.

78

Yin had seen many men die wounded and terrified in battle. She had seen their eyes glaze over and their limbs stiffen and their faces cave in. The body of her wizard, however, was in death as it was in life, except, of course, that it was motionless, sightless, breathless, and clearly devoid of *qi*. Standing beside his grave in the biting wind, she felt as if half of her was missing. She wondered how his faithful followers would possibly honor his request to return her to her island, but her brain was too fogged by cold and loss to think clearly.

Hearing a noise behind her, she turned to see the old man who had caught her attention during Long Ears' goodbye.

"You recognize me, don't you?"

I do.

"And you're not surprised that I can hear your thoughts."

A little, but then again, not really. What do people call you?

"I go by Tsung."

"You don't use the surname Li?"

"Why would I want anything to do with that name?"

There were circumstances you don't understand.

"I understand that my father abandoned us. I understand that my mother died hating you as you hated her."

I envied her; I never hated her.

"And she envied you. Ironic, no?"

Yes.

"She never had another man."

Yet she had you. Why did you take so long to come here?

"I wanted to wait until my mother was gone. She lived almost as long as he did."

I'm sorry you didn't come sooner. He would have welcomed you with an open heart.

"But he wouldn't have told me the location of the library."

Library?

"You take Long Ears' son for a fool? Tell me where to find his precious scrolls and bones."

Now is not the time for such information to come forth.

He reached behind him, produced a spade, and raised it threateningly. "What gives *you* the right to make that decision, you stinking beast? Tell me where it is!"

His sudden ferocity startled her.

Better lives than mine have been lost keeping that secret.

Foaming with rage, he began stabbing the shovel into the ground. "Tell me!"

Yin moved in on him, trying to push him over. *You would desecrate your own father's grave? Stop that!*

He fought back with the bronze shovel, banging it on her shell. She withdrew her head and limbs.

"I hate you!" he screamed. "I hate both of you."

Hate me if you wish, but leave your father out of it. Never has a man given more to others.

"Not to me! Not to my mother! He destroyed us."

Ransoming the library cannot return lost years to you.

"Ransoming? I don't want to ransom it; I want to burn it!"

Burn it? Why would you want to do that?

"Because he loved it!"

His blows were hard enough to chip her shell. She worried

about the carvings she bore. Mindful of the danger, she stuck her head out and bit him. He dodged, but she caught a bit of his robe in her beak. When he pulled away it tore, revealing a tail longer and more fully formed than his father's.

"Bitch!" he screamed, tucking it back in.

He shoved the blade of the shovel beneath her and with one great heave levered her onto her back. She waved her legs wildly, but out there on the flat ground there was nothing against which to push. He began to dig again, furiously, gasping against the cold, his hate driving his old body.

Why are you digging?

Ignoring her completely, he kept at his work. The spray of cold, damp soil coming out of the hole littered the ground like baby tortoises. In the hour it took Tsung to reach his father's corpse, no help arrived, as the disciples were to a one attending a ceremony at the platform. When at last Yin heard the shovel meet something soft, she winced.

"Tell me where the library is or you go in here with him."

Not a chance.

Dripping dirt, Tsung climbed creakily out of the hole and threw down the shovel.

"Tell me."

No.

He grabbed her rear legs and yanked her toward the pit.

"You never dreamed it would end this way, did you? You thought you could just live with him without consequences. You probably wished us dead as my mother wished you. Well, we might have died if General Sun hadn't been such a hero. He saved us, even though it cost him his own life. Loyal to the end, that clever bastard was. Now tell me where to find the library!"

No.

"Last chance."

LOVE BECOMES HER

No matter what you think, your father loved you. His whole life was about love.

"Don't you dare speak that word to me!" he screamed.

It's the only word I care about. It's the only thing I really know.

In response, Tsung loosed a furious scream and shoved Yin into the hole. She landed on her back. Struggling to breathe, she felt the full spades of dirt thud onto her plastron. She hissed and strained as the moonlight grew dimmer, but the weight of the dirt was too much. It wasn't until the last chunk of frozen ground shut out the sky that she managed a vertical position. Even then she didn't stop straining. In total, frigid darkness she continued to grasp and claw and push and wiggle until at last, she lay atop her wizard's body and put her legs out to embrace him.

She thought she could hear Tsung's maniacal laughter, but through all that silent dirt she couldn't be sure. Fighting for each breath, she conjured an image of Prince Shen, guileless and wise beyond his short years. She forced a recollection of his familiar flute music, intricate, sublime, full of spiral patterns and returns, of reversals and advances, of the sweetest melodies and the most fearsome crescendos. She remembered her beloved island, still a brilliant gem glowing in her mind's eye, and her dear Wang Yi dying alone in the cave. She thought of Ma Long's odd but somehow righteous path, of her first ride down the Yellow River in the care of a fat boatman, and of brave General Sun, a hero to the end. She thought of Ding Lok and his boy, and of glorious Queen Qin Jiang. She thought of kind old King Ling and his fancy for dancing girls. Most of all she thought of her wizard's beloved face and soothing voice. She tried to tell herself that the weight of the earth upon her was in fact the grip of his strong, warm legs as he sat astride her back. Sustained by his love, and with no idea how long that love would last, she understood everything.

About The Author

Yun Rou has been called the "Zen Gabriel Garcia-Marquez" for his works of magical realism, many set in China. Born Arthur Rosenfeld in New York City, he received his academic background at Yale University, Cornell University, and the University of California and was officially ordained a Taoist monk in Guangzhou, PRC. His award-winning non-fiction works on Taoism bridge science, spirituality, and philosophy, while his novels have been optioned for film in both Hollywood and Asia. Yun Rou lives in the American Southwest and travels frequently and extensively in the Far East.

yunrou@icloud.com
www.monkyunrou.com

Made in United States
Orlando, FL
17 August 2024

50442429R00192